P9-CRW-905

KLANWATCH

KLANWATCH

BRINGING THE KU KLUX KLAN TO JUSTICE

Bill Stanton

GROVE WEIDENFELD
New York

Published by Grove Weidenfeld
A division of Grove Press, Inc.
841 Broadway
New York, NY 10003-4793

Published in Canada by General Publishing Company, Ltd.

Due to limitations of space, permissions and credits appear on page 261.

Library of Congress Cataloging-in-Publication Data
Stanton, Bill.
Klanwatch : bringing the Ku Klux Klan to justice / Bill Stanton. — 1st ed.
        p.   cm.
    ISBN 0-8021-1327-3 : $19.95
    1. Ku Klux Klan (1915–   )   2. Klanwatch project.   I. Title.
        II. Title: Klanwatch.
    HS2330.K63S73   1991
    345.73'025—dc20
    [347.30525]   90-25645
                            CIP

Manufactured in the United States of America

Printed on acid-free paper

Designed by Irving Perkins Associates

First Edition 1991

1   3   5   7   9   10   8   6   4   2

for Garry

Preface

IN THE early 1970s the Ku Klux Klan was written off for dead. Down to a paltry fifteen hundred members—far below its modern peak of fifty thousand during the civil rights era—the so-called hooded order appeared to be on its way to oblivion. Twice previously since its founding in the 1860s, however, the KKK had seemed headed for extinction, only to stage remarkable revivals. And so it was that history seemed to repeat itself as the decade of the 1970s wore on. Gradually, almost imperceptibly at first, the KKK made its way back from the brink. Few in the civil rights community, or anyone else for that matter, took the resurgence very seriously at first—until May 26, 1979, that is.

That day a mob of approximately one hundred robed Klansmen attacked a Southern Christian Leadership Conference march in Decatur, Alabama, seriously injuring several demonstrators and sending a wake-up call to activists around the country. Six months later the killings of five anti-Klan protesters in Greensboro, North Carolina, underscored in the starkest terms the threat the KKK once again posed. By then it was clear to virtually everyone: The Klan was back.

I was employed as a paralegal at the Southern Poverty Law Center (SPLC) in Montgomery, Alabama, when the Center—a private, non-profit civil rights law firm—took up the fight against the KKK in the wake of the Decatur episode. For much of the next decade, until September 1987, I worked on the Center's Klanwatch Project, first as an investigator, then as director of the multipronged anti-Klan program, which filed lawsuits, published educational materials, and monitored the KKK nationwide.

Our efforts to launch a broad-based attack on the Klan, something that had never been done before, produced some notable successes: A documentary we commissioned received an Academy Award nomination, and a history of the KKK we wrote for high school students (and placed in every public high school in the country) was acclaimed by scholars and educators alike. But it was our litigation against the KKK that proved, perhaps, to be the most important component of our work. Using federal civil rights laws seldom employed since their passage by the Reconstruction Congress, Center attorneys filed lawsuits against the Klan all over the South on behalf of the victims of KKK violence, resulting in the dissolution of one Klan faction and the bankrupting of another. Along the way we cracked a conspiracy the FBI had been unable to solve and uncovered evidence that led to the convictions of more than two dozen Klansmen on charges ranging from civil rights violations to murder.

This book recounts some of our experiences in bringing the Klan to justice. I have written it not merely because the stories are interesting or poignant but because they are enlightening as well. They reveal much about the contemporary South: how far it has come since the sixties in terms of race relations and social and economic justice and how far it yet has to go.

Bill Stanton
December 5, 1990

KLANWATCH

Chapter One

IT WAS the Desperate day of the Wonderful week of the Furious month of the year 114 A.K. All across the Alabama Realm of the Invisible Empire, Ku Klux Klansmen were gathering in twos and threes to head for Decatur, an industrial town of forty thousand people located just south of the Tennessee state line. Word had come down from the grand dragon, through his titans, to the exalted cyclops of virtually every klavern north of Birmingham: "Stop the niggers."

And so they came, a hundred strong, armed with ax handles and baseball bats, long guns and pistols, tire tools, tree limbs, two-by-fours, a machete, a police nightstick. According to plan, they met north of town at a roadside park on the Tennessee River to await further instructions.

A mile or two away, under an almost speckless sky, the first black protesters were just beginning to arrive at Wayman Chapel African Methodist Episcopal Church for their march.

In what the Klan called the alien world, it was Saturday, May 26, 1979, a little more than a year to the day since the arrest of a young, mentally retarded black man on rape charges had touched off an

3

unprecedented wave of protests in Decatur's small black community. The protesters contended that twenty-six-year-old Tommy Lee Hines was innocent and that the police, in their haste to solve a string of black-on-white rapes in Decatur early in 1978, had gotten the wrong man. Time and time again during the ensuing months, demonstrators had taken to the streets, sometimes by the hundreds, but all the demonstrations had failed to gain the young man's freedom. With the coming of fall Tommy Lee Hines, a special education student with a mental age of six years, had gone on trial in nearby Cullman before an all-white jury and, amid an ugly lynch mob atmosphere, been convicted. The protests had gone on.

Now, to commemorate the one-year anniversary of what many blacks perceived to be a flagrant miscarriage of justice, Hines's supporters had proclaimed May 26 "Free Tommy Lee Hines Day" and had scheduled a noon march to the Morgan County Courthouse in downtown Decatur. Dr. Joseph E. Lowery, the president of the Southern Christian Leadership Conference (SCLC), had come from Atlanta to lead it. Officials of the civil rights group had been in Decatur since shortly after Hines's arrest to help the black community organize itself. Blacks made up only about 15 percent of the town's population—a noticeable presence but too small to wield political power—and heretofore they had never asserted themselves.

While the marchers continued to trickle into Wayman Chapel, over at Lakeside Park the Klansmen milled around restlessly, waiting for the word to head into town. In spite of its name, the park was actually situated on the northern bank of the Tennessee River, directly across from Decatur. Locals simply called it the pumps because of a flood control pumping station there. Built for picnickers and fishermen, it had come to serve frequently in the last year as a staging area for the newly resurgent KKK, an easy-to-find landmark for the hundreds of Kluxers who periodically converged on the Tennessee Valley community from all over the northern half of the state.

A few of the Klansmen, eager to get on with the task at hand, had already donned their robes and hoods. One was passing out ax handles. Another—twenty-four-year-old David Kelso, the exalted cyclops, or president, of the Decatur klavern—was carving a club

4

out of a tree limb. Here and there, scattered around the park, other Kluxers huddled in small clusters, talking among themselves. Few, if any, had belonged to the Klan in the 1960s, for it was a fairly young group, with the bulk of its members in their twenties and thirties. In a break with the past, a surprising number had long hair or beards. There were even several women.

Not far from the entrance to the park a group of about ten or fifteen Klansmen lingered in the bright sunlight around the tailgate of a pickup truck, taking turns letting a newspaper reporter photograph them with a life-size effigy of Hines. The stuffed figure, strung up by the neck, was dangling from a horizontal bar suspended above the bed of the vehicle by two wooden posts apparently meant to resemble a makeshift gallows.

Sometime before noon a big, burly man with a slightly ruddy complexion and thinning greased-down hair called the Klansmen together under a nearby shade tree. This was Ray Steele, the newly appointed titan, or regional leader, for the northern Alabama Ku Klux Klan. In the absence of Roger Handley, the grand dragon, or state president, Steele, a middle-aged truck driver, was the highest-ranking Alabama Klansman present that day. Like many northern Alabama whites, he was tired of the endless demonstrations on Hines's behalf, and he was ready to do almost anything to bring them to an end.

A few days earlier Steele had gone over the route of the march and concluded that the best place to stop it was at a dogleg in the street only three or four blocks from the courthouse, where Bank Street turned into Lee. Several factors made the location desirable: It was open and accessible, with room for a staging area; it gave the Klansmen an unobstructed view of the marchers as they descended Bank Street hill; and its location was downtown, not in a black neighborhood, so the police would be less inclined to look on the KKK's presence as invasive. The plan was simple: Steele was counting on the symbolism of stopping the anniversary march, and the humiliation factor, to end the Hines protests once and for all.

But while simple, Steele's strategy hinged on an important assumption: that the KKK could stop the march without prompting a response from the police, who were sure to be on hand to provide at least minimal protection for the demonstrators. For Steele, this would mean walking a fine line. Cross it, and he risked the arrest of his members; come up short, and the Klan would not only fail to stop the march but would lose face, and so would he.

If the past was any indicator, however, the Klansmen would encounter little or no resistance. During the previous year the police had seemed cowed by the KKK. On several occasions Decatur police officers had failed to enforce the law against Klansmen who had not only violated it but even flouted it. Still, to be on the safe side, Steele ordered his men to put their rifles and shotguns in their trunks, so as not to invite police interference. That didn't stop one or two Kluxers from carrying handguns, however.

When he finished his last-minute instructions, Steele gave the order to move out, and a motley caravan of twenty or thirty cars and pickup trucks of varying makes and conditions drove across the bridge into Decatur. In another five minutes it had snaked through the streets of the northernmost part of the city and arrived at the corner of Bank and Lee. It was almost noon. The marchers were nowhere in sight.

At Wayman Chapel Church it had become obvious to SCLC officials that the turnout for the demonstration would be less than they had hoped. Only fifty or sixty people had shown up, and many of them were teenagers. It was a far cry from the crowds of four or five hundred that had marched on the Morgan County Courthouse in the days immediately following Hines's arrest. But, then, a lot had happened in the intervening twelve months to intimidate all but the staunchest of Hines's supporters: A pair of Klan rallies estimated at five thousand and ten thousand people, the staging of a well-attended cross burning on the lawn of Decatur City Hall, the blocking of a march to Cullman and the abduction and beating of a black preacher there; and armed KKK motorcades through black neighborhoods, to name a few.

Finally, after a delay of about an hour, the marchers began their mile-long trek downtown, led by the fifty-four-year-old Lowery and other local and state SCLC officials. A cluster of reporters and photographers from area newspapers and television stations tagged alongside them. The Hines matter had been the number one news story in northern Alabama during the past year, and some members of the press corps were comparing it with the famous Scottsboro Case, which had riveted national attention on northern Alabama during the 1930s. Not since the highly publicized retrials of several of the Scottsboro defendants in the old Morgan County Courthouse had Decatur been engulfed in such controversy.

As the marchers set out, they were in a spirited mood. Many of them wore newly printed T-shirts emblazoned with Hines's likeness, and as they paraded they chanted "Free Tommy Lee" or sang old standards of the civil rights movement, songs such as "Ain't Gonna Let Nobody Turn Me 'Round."

Even in the face of widespread white vigilantism, the protests by Hines's supporters had remained free of violence and remarkably free of confrontational rhetoric. The campaign had consisted of all the elements of nonviolent direct action: sit-ins, marches, mass meetings, and picketing. Before each march or demonstration SCLC officials routinely had appealed to anyone carrying a weapon either to leave it behind or not to participate. Typically the request produced a pistol or two or several knives.

But May 26 was different. Not that the request wasn't made—it was, and several weapons were turned in as a result. However, unknown to Dr. Lowery or the Reverend Arthur Turner, the local SCLC chapter president, several young Hines supporters who were to serve as parade marshals had slipped rifles into a car that would accompany the march. The members of this volunteer security team had grown angry and disillusioned over the repeated failure of local and state law enforcement agencies to provide adequate protection. Twice in the history of the Hines case small groups of protesters had been terrorized by white mobs in nearby Cullman; on both occasions it was the protesters who had been taken into custody—none of the vigilantes had been arrested.

It was as the demonstrators turned onto Bank Street, the halfway point of the march, that the Klansmen first came into view a few blocks down the hill. Clad in white from head to toe, with only their faces, hands, and shoes showing, the Kluxers were a sobering sight, even at a distance. As a precaution, several of the older marchers whisked their younger counterparts out of the demonstration and placed them into the cars of supporters trailing along behind it.

Because it was Saturday and Bank Street was not a particularly busy retail area, there were few pedestrians about, black or white, and the procession descended the long, sloping hill toward the intersection under the gaze of just a handful of shopowners and their employees. The only thing separating the marchers and the Klan at this point, besides asphalt, was a thin line of police and Morgan County sheriff's deputies strung out across the street at the bottom of the hill, at the point where Bank doglegged to the left. Curiously, a half mile away, out of view, a squad of about twenty Alabama state troopers stood at the ready, armed in riot gear. Their commander, Captain Ben Gamel, expected trouble, but he was not about to violate police etiquette and inject his men into the situation without an invitation from Decatur Police Chief Pack Self, and he had received none.

As the blacks drew nearer to the intersection, the Klan members became increasingly agitated, raising a chorus of taunts and racial slurs that clashed with the songs and chants of the marchers. Angry shouts of "Stop the niggers," "Kill the niggers," "Nigger, you ain't goin' past here" filled the air and resounded off the surrounding buildings. A block short of the intersection one of the women in the march fainted, and several other demonstrators fell out of line to assist her.

Just as the first marchers reached the dogleg, dozens of Klansmen, clubs held high, surged forward to block the marchers' path, as if on signal. But at that point something happened that the Klansmen hadn't counted on: The police stood their ground. Angered by this unexpected resistance, the Kluxers began scuffling with the lawmen in an attempt to get to the marchers. The officers, outnumbered by at least two to one, fought back. Without riot equipment or tear gas, though, their efforts were futile.

They did manage to open a narrow corridor next to the curb, however, and seeing the opening, one of the parade marshals shouted over a bullhorn for the marchers to form a single line to pass through the cleared-out area, from which they would have been able to emerge and continue their walk to the courthouse. But it was too late; a handful of Kluxers erupted through the police line and the corridor collapsed. The demonstration ground to a halt. There was little the protesters could do but step back off the pavement and watch as the police battled to restore order.

Then, without warning, gunfire broke out in the middle of the intersection, and in an instant all-out chaos descended over the scene. By the time the shooting ended, a minute or so later, two

Klansmen and two marchers had been seriously wounded, and the Hines case had entered an entirely new phase.

That night it seemed as if the lid might blow off completely. Two white-owned grocery stores in the black section of town were fire-bombed, and fire fighters sent to battle one of the blazes found themselves dodging sniper bullets. Two other stores owned by whites were fired upon, and one was looted.

In the space of a few short hours Decatur was thrust into the glare of the national spotlight. The next morning the South's worst racial confrontation in almost a decade landed the community squarely on the front pages of the nation's newspapers. Reporters from all over the country began pouring into town.

With Decatur's image clearly at stake, the city's white leadership—which had never taken a forceful stand against the Klan—was finally moved to act. As if with one voice, white political and civic leaders reflexively sought to divert attention from their handling of the year-long community crisis by blaming both the Klan and the SCLC for the eruption of violence. Mayor Bill Dukes, a former public relations professional, was the point man in this effort, which skillfully portrayed the community as an innocent victim caught between two groups of outsiders interested only in their own aggrandizement. White civic clubs and business associations, which earlier had refused to touch the case, now rushed to pass resolutions deploring the violence, and the local paper, while conceding shortcomings in the white establishment's response, made out the SCLC and the Klan to be equally blameworthy. Decatur's image-conscious white leadership was closing ranks to defend the city's good name.

As slick as the campaign was, it might not have succeeded except for one critical fact: For the first time since Hines's arrest, one of the young man's supporters had been charged with an overt act of violence. In fact, three blacks had been arrested in connection with the Bank-Lee incident. Two of them were parade marshals, who had retrieved their rifles from the security car after the marchers were attacked and who were charged with violating an ordinance banning guns near demonstrations. The third was a forty-nine-

9

year-old City Hall maintenance worker named Curtis Robinson, who was accused of assault with intent to murder in the shooting of David Kelso, the exalted cyclops. Despite the fact that several Klansmen had also been arrested—three for disorderly conduct or assaulting a police officer, and a fourth for discharging a gun within the city limits—the SCLC had lost the moral high ground.

Two weeks after the attack, on June 9, 1979, approximately fifteen hundred civil rights activists from around the South converged on Decatur to finish the march and to make a witness against violence and intimidation. Protected by hundreds of law enforcement officers and National Guardsmen, they completed the aborted march—to the jeers of 250 robed Kluxers looking on. And this time, with downtown Decatur turned into an armed camp—complete with armored personnel carriers and military helicopters—violence was averted.

The huge turnout of pro-civil rights demonstrators saved face for the SCLC, but it merely played into the hands of those behind the propaganda campaign since the vast majority of the participants were not residents of Decatur. Mayor Dukes took care to point this out to the legion of journalists on hand. And when the reporters filed their stories from the special media center the mayor had set up on the top floor of City Hall—provisioned with coffee and doughnuts and staffed with a former beauty queen handing out promotional literature—their accounts conformed in key respects to the "official" version of events.

Had it not been for a phone call placed from Decatur to Montgomery several days later, the story might have ended there.

Chapter Two

THREE HOURS south of Decatur by car lies the city of Montgomery, the capital of Alabama. Located on the northern rim of the Black Belt, the strip of rich, black topsoil that stretches in a narrow band across the Deep South and was the heart of the region's old plantation economy, the city is known variously as the Cradle of the Confederacy or the Birthplace of the Modern Civil Rights Movement, depending upon your convictions.

In February 1861 the first Confederate Congress met there, and the city subsequently served as the Confederacy's first capital until the seat of the fledgling rebel government was relocated to Richmond later that year. The order to fire on Fort Sumter was sent from a telegraph office at the foot of Dexter Avenue, the city's main street.

Nearly a century later the opening salvo of the civil rights movement was fired only a block away when a black seamstress named Rosa Parks refused to give up her seat on a city bus to a white man. Although she was arrested for violating the city's segregation code, her quiet defiance of the Jim Crow system ignited a successful yearlong boycott of buses that galvanized blacks all across the South and catapulted the twenty-six-year-old Martin Luther King, Jr., to national prominence.

From the standpoint of symbolism alone, the Southern Poverty Law Center couldn't have been located in a more appropriate setting: Montgomery was the symbol of white repression and black self-liberation rolled into one.

Founded in 1971, the SPLC was a civil rights organization, although significantly different from the Southern Christian Leadership Conference, Dr. King's old organization, or the Student Nonviolent Coordinating Committee. The Center was a creature of the post-civil rights era. As its name suggested, it was an education and advocacy group as well as a law firm; its primary weapon, the lawsuit rather than the sit-in. And it was predominantly white. Its founders, Morris S. Dees, Jr., and Joseph J. Levin, Jr., were young white Montgomery lawyers who were politically liberal and concerned with social justice but had never marched or protested during the sixties. They shared a view of the law as a vehicle for social change, however, and a belief that the second phase of the struggle for equality in the South would have to be fought in the courtrooms.

Although in existence for less than a decade, the SPLC by 1979 had compiled an impressive track record. Lawsuits pressed by its attorneys had forced the Alabama Department of Public Safety to hire the first black state troopers in the agency's thirty-nine-year history, desegregated the quasi-public Montgomery YMCA, compelled the reapportionment of the Alabama legislature along one person–one vote lines, brought a halt to the involuntary sterilization of young black girls by a white Montgomery doctor, obtained better governmental services for poor black families in a number of Southern communities, and forced several communities to switch to district representation from at-large systems that discriminated against black candidates.

In addition, the Center had helped set up a law school at a mostly black Birmingham college to offset the effects of historically racist admissions practices at the University of Alabama School of Law. At the time, in the mid-1970s, there were only about fifty black attorneys to serve the needs of the state's one million black citizens.

By 1979 the SPLC had grown from a two-lawyer operation to a staff of five full-time attorneys and more than a dozen support personnel with an annual budget of about a million dollars. It was recognized as a leader in the struggle for civil rights and economic justice in the South.

The guiding force behind the organization was Morris Dees, a tall, curly-haired Southerner with a soft-spoken manner that masked a prodigious drive. Apart from his reputation as a civil rights lawyer, Dees, who was in his early forties, was already widely known in political circles as a national Democratic party activist. By virtue of an earlier career in specialty book publishing, he was also a millionaire several times over. In the conservative, old-money milieu of Montgomery, his accomplishments—and his sometimes flamboyant style—made him a high-profile figure, if not an especially popular one.

Born in 1936, Dees had grown up on a farm in rural Montgomery County, the eldest of five children. His youth was shaped by rural life in the Deep South: the regimen of daily chores, the camaraderie of a large, extended family, the vicissitudes of the price of cotton, and the complexity of black-white relations.

Early on he demonstrated the qualities of industry and ambition that were to characterize him as an adult. He began buying and raising his own livestock as part of a Future Farmers of America (FFA) project in junior high school. Before long, he had developed it into a major farming operation: 150 pigs, hundreds of chickens, and a small herd of brood cows. In his final year in senior high school he made a profit of ten thousand dollars—no small amount of money in those days—and was named Star Farmer of Alabama by the state chapter of the FFA. Yet despite the long hours he put in farming, he still managed to bring home mostly As.

Although Dees's father was a segregationist, he was a racial moderate by the standards of the time, and he taught his children to treat black people with respect and dignity. Little things—like his habit of drinking from the same cup of water as his black field hands—planted in the younger Dees the seeds of rebellion against what was euphemistically known as the Southern way of life.

One incident in particular left an impression on him. When Dees was in high school, a farmhand of his father's, Clarence Williams, was arrested and charged with drunk driving after he lost control of his car on a highway east of Montgomery. Although knocked senseless, Williams was stone sober when a state trooper happened along.

The trooper, finding Williams in a daze, assumed he had been drinking and took him into custody. When Williams remonstrated, he was cited for resisting arrest. Worried that he might lose his license, or worse, Williams confided his troubles to the young Dees, who volunteered to go before the justice of the peace (JP) and explain what had happened, confident he could intercede on his black friend's behalf and straighten things out.

Dees thought all he had to do was appear before the JP, vouch for Williams's reputation, and that would be the end of it. But he had discounted the fact that the trooper was white, too, and the JP got paid only if he found Williams guilty. At the end of a perfunctory trial in the incongruous setting of a country store where the JP held court, Williams was convicted on both charges and slapped with a heavy fine that took him months to pay off. The verdict profoundly affected Dees. (Years later he brought a suit that resulted in the abolition of the justice of the peace system.)

It was another racial incident that occurred soon after Dees had entered the University of Alabama that permanently altered his view of equality and justice, and that was the attempt of Autherine Lucy to enroll there. Lucy, a bright, attractive young woman from Birmingham, sought to become the first black student to attend the institution in the wake of the *Brown* v. *Board of Education* decision. Her matriculation one February day in 1956 touched off Klan-led riots on the Tuscaloosa campus, riots which Dees witnessed. It was the first time he had been confronted face-to-face with the raw reality of mob violence, and he was repulsed. The young woman's suspension and subsequent expulsion by university officials played on his growing sense of sympathy for the underdog.

It was while Dees was an undergraduate at Alabama that he initially made his mark in the business of direct-mail solicitation, the source of his future wealth. His start in the business came about by accident when his mother sent him a homemade cake his freshman year to mark his first birthday away from home. Touched by her thoughtfulness, Dees saw in her act of motherly love the potential to turn a profit. His idea was to approach the parents of his fellow freshmen and offer to do the same for their sons and daughters: to deliver a freshly baked birthday cake to each student on his or her special day.

Thus was Bama Cake Service born. Dees composed a form letter explaining the offer and sent out a test mailing to a sampling of parents, a quarter of whom wrote back with affirmative responses. In a field where a positive response of 1 percent constitutes success, Dees had demonstrated an uncanny ability to motivate people through the mail. In the course of his years at the university he subsequently realized a profit of several thousand dollars annually from the cakes, and he used the money from that and other equally enterprising ventures (a holly wreath business he and a partner ran one Christmas cleared ten thousand dollars) to pay his way through college and law school.

Although Dees was graduated from law school in 1960,* he did not join in the civil rights struggle right away. Married and with two toddlers to support, he was intent first on becoming financially secure, and upon his return to Montgomery he and Millard Fuller, a fellow law school graduate and his business partner, hung out their shingle and launched their legal careers under the name Dees & Fuller. Meanwhile, they continued to pursue business ventures through their direct-mail company, Fuller & Dees. Eventually Fuller & Dees, the more profitable enterprise, won out.

Dees's decision to put his legal career on hold came in 1962, after a schoolgirl walked into his law office selling cookbooks as part of a fund-raiser for the local chapter of the Future Homemakers of America (FHA). Dees happened to overhear the teenager making her sales pitch to his receptionist and strolled up to the lobby to have a glance at the book. As he leafed through it, he noticed that the recipes were from home economics teachers and that the volume was already in its second printing. Dees's mind raced ahead. If he gathered the recipes of home economics teachers from across the country, he could sell them to FHA chapters nationwide for use as a fund-raiser, and both parties would benefit.

The key was to find an editor and assemble an advisory board that would lend the project credibility. The logical choice was the editor of the original book, the director of the vocational home economics program for the Alabama Department of Education. Dees contacted her and brought her on board. Together, they as-

---

* Attending school year-round, he finished two years ahead of his class.

sembled an advisory panel of home economics supervisors from several states. Then Dees sent out a letter over his editor's signature to the head of the home economics department of every high school in the country, soliciting their favorite recipes. The cookbook was compiled, and in September 1962 Dees mailed a free copy of *Favorite Recipes of Home Economic Teachers of America* to the head of every FHA chapter in the United States. In the first year nearly half a million copies were sold. Soon Fuller & Dees was shipping five million cookbooks and other specialty publications a year. By 1966, the year Dees turned thirty, both he and Fuller had become millionaires. About that time Fuller had a religious experience, sold his share of the company to Dees, gave his money away to charity, and moved to Georgia, where he later founded Habitat for Humanity, a nonprofit organization that constructs and renovates housing for poor people around the world. A year or two later Dees sold out to the Times-Mirror Company, the parent corporation of the *Los Angeles Times*, for six million dollars, and turned his attention back to the law.*

In 1970 Dees met Joe Levin, a progressive lawyer a few years younger than himself, and they subsequently formed their own law firm, Levin & Dees. By some standards the two were unlikely partners: Dees the businessman and supersalesman with his Baptist roots in rural Montgomery County; Levin from a comfortable Jewish background in the city. The men quickly realized they would need outside funding to allow them to pursue the cases they wanted to handle, since most of their potential clients couldn't afford to pay them, and there were no provisions in federal law at the time for the awarding of attorneys' fees in civil rights cases. Out of this quandary the concept for the SPLC emerged, and Dees's direct-mail business background was the key to it. In establishing the Center, Dees used the same approach that had worked so well in selling the cookbook idea to the home economics teachers. To gain credibility with poten-

---

* Dees had previously found time to do some work for the American Civil Liberties Union (ACLU) on a volunteer basis. In one case he had represented a college student expelled for writing a school newspaper editorial critical of Governor George Wallace. He also had handled a suit on behalf of a black teachers' group opposing the construction of a branch campus of predominantly white Auburn University in Montgomery, since another state school, mostly black Alabama State University, was already in the city, and the new institution would serve only to promote continued segregation in higher education. He won the first suit but lost the second.

tial supporters, he asked Julian Bond, the Georgia state senator, to serve as its president, a largely honorary position, and pulled together an advisory council of civil rights era luminaries, including Fannie Lou Hamer, John Lewis, and Charles Evers. With a solid organization in place, he was ready to go to the public to ask for support.

The results of the test mailings were encouraging, but the big break for the SPLC came late in 1972. Dees, a vigorous opponent of the Vietnam War, had volunteered the previous year to raise funds for George McGovern's presidential bid and had become the campaign's chief fund-raiser. Although his candidate lost by a landslide, Dees helped raise an astounding twenty-four million dollars for him through the mail. It was the first time direct-mail solicitation had played such a major role in presidential politics, and Dees's success—one letter drew a 15 percent response—astounded the political fund-raisers of the old school.

Dees had worked without pay in the campaign, and once the election was over, he asked McGovern's permission to send a prospecting letter about the SPLC to the senator's more than six hundred thousand donors. McGovern's backers not only had sound liberal credentials but had shown a willingness to support their cause financially, and Dees believed many of them would respond to the SCLC appeal. McGovern consented, the mailing was sent out, and the senator's contributors came to make up the Law Center's initial donor base.

Of all the cases the Center was associated with during its early years, the best known was that of Joanne Little, the twenty-one-year-old North Carolina black woman who was charged with capital murder in 1974, after she had stabbed a jailer to death with the ice pick he had used to force himself on her. After the incident, convinced the white authorities would never believe the circumstances that led to the killing, she fled the empty jail. Although she reconsidered and surrendered a few days later, the prosecutor brought murder charges against her and announced his intention to seek the death penalty.

Dees read about the case in the *New York Times* and contacted Little's local counsel to offer the Center's assistance with her defense, joining several other attorneys who had already volunteered to help. The SPLC funded a massive defense effort on Little's behalf, and the case became a liberal cause célèbre. She was acquitted in a controversial, highly publicized trial in 1975. Ironically, Dees watched most of the proceeding from the sidelines, having been tossed out of the case by the presiding judge. His ejection came after a crucial defense witness, who had given him a prior statement, changed her testimony on the stand. When Dees tried to persuade her to retake the stand and testify to what she had originally told him, she accused him of suborning perjury. Dees was absent from the counsel table for the remainder of the trial but stayed in touch with the defense team by phone.*

As the Center's reputation grew, so did Dees's. In 1976 his stock in the national Democratic party shot up some more when he raised millions of dollars through the mail for Jimmy Carter, then an unknown Georgia governor running for the White House. But while Dees's precedent-setting lawsuits and direct-mail prowess won him widespread acclaim in the nation's legal community and among political activists and liberals, they won nothing but animosity for him at home. In a 1975 article *Time* magazine called him the "second most hated man in Alabama," runner-up to a Montgomery federal judge whose pro-civil rights decisions during the 1960s had earned him ostracism and death threats. Dees's life had never been threatened—yet—but he was reviled for essentially the same reasons as the judge: He was viewed by many Alabamians as a "nigger lover."

When the telephone rang at Rolling Hills Ranch a few weeks after the Decatur incident, Dees was just sitting down to dinner. At forty-two he still had a youthful air. Tall, athletic-looking, with sandy-colored hair, he could have passed for several years younger. Although a workaholic, he still took time out for regular exercise, and he prided himself on eating well and keeping fit. For Dees, the two activities—work and physical fitness—were two sides of the same coin; each held out the hope for a little bit of immortality.

Dees's home was large but not ostentatious, a low, rambling ranch

---

* In fact, Dees was arrested for suborning perjury, but the charge was dropped after he obtained an affidavit from a law enforcement officer who had been privy to his conversation with the witness and who confirmed Dees's version of the events. Despite the dismissal of the charge, the judge refused to permit Dees back in the case.

house set on a knoll in the middle of a huge estate a half hour's drive south of town. An avid tennis player, he had had a fenced-in court built at the edge of a cow pasture out back and, of course, a swimming pool for the sweltering summer afternoons that often stretched (despite what the calendar might say) from mid-May to mid-October.

The phone call was from Clint Brown, the director of the federal government's Legal Services office in Decatur. Dees and Brown had known each other for several years and had worked together on some civil rights cases when Brown, who was in his mid-thirties, had been in private practice in Mobile. Although their relationship had at times been stormy, they respected each other's abilities.

Brown wasted no time in getting to the point. He wanted to know if Dees would be interested in representing Curtis Robinson, the City Hall maintenance man charged in the shooting of Klansman David Kelso. Robinson had come to Brown's office that afternoon looking for legal help, not knowing that the agency's guidelines prohibited Legal Services lawyers from handling criminal cases. The criminal defense attorney in Brown had wanted to hear him out, and once he had, he was convinced that Robinson had acted in self-defense and promised to find him a good lawyer.

Dees was hesitant. The Law Center's small legal staff already had more work than it could handle, and he knew there were plenty of good attorneys around, black and white, who would be willing to take the case; in that respect, the South had changed greatly since the civil rights era. He hedged.

At that point, Brown did the only thing he knew to do: He handed the phone to Robinson, who was seated across the desk from him. Though momentarily startled, Robinson took the receiver, introduced himself, and launched into an impassioned plea for help. He obviously struck a responsive chord because when he finished, Dees consented to go to Decatur to look into the case.

At the time, June 1979, I was the Law Center's only paralegal, and a fairly green one at that. Despite my inexperience, Dees asked me to accompany SPLC Legal Director John Carroll and himself on the trip. Should they decide to represent Robinson, as seemed likely, they would need someone to do the pretrial legwork in the case: finding and interviewing witnesses; filing court documents; tending to the many details that go into forming the foundation for a successful trial.

A few days later, the three of us met at the Law Center at about 7:00 A.M. and were soon on the road, sweeping north along Interstate 65 in Dees's peach-colored Mercedes. It was a solid three-hour drive to Decatur, and Dees had told Brown to expect us before noon. We pulled into town early and drove straight to the Legal Services office. Robinson, who was getting off work to meet us, had not yet arrived.

We took advantage of his absence to learn more from Brown about the case. Summarizing for us what Robinson had told him, Brown went on to fill in some context on the Hines protests. Although there had been statewide news coverage of the events, we were not particularly familiar with the details of the yearlong conflict that had led up to the May 26 incident.

Brown's first piece of advice was to get the case out of the county. He noted that the community was deeply polarized along racial lines, and he believed Robinson could not get a fair trial there, especially in light of the resentment many whites felt over the negative publicity the confrontation had generated nationally. He had harsh words for Decatur's white leadership: The politicians who apparently had been afraid to speak out against the Klan for fear of alienating white voters, the business and civic leaders—including the all-important religious community—who had all but buried their heads in the sand, hoping the controversy would go away. In Brown's view, much of the responsibility for the violence could be attributed to their collective failure to take a firm stand against the KKK.

Brown had also collected some newspaper clippings for us about the incident, and he gave these to us. Scanning them, we learned just how close Decatur had flirted with real tragedy; as it turned out, there could easily have been four fatalities. The bullet that hit Kelso, for instance, had lodged only centimeters away from his heart—the difference between attempted murder and murder charges for Robinson. By the same token, both blacks wounded in the gunfire also had had close calls. Bernice Brown, a young woman in her twenties, had been struck by a bullet that entered and exited her mouth and left her with a lisp, and Larry Smith, thirty years old, had been hit in the temple. Evelyn Lowery, the SCLC president's wife, had narrowly escaped injury herself, or worse, when a bullet pierced the windshield of her automobile right at the level of her head. She had been following the marchers to help transport them back to the church after the rally at the courthouse.

Buried at the very bottom of one of the articles was a paragraph in which the reporter mentioned overhearing Ray Steele, the Decatur titan, make a reference at the pumps to the KKK's plan to block the march—important information that seemed to suggest that the Klan had provoked the incident.

When Robinson and his wife, Eva, arrived, our conference with Brown broke up, and we emerged from his office to meet with them. For someone nearing fifty, Robinson looked remarkably fit— slightly under six feet tall, still trim around the middle, with a youthful face. He was an extremely outgoing person and made an all-around good first impression. It was difficult to believe he was guilty of assault with intent to murder. Brown showed Dees and Carroll into a large conference room at the back of the office; for nearly an hour they huddled with the Robinsons to hear their story firsthand. When the four of them came out, Dees was very upbeat, and I sensed we had a new client. "Anywhere else but the South," Dees said later, "Robinson would be pressing charges rather than having to defend against them."

From the account Robinson had given, it sounded as if his arrest was a classic case of having been in the wrong place at the wrong time. Saturday, May 26, had been the start of the long Memorial Day weekend, and Robinson and his wife had planned a family outing for themselves and their five young children on the Tennessee River. The Robinsons were relatively poor, but Curtis had indulged himself the luxury of a small secondhand motorboat, and he liked to take his family for rides in it during the warm months. He had christened it the *Red Goose*, the nickname by which he was widely known around town.

Before going down to the river that day, however, Robinson had to take care of a chore at City Hall. As foreman he had to check the boilers on weekends to make certain the air-conditioning system was operating properly. Rather than put off the task until he returned from the outing, he decided to take care of it beforehand.

With the kids in the backseat and his wife in front, Robinson and his family headed downtown in their car sometime after noon. On the way there they happened upon the marchers. Captivated with the spectacle of the demonstration, Robinson's children begged their father to join in behind the procession; he did so, unaware that dozens of armed Klansmen were waiting along the parade route only a few blocks from the courthouse.

He never fully appreciated the seriousness of the situation until it was too late, he said. By the time the march reached the intersection of Bank and Lee streets, it was impossible for him to turn around—what with several other cars behind him—and soon afterward the KKK attacked. His car was quickly engulfed by hooded figures, and one Klansman reached through the window and began to assault him. In the backseat the children wailed in fear. Amid the chaos Robinson tried to fend off the blows while grabbing his pistol from the console between the seats, but the Klansman succeeded nevertheless in dragging him out of the car. At that point, Robinson said, he yelled to his wife to get the children to safety, and as he landed on the pavement, the gun accidentally discharged. Eva Robinson slid behind the wheel and sped away with Klansmen pounding on the car from all sides with their clubs.

As the pistol went off, a full-scale gun battle broke out in the intersection, and Robinson began running up Bank Street, fleeing for his life alongside the other marchers. He ran so hard that he lost the house slippers he had been wearing. Eventually, a motorist recognized him and gave him a lift back to the black section of town, where he soon found his family, terrified, but otherwise unhurt. His car was quite another matter, though. One of the tires had been shot out, and a headlight was broken. In addition, the hood was dented in several places where the Klansmen had struck it with their clubs.

Robinson was upset, and the next day he called the police to report the incident. The police department was located in City Hall, and Robinson knew one of the detectives by name, so he asked to speak to him. But the officer was preoccupied with the investigation and was unable to make time to see him. On Monday, May 28, however, that same officer came to Robinson's house in the evening and placed him under arrest.

Dees, Carroll, and I talked further with Brown and then headed back to Montgomery. There was no shortage of irony in all this. A

year earlier Dees had been approached about the SPLC's representing Tommy Lee Hines. At that time he had said no—for many of
the same reasons he had enumerated on the phone to Clint Brown.
Now here we were about to become immersed in the Hines affair
after all, for the Robinson case was merely an extension of it.

On the way home Dees began drawing up a list of things to do. He
wanted an aerial photograph of the Bank-Lee intersection; the
names of the marchers, the Klansmen, and the police; newspaper
clippings; ballistics reports; photographs. It was obviously going to
be a no-holds-barred investigation—the kind Dees was known for.

After notifying the court of his appearance in the case as the
attorney of record, Dees immediately filed a request for a preliminary hearing. Under Alabama law, a person arrested for a crime but
not yet indicted by a grand jury has the right to ask for such a
hearing for the purpose of learning the facts about the charges
facing him and to confront the state's witnesses. If utilized, it can be
an important defense tool because the accused (or his attorney) has
the right to question the state's witnesses but is under no burden to
put any of his own on the stand. And if the state fails to make its
case, the judge presiding over the hearing may dismiss the charge.
The state is, therefore, under considerable pressure to reveal its key
evidence.

This, then, became our immediate priority: to identify as many
potential state witnesses as possible and subpoena them for the
preliminary hearing so we could find out what their testimony was
going to be. Time was growing short, however; the hearing was
scheduled for July 27, and it was already the middle of June.

I did a quick turnaround in Montgomery, returning long enough
only to put my office in order, confer with Dees, and gather up some
clothes. Within a day or so I headed back to Decatur. It was dark by
the time I got there, and as soon as I crossed over the river bridge
into town, I felt a keen awareness of being alone. I stopped at a
traffic light just beyond the bridge and thought I caught the driver
in the next car stealing a glance at my Montgomery license plate. I
drove across the street to a motel and passed a policeman heading in
the other direction. Had he been sent to conduct surveillance on
me? I pulled up in front of the motel and went in to register. Was the
motel clerk the wife of a Klansman? A secret sympathizer? Would
she notice the SPLC credit card I used?

For the first time I began to understand on a personal level the dynamics of fear that had enabled the Klan to wield influence out of all proportion to its numbers over the years. In town less than ten minutes, I was already beginning to look over my shoulder.

After checking into the motel, I sought to reassure myself. This was 1979, not 1963. Civil rights laws had been passed; a Southerner had won the White House largely on the strength of black votes; men had landed on the moon; the Mets had won the World Series. I climbed the stairs to my room. As I shut the door behind me, the telephone rang. It startled me since I hadn't mentioned to anyone, not even Dees, where I would be spending the night. As I walked over to the bedside table, it occurred to me that it was probably the motel clerk. I picked up the receiver. The only sound was a dial tone.

A rational voice inside me counseled that the phone call was a coincidence, nothing more than a wrong number, and I tried to laugh it off; but a second, suspicious voice pointed up the magnitude of the coincidence. Looking for a diversion, I turned on the television and watched it for a while. Time passed, and nothing else happened, so I finally went to bed. Still, I slept fitfully, and as I lay there, exasperated with myself, I tried to use the time productively by directing my thoughts to the work that lay ahead. Morning eventually came.

According to the instructions I had received from Dees, my first order of business was to identify every person who had witnessed the May 26 attack or played a part in it. That alone could have kept a small army of investigators busy for months. Figures I had seen in the newspapers suggested that the number of potential witnesses was at least two hundred: a hundred Klansmen, sixty marchers, fifty lawmen—plus a dozen or so reporters and photographers.

Had it not been for the excellent photographic record of the event, our efforts might have been doomed from the start. But in the 114 years of Ku Klux Klan history there had probably never been an incident of Klan violence so thoroughly documented on film.

Among the press on hand that day had been three TV crews from Huntsville, the nearest major city, and reporter-photographers from four area newspapers, plus two free-lance photographers. In all, they had taken some two hundred fifty still photographs and several hours of videotape. This mound of images was going to be crucial to our task of identifying the potential witnesses for the state and was very likely to hold the key to Robinson's defense as well.

One by one I began contacting the photographers and meeting with them to look at their pictures. They were a friendly enough group, but the more of them I talked with, the more I began to fear for our case.

From the outset it was apparent that they shared the view of the white community at large that the marchers were at least as responsible as the Klan for the May 26 violence. At one end of the spectrum were those who believed the protesters had brought the attack upon themselves by marching into the face of a Klan mob. Then there were those who thought the marchers bore responsibility for firing the first shot. At least one of the photographers went so far as to suggest that the SCLC had wanted a confrontation with the KKK in order to rejuvenate the Hines protests.*

It was not that the photographers were pro-Klan. They viewed themselves as fair-minded people and objective journalists. They simply reflected, unwittingly, I think, the double standard that existed among whites in Decatur. The Klan could arm itself with ax handles, tire tools, and baseball bats, plant itself in the middle of the street, and attack the police for trying to make way for the demonstrators to pass, yet the marchers were still somehow to blame—first for having exercised their constitutional rights and then for defending themselves when the police proved incapable of doing it.

As for the matter of identifications, the photographers turned out to be of surprisingly little help. While most of them seemed to know the identities of the KKK leaders, very few knew any rank-and-file members by name. As a rule, they had dealt only with the Klan higher-ups, apparently because KKK leaders had wanted it that way.

One self-styled journalist—an offbeat free-lance photographer named Garry Nungester—seemed more informed about the Klan than the rest of the group. Nungester looked like a sixties icon, with thinning, shoulder-length hair and a big, black, bushy beard that half obscured his face. He chain-smoked and wore faded jeans and T-shirts and drove around in a big, blue, gas-guzzling Buick Electra, circa 1970. A member of a prominent Decatur family, he was kind

* During the sixties it was a common refrain among white Southerners that civil rights leaders provoked violence in order to come across as victims.

of the town's resident hippie, apparently—a veteran of the anti-war movement who had dropped out of Tulane to live the countercul- ture life. Until fairly recently he had traveled the Southern arts-and- crafts circuit with his wife, selling handmade jewelry. Shortly after the Hines affair began he had started attending the various protests and demonstrations, taking photographs, and he had become an expert on all aspects of the controversy, particularly the KKK. Clint Brown had cautioned us about him, saying he might be playing both ends against the middle in the confrontation between the Klan and the SCLC, for he seemed to have excellent contacts on both sides of the dispute.

The day of our first meeting he had come sauntering into the law office out of which I was working wearing a weathered old T-shirt with the words *National Democratic Party of Alabama* (NDPA) embla- zoned across the front. If he had worn the shirt with the idea of ingratiating himself with us, he had selected a clever one, to be sure. The NDPA was a mostly black faction of the state Democratic party that had been formed in the 1960s as an alternative to the segre- gated regular Democratic party controlled by George Wallace. Nungester said he had been one of its few white supporters in the Decatur area.

Despite Brown's misgivings, and a few of my own, I began to try to cultivate Nungester as a source. I didn't appear to have much choice; my independent efforts to identify the Klansmen in the May 26 pictures were producing discouraging results.

A few days after that first meeting, Nungester phoned to inform me he had printed up the photos I had ordered from him, and I went over to his home to pick them up. He lived with his wife in a weather-beaten little house on the south side of town, with a hand- some black Labrador retriever named Jomo (after Jomo Kenyatta, the founder of modern-day Kenya). His office, a makeshift affair, was filled with pictures and other memorabilia from his activist days, along with albums and albums of negatives and proof sheets from what appeared to be a substantial file on the KKK.

I asked him to thumb through the photographs with me and see how many people he could identify. He consented, professing to be sympathetic toward us, but I was dismayed by the results. He recog- nized only eight or ten Klansmen in all—a small number, it seemed, for someone who had been following the Klan for a year. I sensed he might be holding back so I pressed him further, but to no avail. When I tried to probe about his work, he deflected most of my questions. He was an enigma.

In the weeks that followed, I met with him several additional times to go over the May 26 photos again or to examine new ones he had taken at subsequent Klan functions. But my best efforts to mine him for information continued to be futile. He told me what he wanted to and nothing more: an identification here, some bit of information there, all helpful tidbits, to be sure. It was frustrating, but he was the best source I had, and I figured as long as I watched what I said around him there was no harm staying in touch. (Once, in what I surmised was an effort to remind me to be security-conscious, he pulled out a photo from a KKK rally showing two top-ranking Klan leaders with their arms around a courthouse switchboard operator.)

In the meantime, I went on to the next item on my checklist: seeking the help of the two top law enforcement officers in the community, Police Chief Pack Self and Sheriff Van Ward. This was not as naive a notion as it might seem. By the late 1970s sympathy for the Klan seemed to be on the wane among white Southern lawmen, and it was rare to hear of a law enforcement officer who actually belonged to the Klan or some other organized white supremacist group. Stricter hiring standards and improved pay had resulted in the attraction of higher-caliber recruits to Southern police forces, especially in the larger cities of the region, and attrition had removed many of the bigots of the civil rights era. Furthermore, the integration of many police agencies had made it more difficult for the KKK to operate inside them as it once had. In light of changed public attitudes and black political empowerment, membership in the Klan had become an extremely risky proposition for anyone in law enforcement. Consequently, Klan conspiracies such as the one involving the Goodman-Chaney-Schwerner murders, which had been carried out with the assistance of personnel from the Neshoba County, Mississippi, Sheriff's Department, had seemingly become a thing of the past.

That is not to say that Southern law enforcement was prejudice-free. In some of the smaller departments around the region and in isolated instances elsewhere, the relationship between the police and the KKK was still pretty cozy. But in general, the situation was far better than it had been just a decade earlier.

I had another reason to call on these particular police officials, though. It seemed logical that after all the embarrassment the Klan had caused them, the chief and the sheriff might be fed up with the Klan. Since Chief Self had been in charge of providing security for the march and the failure to provide adequate protection was clearly his responsibility, I had decided to pay him a visit first. It took only a few minutes to find out how off base my logic was. Self not only refused to identify any of the Kluxers in our photos but even refused to identify his own men. It was a painfully brief meeting. I was dismayed, and I wondered if my failure had been the result of the way I had asked; but I went across the street to the courthouse to see Sheriff Ward and got the same answer. So much for Decatur's finest.

I was making limited progress on another front, however, thanks largely to Robinson. Although he was not a member of the SCLC and had not participated in any of the numerous pro-Hines demonstrations, he knew many of those who had, and he helped me identify them.

But when I began to contact some of the marchers, I encountered lukewarm reactions: Some seemed reluctant to cooperate; others failed to keep appointments or return phone calls. Being white, and a Southerner to boot, I detected in them an underlying skepticism and mistrust toward me. It wasn't hard to figure out why, considering the racially polarized atmosphere in the community, but I didn't know exactly what to do about it.

By this time the SCLC had pulled its controversial organizer, Reverend R. B. Cottonreader, out of town, and in his absence there was no one who could dispel the misgivings that some of the marchers felt toward us. That basically left it up to Robinson, who interceded on my behalf and occasionally took time off from work to accompany me to some of the interviews. He urged people to cooperate with us, and once it became clear that we intended to put on an aggressive defense, we got all the assistance we needed. The catch was, everything had happened so rapidly at the corner of Bank and Lee that the marchers were unable to provide a very detailed account of the sequence of events.

The better I got to know Robinson, the more ironic his situation seemed. Here, apparently, was the consummate family man—happiest when he was at home with his wife and kids, widely liked for his easygoing ways, politically uninvolved—on his way to a holiday outing when circumstances conspired to overtake him, sucking him into a whirlpool of controversy. That the controversy was racial in nature compounded the irony because Robinson strove hard to bridge the gap between whites and blacks, if on a personal rather than a political level. Extremely outgoing, he worked to create good relationships with his fellow white employees and was on speaking terms with Mayor Dukes. Beyond that, he went out of his way to initiate friendships with whites in the community at large, something few black Southerners of his generation felt comfortable doing. His best friend was a white man, and the two of them frequently visited each other's homes. Those kinds of social contacts were rare in Decatur, just as they were in many other Southern communities—and beyond. But Robinson, who had migrated to Cleveland as a young man before returning home to Decatur about 1970, had seen the world beyond Alabama, a fact that accounted, perhaps, for his greater social assertiveness.

About a week into the investigation Dees came to Decatur to try to persuade the district attorney to drop the charge against Robinson or at least permit him to plead guilty to a less serious offense, such as violating the parade ordinance banning weapons at public demonstrations. (Ironically, Robinson was licensed to have the pistol, which he had begun carrying for protection the previous year, when the Klan was holding daily demonstrations at City Hall.) Although the chances for success were slim, Dees was heartened by the fact that Robinson had been allowed to remain on the job despite the seriousness of the charge against him, and he took it as a sign that the authorities might be flexible about settling the case. He decided to take Robinson with him, in the hope that his client's presence might sway the prosecutor's mind.

What made Dees's task particularly formidable, however, were certain racial realities of Alabama politics. Curtis Robinson was a black man who, in the eyes of the white voting public, was charged with trying to kill a white man during a protest on behalf of a black rapist. In a county where whites outnumbered blacks by more than six to one and where less than fifty years earlier lynch mobs had formed to mete out vigilante justice to the Scottsboro "boys," it didn't take a political scientist or a statistician to figure out what course of action was the most politically expedient for the DA to take.

The district attorney for Morgan County was Mike Moebes, a stocky middle-aged man with large jowls and a sandy-colored toupee. He was an aggressive, hard-nosed prosecutor, but his handling of the Hines case had raised serious questions about his fairness.

On the morning of the settlement conference, Dees met Robinson across from the courthouse. Dees's plan was to open the discussion, then make way forRobinson to tell Moebes, in his own words, the sequence of events that led to the discharge of the pistol.

Dees intentionally had not made an appointment, on the theory that it would have been too easy for Moebes to reject an overture over the telephone and that catching the district attorney cold could possibly work to Robinson's advantage. Fortunately Moebes was in his office that day. When he came out to greet his visitors, Dees introduced himself and his client.

Moebes agreed to meet with them and waved them into his office, but before going any further, he sent for Sergeant Kenneth Collier, the detective heading the Decatur Police Department's investigation of the incident. A veteran of nearly ten years on the force, Collier had been one of five officers injured by the Klan on May 26, suffering a broken finger while attempting to place a member of the Klan under arrest.

At Dees's urging, Robinson repeated his story, beginning with the fact that he was headed to City Hall to check on the boilers and concluding with his phone call to the police department on May 27 to report the incident. It was Detective Collier whom Robinson had phoned because he knew the officer through their contact at work and liked him.

When Robinson finished, Dees turned to Moebes and said, "Now, Mike, this just isn't a murder case. Maybe he'll plead guilty to a misdemeanor, but not assault with intent to murder."

Moebes, seated at his desk, looked from Robinson over to Dees and replied, half smiling, "Morris, do you really believe what Curtis said?"

"Well, I haven't got any reason not to believe him."

"Collier," Moebes said, "show him your photographs."

At that point Collier opened a manila envelope he had been holding in his lap. As the detective laid out several pictures across the desk—pictures we had on order from the same photographers but had yet to acquire—Dees got a sinking feeling.

One photo revealed Robinson standing outside his car in a crowd of demonstrators immediately prior to the KKK attack. The picture made it abundantly clear that Robinson had gotten out of his car of his own free will before the clash. A series of four other photographs depicted the scene of the shooting. There were no signs of the Klansman Robinson claimed to have scuffled with. He was standing almost all alone, at least twenty feet from David Kelso, the fallen exalted cyclops. The evidence we had been counting on to prove our case suggested instead that our client was a liar.

Next, Moebes instructed Collier to give Dees a document from his file. It was an incident report by Officer Marlon Owens, a fourteen-year veteran of the Decatur Police Department. The report began by describing his assignment to protect the marchers on May 26. In carrying out his duties, Owens had written, he stationed himself in the parking lot of an abandoned gas station on Bank Street to monitor the demonstration as it came down the hill. After a few minutes the marchers passed in front of him, singing and chanting slogans of support for Hines. Trailing the march were several automobiles; one was driven by Robinson, whom Owens recognized as a worker at City Hall.

As Robinson drove by, the two exchanged greetings. Then, according to Owens's report, Robinson held up a pistol, waved it, and said, "I'm gonna get me a couple of 'em today."

At that point Owens responded, "Red Goose, you better get your butt back home. There's gonna be trouble!"

Stunned, Dees handed the statement back.

"That's the facts, Morris," Moebes said. "We're goin' for assault with intent to murder."

The settlement conference was over.

Chapter Three

Dees was not only stunned but furious as he and Robinson left Moebes's office. There wasn't much Robinson could say. He admitted the obvious—that he had lied about being dragged from his car—but he continued to insist that he had acted in self-defense, and he vehemently denied making the statement attributed to him by Officer Owens. In so many words, Robinson said he had panicked at being placed under arrest, perceiving himself to be the victim in the matter, and that he had decided on the way down to the police station to embellish his account of the incident in order to cast himself in the most favorable light. The only major change he made in his story was to say that he had gotten out of his car as the march came to a halt to see what the commotion was. Minutes later, he asserted, the Klan had broken through the police lines, and when a wave of Kluxers rushed toward him with clubs raised, he pulled his pistol from his pocket and fired—in defense of himself, his family, and the other blacks standing around him.

Dees was understandably a little skeptical, but he accepted Robinson's explanation. From what he knew of the mistrust and fear many blacks still felt toward white law enforcement officers, it was entirely plausible. Furthermore, Robinson had an excellent reputation in the community, had never participated in a previous demonstration, and had only become involved in the May 26 one inadvertently. But if there was one overriding reason that Dees continued to believe in his client, it was the presence of Robinson's family in the car, directly in the line of fire. A man normally doesn't go looking for trouble with his wife and five kids in the car.

Yet Dees was troubled by Sergeant Owens's statement. What motive did the officer have to lie? Dees didn't know, but one thing was certain: Whether Robinson had made the remark or not was now almost immaterial, because Moebes would put Owens on the stand to say he had, and the Alabama jury that would take the word of a black maintenance man over a veteran white police officer would be hard indeed to find. All in all, it had been a disastrous turn of events. The single consolation for Dees was that Moebes had shown his hand.

As a practical matter, the effect of the settlement conference was to heighten the significance of the photographs and videotape. If Robinson had acted in self-defense, there had to be proof somewhere in the pictures, and we had to find it. But as the photos continued to come in, we looked for it in vain, although I did locate one with Robinson's house slippers in it, abandoned a few feet away from his car. At best the pictures illustrated the KKK attack on the police and the efforts of the lawmen to clear a path for the marchers. There were only a handful of photos depicting physical interaction between Klansmen and the protesters, and these showed nothing conclusive. If Robinson was to be believed, the photographers, at least the still photographers, had missed a key sequence of events.

The videotapes posed a problem of a different sort. The television stations wouldn't let us have them without a subpoena, although they did at least permit me to view them. But in the short time I had to examine them one afternoon, I was able to learn little.

There was so much to do during those weeks prior to the preliminary hearing that I practically took up residence in Decatur. I lived out of a motel and worked out of a local attorney's office but spent little time in either place. Usually I was out interviewing witnesses, or trying to identify them, or simply trying to find them. Those I couldn't see during the day I arranged to meet in the evening. The days simply weren't long enough for me to accomplish the things I needed to accomplish.

As I went about my business, I repeatedly crossed the trail of a team of FBI agents sent to Decatur by Attorney General Griffin Bell to determine if the KKK's actions on May 26 had violated any federal laws. A special set of laws known as the Ku Klux Klan Acts, passed by the Reconstruction Congress, made it illegal for anyone to conspire with another person to deny an individual his or her civil rights on account of race. The statutes had been enacted in response to a wave of Klan terror that swept the South following the group's founding shortly after the Civil War. A century later the Justice Department had used those same laws to break the back of the 1960s Klan.

Much was riding on the FBI's investigation, for the civil rights cause in general and for Curtis Robinson in particular. If the agents found evidence of a conspiracy, the federal government would probably have legal jurisdiction to conduct a criminal prosecution against any Klansmen involved; if not, jurisdiction would remain in the hands of state and local authorities, where it had been all along.

The FBI investigation had ramifications for us as well because if it uncovered evidence that the Klan had engaged in a conspiracy to block or attack the march, our job of convincing a jury that Robinson had acted in self-defense would be made considerably easier.

The KKK was still going strong all over northern Alabama, although true to its name, the "Invisible Empire" was nowhere to be seen in Decatur except when it wanted. So far as I knew, I had yet to see a Klansman in the flesh. But nearly every weekend there was a rally or some other Klan function somewhere within a ninety-mile radius of the town. One weekend in late June, while I was out of town, several hundred Kluxers and their sympathizers gathered in a field on the outskirts of Decatur for a nighttime rally and cross burning. According to the *Decatur Daily*, the cross was sixty-six feet tall. The story about the rally also told of a special ceremony conducted that night by members of the KKK Youth Corps, a sort of junior Klan for teens. In a protest meant to symbolize the Klan's opposition to mandatory school busing, several of the young Klansmen in training had set fire to an old yellow school bus the adult members had obtained for the occasion.

On July 7 I attended my first Klan rally. The site was just over the border in southern Tennessee, near a small community called Estill Springs, not far from the famous Jack Daniel's distillery. There had been rallies closer to Decatur, but I was worried about being recognized and thought I would be safer the farther from Decatur the rally was held. (Later I learned that my logic didn't necessarily follow, that Klansmen frequently drove a hundred or two hundred miles to attend Klan functions.) I went alone, but with the belief that Garry Nungester would be there (he attended most Klan functions in the area), and that gave me an added sense of security.

By the time I arrived at the rally site, a large open field, it was already dusk, and the meeting was getting under way. There had been no mistaking it for anything else as I drove up: the towering cross, unburned, standing in a darkened corner of the field; the robed, hooded figures walking about or standing in groups of twos and threes; the flatbed truck draped with Confederate flags; the whole scene bathed in the dim light of a dozen or two generator-powered light bulbs hanging from a wire strung above the truck bed. The scene was real, but it looked like so much historical film footage to me. I couldn't believe my eyes.

Lawmen were everywhere, and I don't think I was ever so glad to see them as then. Although they were on hand principally for traffic control, I viewed them as my refuge of last resort, in case I got into a jam of some sort.

I found my way to a parking place and got out of the car, leaving my wallet behind since it had my driver's license and SPLC credit card in it. I felt extremely self-conscious. For fear I wouldn't look the part of a Klan sympathizer, I had bought a plain baseball cap and dressed down as much as possible, but I didn't feel convincing in the role I had chosen to play.

There must have been 200 or 250 people in attendance—not a large crowd by Decatur standards, where rallies the previous summer had drawn throngs in the thousands, but the Klan was just then gaining a foothold in Tennessee. Fifty of the people were dressed in the traditional robes and cone-shaped hoods. In another setting they might have looked like buffoons, but in their own element, under a dark Southern sky, they looked sinister enough to give anyone pause. Only their faces were exposed. In Tennessee, as in most other Southern states, it was illegal for Klansmen to wear their masks in public; the local sheriff, interpreting the law liberally, had apparently adopted the view that this indeed was a public rally, even if it was being held on private property.

Other members of the crowd wore Klan T-shirts. These were light blue with dark blue trim around the collar and sleeves, with the figure of a hooded horseman and the words *Invisible Empire, Knights of the Ku Klux Klan* on the front.

The crowd looked predominantly lower- to lower-middle-class—gone were the days, apparently, when the Klan could draw from the ranks of professionals. There were people of every age-group, including tots in the company of their parents, but the average age of the adults was about thirty-five. My attention was drawn immediately to the number of children there, and I suddenly began to understand the staying power of the KKK and how it was transmitted from one generation to another, like some hereditary disease. The kids of Klan members, it seemed, hardly had a chance to grow up into anything but bigots.

What impressed me most about the people I saw, though, was how very ordinary they looked. They were mothers and fathers, truck drivers and waitresses, construction workers, store clerks, and housewives. For the most part, they didn't look like evil people. Some had a beaten-down appearance about them; others looked hard. But a surprising number seemed friendly. Among this latter group there was an element of socializing, and it was clear to me that whatever else the rally was, for some it was partly a social occasion.

The first speaker was introduced as an eighty-three-year-old former radio evangelist and chaplain of the Huntsville klavern, Reverend J. M. Drummond. A Klansman of fifty years, Drummond was from the fire-and-brimstone wing of fundamentalist Christianity but with an unabashedly racist twist: His God was a God for whites only. For blacks and Jews he had nothing but utter contempt. In Drummond's hierarchy blacks were an inferior race, but Jews were the real enemies because he believed they were engaged in a plot to rule the world and subjugate or destroy white Christian culture in the process. Blacks and other people of color were just their pawns in this cosmic conspiracy.

Drummond saved his most vitriolic denunciations for those he called "white niggers"—the white judges, lawyers, social workers, ministers, reporters, and other "liberals" who supported the civil rights agenda and who, according to his worldview, were playing into the hands of the Jews. He described them as racial traitors. Drummond's bizarre theology, which included the view that Jews were the descendants of Satan, also encompassed the belief that there was a Ku Klux Klan in heaven, and he cited Scripture to corroborate his views. The ironic thing about his tirade against the Jews was that most members of the crowd had probably never knowingly met a Jew in their lives.

However much the crowd understood of Drummond's speech, it cheered him on enthusiastically, particularly the references to blacks and "white niggers," which caused me some unease. On one level I felt pity for the poor, uneducated mechanic or construction worker who bought in to Drummond's cosmology, but it didn't take much imagination to see one of the spectators going off and acting out the hatred embodied in Drummond's rhetoric against the first black person he came across.

On this clear, comfortable summer evening, however, Drummond was only the stage setter for a young Louisianan named Bill Wilkinson, the imperial wizard, or national leader, of the Invisible Empire, Knights of the Ku Klux Klan (IEKKKK), one of three national Klan groups then operating in the country.*

The thirty-six-year-old Wilkinson was the rising star of the Klan, a new generation of KKK leader who had been only coming of age during the pitched battles of the civil rights era. Smoother and more sophisticated than his predecessors of that period, he combined the qualities of the classic good old boy with those of a populist politician and a savvy PR man. The end product was a slick but personable spokesman for white supremacy—and an increasing level of racial unrest throughout the South.

Spurred by what he said were concerns for the future of his two young sons, Wilkinson had joined the KKK in 1974 in his home town of Denham Springs, Louisiana, where he worked for a cement manufacturer and ran an electrical contracting business on the side.

---

* The contemporary Klan was comprised of three major factions and a score or more splinter groups operating on a very localized basis. The main factions were the United Klans of America, established in 1961, the oldest and believed to be the largest of the three, with perhaps four thousand members; the Knights of the Ku Klux Klan, founded in the early seventies, with roughly two thousand members; and the Invisible Empire, Knights of the KKK, which was organized in 1975, when Wilkinson split off from the Knights and started his own group. In 1979 it had an estimated twenty-five hundred to three thousand members. The UKA was headquartered near Tuscaloosa, Alabama. The other two factions were based in Louisiana.

After only a year or so, in the manner of many an ambitious young Kluxer, he resigned his membership to form his own Klan and named himself its imperial wizard. But success did not come right away. Prior to 1978 Wilkinson's chief claim to fame was the fact that an incensed spectator had rammed a small foreign sports car into his podium during a rally in Plains, Georgia, shortly after Jimmy Carter's election. Bodies went flying everywhere, several people were injured, and the incident made national headlines.

Wilkinson's big break came in the summer of 1978, when a handful of white men from Decatur, angered by the demonstrations on behalf of Tommy Lee Hines, invited him to organize a Klan chapter there. The community soon proved fertile ground for his struggling organization. Within six weeks of the invitation the IEK-KKK held its first rally, attracting a crowd estimated at between two thousand and five thousand people. A second rally a month later drew from five thousand to eleven thousand, according to widely varying newspaper estimates. These were the biggest Klan rallies the country had witnessed in more than a decade, and in light of the fact that Carter's election had seemed to herald a New South, they put the cigar-chomping young imperial wizard in the media spotlight. Wilkinson in turn parlayed the press coverage into further recruitment gains around the region, and the movement began to snowball. In only about a year membership in his group had swelled from a few hundred to a few thousand, most of them right there in the Tennessee River valley. For a while Decatur became the hub of his operations.

Wilkinson's meteoric rise was not attributable to the Hines case alone, though. Quite calculatedly he was tapping into a growing nationwide white backlash against affirmative action, school busing, and housing integration, a backlash being fueled by the hard economic times: inflation and interest rates in the double digits; unemployment high and apparently headed higher. The secret of Wilkinson's success lay in his ability to convince a new generation of young white males that in the post-civil rights era the Klan could do something about these matters.

Standing in the middle of a cow pasture on a Saturday night in the summer of 1979, I thought that I developed some insight into Wilkinson's appeal. It was not, as I had imagined it might be, that he was a dynamic and forceful speaker; he was passable, but the

Klan had more effective orators. Nor was it simply an invitation to vigilantism, although that was very much a component. Rather, Wilkinson's appeal was something intensely personal and intangible: It was his ability to inspire his listeners to believe that if they only banded together with him ("Come join us," his posters read, "and we will send our message to Washington"), they could change their lives for the better. He gave his frustrated supporters a measure of hope. The irony was—as it always was with scapegoating Klan leaders—that the race-baiting solutions he proposed for improving their lot would not have addressed the issues that had made many of them genuine victims in their own right: poverty, a notoriously weak public school system, and crass economic exploitation.

As Wilkinson spoke, several robed Klansmen circulated through the crowd, passing out membership applications. A number of people accepted them, and a few filled them out on the spot. Two or three other Kluxers took up donations in rubber buckets.

To my surprise, the speech was more political than I had expected. With its emphasis on affirmative action, immigration, and violence in the schools, it resembled the stock campaign speech of many conservative politicians, save for the racial slurs sprinkled throughout it. As for the send-our-message-to-Washington theme, I recognized it right away. It was straight from George Wallace's presidential campaigns of the late sixties and early seventies.

For whatever reason—the relatively small attendance or the fact that the Klansmen felt naked without their guns, which the sheriff had prevented them from carrying—the rally ended up being rather brief. When Wilkinson finished his speech, he announced that the meeting would conclude with the Klan's traditional cross burning ceremony, which he referred to as a "cross lighting." From his remarks it was clear he was on the defensive about whether the burning of the cross constituted a desecration, as some Christian leaders (the few who publicly denounced the KKK) had charged. Wilkinson defended the ceremony by insisting that it symbolized the Klan's belief that Christ was the light of the world.

To judge by the crowd's reaction, the cross burning was the highlight of the evening. At Wilkinson's command, the fifty robed Klan members converged on the cross, and each picked up what appeared to be a three- or four-foot-long stick from a pile stacked near its base. They formed a wide circle around the cross, facing inward, at perhaps a twenty- or thirty-foot radius. It was then that I noticed the wide variety of uniforms the Kluxers were wearing. They all had white robes, but several also had small black collars, like the kind on a sailor's uniform. Two or three had red collars, and there was at least one green collar. Wilkinson's collar was a pretty royal blue. Those with the colored collars had matching stripes on their sleeves. According to what Nungester had told me, these insignia indicated rank: black for local office; red for regional; green, state; and blue, national.

Over to one side of Wilkinson, the only other Klansman inside the circle lighted the stick he was holding, and it burst into flame. Slowly, silently, the circle of Klansmen began to rotate by him, each lighting his torch from the original flame. It was an eerie and colorful sight, and despite Wilkinson's protestations, it struck me as quite pagan.

When all the torches were ablaze, the rotation stopped, and Wilkinson, facing the cross, addressed the members of the circle. "Behold, the fiery cross still brilliant," he said. "All the troubled history failed to quench its hallowed flame."

He barked out several commands, and the Klansmen alternately raised and lowered their flaming torches in unison. The sudden motion produced a great rush of air that was audible to those of us in the crowd standing just a few feet away. Wilkinson took his own torch and lighted the cross, which had been swathed in diesel-soaked burlap bags to make it flame up dramatically. As tongues of fire leaped up the post and spread out over the horizontal piece, Wilkinson said in a lilting voice, "In the fiery cross I glory/Beneath the sacred glow my oath was made/It shall ever live in song and story/I swear its light shall never fade."

The Klansmen in the circle stepped forward and piled their torches at the base of the cross. The flames jumped skyward again. The rally was over.

"You're not one of them, are you?" a woman's voice behind me said.

Startled, I turned around. The woman, dressed in jeans and a long-sleeved shirt, with all kinds of photographic gear hanging from her shoulders, was clearly talking to me.

"What?"

"It's obvious you're not a Klansman. What are you doing here?"

All my carefully scripted lines—the responses I had thought out and rehearsed so as to be fully prepared in the event my identity was challenged—suddenly left me. The thing was, I hadn't expected my inquisitor to be a female photographer. Shamelessly I spilled my guts.

My future clearly was not in espionage.

On Monday I returned to the business of preparing our final witness list for the preliminary hearing, which was now less than three weeks away. By the time I finished, there were approximately seventy names on it: police officers and sheriff's deputies, newspaper and television reporters, Klansmen. We filed the list with the Morgan County clerk of court and asked him to have the sheriff serve the subpoenas, according to procedure.

Several days passed. Nothing happened.

The first inkling we had that something was amiss was when no one phoned to complain about being subpoenaed. Invariably someone did, and with seventy subpoenas out, we were expecting a hail of complaints. I called two or three friendly witnesses to see if they had been served; they hadn't. When I called the clerk's office to see what was wrong, all I got was the runaround.

Very shortly we discovered why. On July 25, two days before the hearing, Robinson was indicted. Moebes apparently had gotten word of the size of our witness list via the courthouse grapevine and had decided to block our attempt to learn anything about the case by impaneling a special grand jury to indict Robinson. With the handing up of the indictment, the preliminary hearing was now a moot point; there wouldn't be one, since its sole purpose was to determine in a more neutral setting than a grand jury session whether or not there was sufficient evidence to bring charges.

There was nothing illegal about Moebes's actions; a preliminary hearing was not a right under the law but a privilege. It was a question, rather, of fairness. Not everyone requested a preliminary hearing, but when a defense attorney sought one on behalf of his client, it was considered good form (and professional courtesy) for the prosecutor to grant it.

Dees was incensed, and he vented his frustration to the press, partly in an attempt to garner public sympathy for Robinson. "This rushed indictment of Mr. Robinson appears to be an attempt to prevent Mr. Robinson from learning the facts of the case before he is put to trial," he told the *Huntsville Times.* "This is a shabby attempt to undercut Mr. Robinson's constitutional rights."

Although Moebes countered that the grand jury was convened because of a heavy caseload and that fifty other cases had been considered at the same time, his explanation didn't completely wash: It failed to account for why the subpoenas had apparently never left the courthouse. It was a remarkable coincidence. Down South we called it home cookin'.

Decatur was fast gaining a reputation for such courthouse she-nanigans. The previous year Tommy Lee Hines had been the victim of the very same thing. After suggesting to reporters that the case against Hines might not be presented to the grand jury for several weeks, Moebes called a special grand jury into session and indicted him the very next day. To top it off, Moebes then asked Hines's attorney to bring his client to the courthouse but didn't tell him why. When Hines arrived, Moebes had him taken into custody and whisked away to the state mental hospital for a competency exam. Even the sheriff—whose duty it was to carry Hines to the hospital—was reportedly caught off guard by the ploy.

But an even more blatant example of home cookin' occurred after Hines's lawyer had filed a motion to have the trial moved out of Decatur because of extensive pretrial publicity. Morgan County Circuit Judge Richard Hundley took the motion under advisement and then granted it—after a fashion. From Morgan County, with a black population of approximately 14 percent, the judge ordered the case sent to Cullman, the county seat of one of the most baldly racist communities in the state. Blacks constituted less than 1 percent of its population, and until the 1960s signs had been posted at the county line reading, NIGGER DON'T LET THE SUN SET ON YOUR HEAD IN CULLMAN COUNTY ALABAMA. In 1978 most of the county's blacks still lived in a place called the Colony, an enclave where former slaves had taken refuge after the Civil War.

As fate would have it, the same Judge Hundley was assigned to hear Case No. CC79-0445H of Morgan County Circuit Court, *State of Alabama* v. *Curtis Robinson.*

Chapter Four

As A bellwether of future events, the hurried-up indictment of Curtis Robinson did not bode well for our chances of winning an acquittal. To the problem of picking an impartial jury in a highly charged racial atmosphere was now added that of playing against what appeared to be a stacked deck. For these reasons, we decided to seek a change of venue. Outside northern Alabama, far removed from the passions stirred up by the Tommy Lee Hines case, we thought we stood a fighting chance of finding twelve unbiased jurors who could be persuaded that Robinson had acted in self-defense.

To make the most compelling case possible for moving the trial, Dees decided we should go back to the date of Hines's arrest and document every single public act of protest or counterprotest staged throughout the yearlong history of the Hines affair. Even though Robinson had not been demonstrating on Hines's behalf on May 26, Dees knew that any jury picked in Decatur would assume he had been, and he believed the court, therefore, should take the whole panorama of protests into consideration when deciding whether to move the trial.

For me, this would mean a tedious, time-consuming search through the Decatur and Huntsville public libraries and a year's worth of old newspapers. Before I managed to get started, though, something utterly astonishing happened. On August 11 and 12 Wilkinson and nearly two hundred of his followers were arrested just inside the city limits of Montgomery as they tried to march on the Capitol without a permit.

The arrests were the result of a PR stunt gone awry. In his quest for publicity—which, Wilkinson and other Klan leaders of the post-civil rights era had learned, served to attract new members—the imperial wizard had struck upon the idea of staging a reenactment of the 1965 Selma to Montgomery voting rights march to dramatize the "plight" of white people suffering from reverse discrimination.

For the first couple of days everything went according to plan. Reporters and photographers swarmed all over the march, drawn to it, as Wilkinson had undoubtedly known they would be, by the irresistible irony of one of America's most violent organizations mimicking one of history's great nonviolent protests. Wilkinson had scored a public relations coup. But even as the ragtag bunch of Klansmen marched through the sizzling cotton fields of the Black Belt, retracing the route Dr. King and a handful of activists had taken fourteen years earlier, trouble was brewing down the line. A dispute had erupted between IEKKKK leaders and Montgomery officials over the city's parade permit law. The Klansmen insisted they had complied with the law as it had been explained to them; the city said they hadn't—and refused to issue a permit for the Klan to march from the city limits to the Capitol downtown. Neither side appeared willing to back down.

Wilkinson called the city's bluff, and on Sunday morning, August 12, he and his hooded followers marched down U.S. Highway 80 on the final mile of their walk from Selma and peacefully surrendered to the police on the outskirts of the city.

The first court date in the case—apparently the largest single bust in KKK history—was docketed for later that month. When Wilkinson returned to Montgomery to attend it, Dees set up a meeting with him through the imperial wizard's local counsel, who happened to be one of Dees's friends. Dees was still eager to settle the Robinson case, especially in view of the new evidence that had come to light in his meeting with Moebes, and it had occurred to him that there might be another way to go about it, via Wilkinson.

The meeting took place in a Montgomery restaurant. Besides Dees and Wilkinson, the only other person there was the KKK's Alabama grand dragon, or state president, Roger Handley. After a few minutes of small talk—there wasn't much to say—Dees put forward his proposal. It called for the Law Center to pay three thousand dollars' worth of the injured Klansman David Kelso's medical bills (which, considering his nearly monthlong stay in the hospital, were estimated at several thousand dollars) in return for Kelso's help, and the Klan's, in persuading Moebes to reduce the attempted murder charge against Robinson to a misdemeanor. Wilkinson listened with apparent interest to the proposal and then agreed to carry it back to Kelso to let the wounded Klansman decide.

A short time later the answer came back: no deal. Nor, unfortunately, did the episode end there. Somehow (presumably from a highly placed KKK source) a reporter for the *Huntsville Times* found out about the proposal, and the paper printed the story. Wilkinson not only told of the settlement offer but also claimed that Dees had indicated that he knew of impending federal indictments against thirty-one Klansmen involved in the May 26 incident and that he could get the indictments dropped if Kelso and the Klan would agree to his terms.

Dees was stung by the disclosure of the conversation, even though he had done nothing wrong. He had made the overture to Wilkinson in the belief that it was in the best interests of his client. He knew he risked being accused of selling out the larger cause if the settlement offer ever became public, but he also knew that Robinson was facing a serious prison term if convicted on the attempted murder charge. Dees thought that if he could settle the case for something less, he should. The fact that the reporter got wind of the story caught him by surprise, however. He denied the allegation about the indictments, and to his great relief the story didn't receive much play. Still, he had been "had," and he knew it.

Meanwhile, I returned to northern Alabama to begin the process of scouring the *Huntsville Times* and the *Decatur Daily* for stories connected to the Hines case. Some four hundred articles later (on the average, a publication rate of about one story per day), I emerged, bleary-eyed, but with a keener understanding of what all the turmoil had really been about: Decatur's black community had been struggling to break out of a kind of time warp it had been stuck in since the 1960s.

One of the shortcomings of the civil rights movement was that even though it transformed the South as a whole, it left many cities and towns in the region only nominally affected. This was particularly true in communities where blacks constituted less than a quarter of the population. Being so much in the minority, they were far less likely to organize and press for change, and where they didn't actively press for it, change was at best slow in coming. (It often didn't come at all.) By the time the civil rights movement began to fizzle out in the late 1960s, blacks in these communities had the right to vote, the right to ride in the front of the bus, and the right to eat and lodge in establishments previously off limits to them, but little more (and in many places even these rights were theirs only on paper). The fundamental balance of power between the races had not been materially altered.

Decatur, with its approximately 15 percent black makeup, was a part of this other South.* Though only ninety miles from Birmingham, one of the key battlegrounds of the civil rights era, Decatur during the 1960s experienced none of the strife that made its sister city to the south synonymous with racial acrimony. There were no protests and no demonstrations in Decatur, no police dogs or water hoses, and integration—albeit of the most minimal, token sort—occurred without incident.

By the latter part of the 1970s the consequences of the black community's failure to demand real change, and of the white community's failure to countenance it, were plainly evident. The city had one black policeman on a force of seventy sworn officers and no black fire fighters. There were no black elected officials and only a handful of appointed ones. None of the city's thirty-eight polling places was located in a black neighborhood. The school system was about to be hit with a federal court order mandating busing. In the

* It would be inaccurate to say the civil rights movement bypassed Decatur. During the mid-1960s Dr. King made overtures to the city's black leadership, proposing a program of demonstrations to advance the cause of civil rights locally. However, he was rebuffed.

private sphere the mainline civic clubs and churches were virtually lily-white, and social contacts between the races were few.

As I uncovered these facts during the course of my research, I came to the conclusion that the tensions generated by the Hines case had not been the cause of racial polarization in Decatur so much as a symptom of it. There was no other way to explain why the arrest of a rape suspect should suddenly galvanize the community's black population, with its history of submissiveness, or why a series of peaceful, nonviolent demonstrations should prompt such a hostile, even violent reaction from the city's whites.

Underlying the mass meetings and protests that began almost immediately upon Hines's arrest were deep but invisible racial divisions in the community, divisions of which Decatur's whites, who had taken a kind of paternalistic pride in the absence of conflict in their city during the sixties, were seemingly oblivious. For proof of their existence, however, one had to look no further than the way blacks and whites reacted to the news, and the circumstances, of the controversial arrest.

Hines had been picked up by the police on May 23, 1978, after residents of a mostly white downtown neighborhood complained that a black man had been "loitering" in the area and had been observed peering into the window of a downtown office building. Two officers responded to the call and took Hines into custody. He put up no resistance, and the officers transported him the short distance to the police station. There, without the benefit of counsel, he was questioned at length about the three unsolved black-on-white rapes that had recently stirred fear within the white community. During this interrogation he was said to have confessed to all three. There was no physical evidence against him, and the police decided not to conduct a lineup for the three victims before formally charging him. The charges thus were based solely on his confession. Prior to his being picked up, he hadn't even been a suspect in the case.

Despite the dubious confession and the fact that the newspaper reported Hines's status as a student at a school for the mentally handicapped, whites greeted the arrest with an almost audible sigh of relief, their somewhat shaken faith in the police restored. In the black neighborhoods to the northwest, however, where confidence in law enforcement was not the implicit article of faith it was else-

47

where in the community, friends of the Hines family were stunned. They knew the accused as a simple but polite young man who not only could not drive a car—as at least one of the victims maintained her assailant had done—but couldn't even ride a bicycle. Within hours of his arrest they had begun to organize. The first step they took was to schedule a meeting at the Hines family's church for May 25, two days later. In view of the haste with which it was set up, the turnout of eighty people at the meeting was an impressive show of support, at least for Decatur. At that point, forty-eight hours after Hines had been taken into custody, it was becoming clear that the arrest had struck a deep chord within many of the city's black residents. Ironically, the arrest that Decatur police had hoped would quell growing unease in the white community was about to touch off an unprecedented protest among the community's historically docile black population.

Racial lines were being drawn fast. Sweeping the black community was support for Hines and for a program of protests in his behalf, fueled by years of pent-up resentment and the prospect of help from the Southern Christian Leadership Conference, whose officials had been invited from Atlanta to assist in the organizing drive. Soon unease among whites, which had dissipated briefly with Hines's arrest, began to resurface. With a vocal march by an estimated five hundred black people from the church to City Hall on May 29, the situation was transformed into a full-blown community crisis.

But Decatur was caught in a classic catch-22: The only way to defuse the crisis was to draw on the community's reservoir of racial goodwill, yet because of Decatur's racial dynamics, which had given rise to the crisis in the first place, the reservoir was perilously low. Nor was there any formal mechanism for handling race-related disputes such as a human relations council. The situation seemed to cry out for strong political and civic leadership. As it turned out, that, too, was in short supply.

In May 1978 Bill Dukes was in his third year as the mayor of Decatur. A basically well-intentioned man, Dukes was no Bull Connor (the Birmingham police commissioner who had met black protests in 1963 with attack dogs and water hoses), and to his credit, he met with protest leaders on more than one occasion in the early days of the conflict. The meetings accomplished little, however, partly

because the protesters put forward a demand he was legally power-
less to fulfill (Hines's release) and partly because of his own failure
to seize the leadership initiative by addressing the inequitable conditions that had fueled the crisis. A former public relations man at
the local Monsanto plant (the giant synthetics manufacturer), Dukes
was a promoter and booster but not a decisive leader. After the
initial meetings with the leaders of the protests, he receded into the
background and did not play a major role in future developments.
His timidity, combined with the failure of white civic and religious
leaders to make concerted attempts to mediate a solution to the
conflict, left a serious leadership vacuum.* As predictably as a law of
physics, an outside force rushed in to fill the void: a newly resurgent
Ku Klux Klan. Largely dormant in the area since the late sixties, the
KKK was in the early stages of a revival in neighboring northern
Mississippi, and it soon spilled across the border.

It had been only a matter of time until vigilantism reared its
head. Demonstrations by Hines's supporters were occurring on a
daily basis, and led by the skillful organizers of the SCLC, they were
succeeding in disrupting the orderly conduct of the community's
business. After the big march on May 29 a picket line was set up
outside City Hall. It was followed by a sit-in in the City Hall lobby.
Fanning out from downtown, the demonstrators took their protest
to several shopping centers and then to a public park. As the
protests thus escalated, the initial shock that gripped many whites
over the unexpected show of black activism successively turned to
fear and finally to anger. (More than a little of this growing dissat-
isfaction was directed at Mayor Dukes and the police for not cracking down on the protesters.)

The first sign of KKK activity appeared less than three weeks
after Hines's arrest, in the form of a charred small wooden cross
found in a vacant lot across the street from the courthouse. The
June 13 *Decatur Daily* ran a photograph of Officer Marlon Owens

---

* A handful of concerned whites came forward on their own to form an interracial council
with several black citizens, but it lacked the full backing of the community's white leadership
and was, despite individual members' good intentions, largely ineffectual. One incident in
April 1979 illustrated the timidity that characterized the council's response to the ongoing
racial crisis. Meeting for its regular monthly session just two or three days after the home of a
black family in a mostly white neighborhood had been rocked by a shotgun blast, the group
never discussed the attack in more than an hour of deliberations. As the meeting was nearing
adjournment, Clint Brown, the Legal Services director, called the council to task for dodging
the issue. Only then was the matter brought up for consideration.

and another policeman removing it. One morning about a week later another cross was discovered, still burning, in a park. This time the perpetrators left their calling card: an official KKK recruitment flyer, professionally printed in bold red block letters. It said, "Save Our Land Join the Klan." Near it was a handwritten sign: MAYOR, LOOK, IF YOU CAN'T, WE CAN.

The situation was deteriorating day by day.

For its part the SCLC constantly reaffirmed its commitment to nonviolence, and its leaders sought to allay fears in the white community over the aims of the protests. In a speech to three hundred blacks on June 21, Dr. Lowery was quoted by the *Daily* as saying, "We've come not to scare Decatur to death. Instead, we've come to challenge her to a new life of justice and equality. . . . An eye for an eye and a tooth for a tooth will leave all of us blind and snaggle-tooth."

White attitudes had hardened, however, and several days after Lowery's speech the first of the physical attacks against the protesters occurred. The initial incident involved the ransacking of a tent encampment Hines's supporters had erected on the lawn of City Hall. The perpetrators also burned a small cross on the courthouse lawn, but neither incident resulted in an arrest—or even a condemnation from the authorities. Over the ensuing weeks, threats and acts of vigilantism against the protesters increased and took a more serious turn. On one occasion, according to an article in the *Daily*, a motorist veered directly toward a group of marchers only to swerve away at the last minute. The paper reported that police officers stood idly by. In yet another case a black youth was chased into the police station by Klan supporters yelling threats. Once again the police took no action, and community leaders remained mute.

Compared with subsequent events, however, these incidents were only minor. In mid-July, after recruiting quietly for more than a month, the KKK came out into the open, holding its first area rally in fifteen years. It was a resounding success, as was a second one a month later. Shortly after the initial rally, the KKK erected its own tent city on the lawn at City Hall and staged a nighttime cross burning in front of the building, where, surrounded by rifle-toting Klan members and spectators armed with baseball bats and clubs, Imperial Wizard Bill Wilkinson announced, "We are providing vigilante law for Decatur." The astounding thing was not simply the remark but the fact that it was never rebutted by Decatur's political or civic leaders or by Police Chief Pack Self.

Taking silence for consent, the Klan began to run wild. When Hines's trial was moved to Cullman, the KKK followed it there, and in a dramatic foreshadowing of the Bank-Lee incident, a Klan-led mob of two thousand whites twice stopped a march by a dozen Hines supporters from entering the town on the eve of the trial. The demonstrators, including Dr. Lowery, had begun the thirty-five-mile march from Decatur on September 30, two days before the October 2 trial date. On the evening of the second day, soon after entering Cullman County, the marchers were blocked by a crowd of threatening, cursing whites brandishing baseball bats, sticks, and clubs. Someone in the mob had hung a noose over a highway sign, and others had placed a Klan cross along the roadside. Only an escort of eighty riot-equipped state troopers prevented mob violence against the protesters. Despite the formidable show of force, the officer in charge, Major James Fuqua, informed the marchers shortly before sundown that because of the size and threatening behavior of the mob, he could no longer guarantee their safety. At Fuqua's request, the marchers hastily piled into cars for the ride back to Morgan County for the night. When they tried to resume the march the next morning, they found that the mob had reformed at the Cullman city limits and had blocked the highway again. This time the marchers determined to assert their rights by continuing to march. Rather than confront the leaders of the mob, however, the Cullman police placed the marchers under arrest and took them into "protective custody." (The charges were later dropped.)

Hines's trial was conducted in the same lynch mob atmosphere before an all-white jury. Court sessions were attended by unrobed Kluxers, while dozens of other whites, including robed Klansmen and Klan members in T-shirts, stood outside. The imperial wizard gave media interviews beneath a shade tree on the courthouse grounds. Two bomb threats, a large Klan rally, and a number of minor incidents marred the two-week proceeding, according to the newspapers, and on October 13, 1978, Hines was convicted and sentenced to thirty years in prison.

In the wake of the verdict and the frightening displays of vigilantism, support in Decatur's black community for continuing the protests plummeted. Internal squabbling between SCLC officials and Hines's attorney, and accusations of misuse of funds by Reverend Cottonreader, though never proved, further eroded support.

By contrast, the KKK emerged from the trial energized and bolder than ever. One night, less than ten days after the trial had ended, seven Klansmen threatened an interracial couple seated together in a downtown Decatur coffee shop. According to the October 23 edition of the *Daily*, a restaurant employee called the police, who arrived just as the Kluxers were leaving. Questioned about the incident, the Klansmen told the officers that "they objected to seeing a white woman with a black man and that they [the police] should ask them to leave." There were no arrests. In mid-December Bill McGlocklin, a top-ranking Alabama IEKKKK leader, took credit in the *Huntsville Times* on behalf of the Klan for the abduction of an itinerant black minister who had been found stripped and beaten near Cullman. The next day McGlocklin denied any KKK involvement in the incident.

Two incidents a few weeks later, recounted in the same paper, illustrated how thoroughly Decatur authorities were intimidated by the Klan. On February 10 Reverend Cottonreader joined a black man who had been accused of shoplifting food from a west Decatur grocery store and set up a picket in front of the store. News of the protest quickly reached the KKK, and soon seventy-five Klansmen confronted the protesters. The Klansmen tried to intimidate the picketers, then exchanged taunts with a group of blacks, some of them armed, who had gathered at one end of the shopping center parking lot as word of the Klan's presence spread. The police were called to the scene and ordered everyone to disperse. The next day the picketers came back. This time, armed with rifles, pistols, knives, and clubs, two hundred Klansmen descended on the store. Again the police were summoned. In view of dozens of witnesses a Klansman approached the SCLC official and wrapped a Confederate flag around his face. A second Klansman snatched the hat off the other man's head and set it on fire. The police did nothing. Meanwhile, a black customer who had driven up to the store was knocked back inside his car by a Klansman when he tried to get out. Gunshots struck the driver's side of a car driven by another black man, but when he advised an officer that he could identify his assailant, the officer declined to arrest the Kluxer, informing the victim that he would have to go down to the police station to file a complaint. When about twenty blacks gathered nearby, some of them openly armed, state trooper reinforcements were finally called in. Chief Self asked the Klan to disperse, but Grand Dragon Handley agreed to do so only if the picketers followed suit. Self then placed the blacks under arrest and returned to speak with Handley. "I went through with my deal," the paper quoted Self as saying. "Y'all said you would get them [the other Klansmen] and go." Handley then ordered his men to leave. No other arrests were made.

At the prompting of Mayor Dukes, the Decatur City Council a few days later passed a gun ordinance that made it unlawful to carry firearms within a thousand feet of a demonstration, but Klan leader Bill McGlocklin immediately announced his intention to disobey it. "We are not going to respect it," he declared publicly. "The mayor, the police chief, nor anybody else is going to tell us what to carry and what not to carry."

Openly defying the new ordinance, 150 robed and armed Klansmen rumbled through Decatur about a week later in an hourlong twenty-six-vehicle demonstration. The Kluxers displayed rifles, shotguns, and pistols and ran numerous traffic lights and stop signs. On the lead truck was posted a placard that read, MAYOR DUKES IF YOU WANT OUR GUNS YOU COME GET THEM. At least one of the Klansmen was masked, in violation of state law. Police witnessed the demonstration but made no attempt to make an arrest. Later Chief Self explained the officers' inaction by asserting that they had been uncertain whether the motorcade constituted a demonstration.

Nearly three months to the day after that motorcade, members of the very same Klan mob blocked the anniversary march at Bank and Lee streets.

I finished the newspaper project and compiled a report for Dees. The information we gleaned from the articles was to form the basis of the change of venue motion. Beyond its purely evidentiary value, however, the newspaper project also helped put Robinson's actions, and those of the parade marshals who had felt it necessary to arm themselves, in a clearer light. As a result, we started to feel as if we were fighting something bigger than just Robinson's prosecution. The case came to represent an attempt to redress the wrongs done to the entire black community.

During the final months of 1979 events in the Robinson case happened in rapid-fire succession. In October the FBI announced it was closing the book on its five-month investigation into the May 26 incident. The team of special agents sent to Decatur to determine if the marchers' civil rights had been violated had turned up no "prosecutable evidence" (the feds' term) that the Klan had engaged in a conspiracy to disrupt the march. No federal charges would be filed after all. The FBI had interviewed scores of people, racked up hundreds of agent-hours of investigation, and spent untold thousands of tax dollars, only, in effect, to exonerate the KKK. Predictably Klan leaders crowed over the news; at the same time there was a deepening sense of anger and despair in the black community.

Hard on the heels of this discouraging development, however, came news of a very different sort from Nungester, with whom I had remained in frequent contact. He had learned—he didn't say how—that Marlon Owens, the police officer who supposedly had talked with Robinson minutes before the shooting, was moonlighting for a sometime Klansman, Paul Watson, in Watson's small-engine repair shop. And according to Nungester, Watson had been fairly active in the local klavern, participating in the KKK's tent city at City Hall and attending other public functions, so it was unlikely that Owens could have been unaware of his membership in the group. This suggested that Owens might have Klan sympathies and might explain why the police officer had said Robinson made the "I'm-gonna-get-a-couple-of-'em" remark that Robinson strenuously denied. Dees believed it did. He viewed the information as the missing piece in our case.

We had hardly finished examining this piece of news, however, when Robinson called the Law Center several days later, terribly distressed. It seemed that he had been sued by David Kelso for $750,000. For Robinson, who was trying to rear a family of five children on a maintenance man's salary and who lived in subsidized housing, the suit was one nightmare on top of another. Dees assured him the SPLC would represent him in the new case and urged him not to worry.

Actually the civil suit looked as if it were going to turn out to be a blessing in disguise. Realizing that the civil process could be used to conduct discovery (a legal term for formal evidence gathering) in the criminal case, Dees quickly arranged to take depositions under the auspices of the civil suit from several law enforcement officers who had played key roles in the May 26 incident. Denied the preliminary hearing by Robinson's sudden indictment, Dees figured to take advantage of the civil suit to obtain the facts about the case.

On the eve of the depositions, however, Dees had to go to Washington on business connected with his work as chief fund-raiser for Senator Edward Kennedy's presidential campaign, so he asked SPLC Legal Director John Carroll to go in his place. Carroll, a native of Washington, D.C., was an excellent attorney in his own right, graced with a keen legal mind and a razor-sharp wit to match. More important, perhaps, he was able as few other Northern attorneys were to "good old boy" with Southern courthouse officials: to deliver the self-deprecating joke, draw the humorous parallel, invoke the appropriate religious or cultural value that might cultivate in a judge or a juror or a bailiff an unconscious predisposition toward his client (it didn't hurt that he was a huge Crimson Tide fan). What was unusual about Carroll was his ability to feel equally at home arguing an appeal in the U.S. Supreme Court or trying a case before some small-town judge.

On the day of the depositions, the Tuesday after Thanksgiving, Carroll and I arrived at the court reporter's office in Decatur a few minutes before 9:00 A.M. The depositions were to begin at 9:00. Everything seemed set. At 8:57, however, Mike Moebes abruptly appeared and without so much as a smile handed Carroll a slip of paper. It was an order from Judge Hundley permanently barring us from taking testimony from any of the police officers. Moebes had cut us off at the pass once again. After learning of our plans to take the officers' depositions, he had gone to Judge Hundley and requested a stay. Judge Hundley had granted it *ex parte*, meaning he hadn't provided us an opportunity to respond to Moebes's objection. Although there was nothing improper with the order itself or even the fact that Moebes had sought it, the manner in which it had been sought and granted smacked of collusion.

As more and more time passed without a trial date being set, Dees came to the conclusion that Hundley had decided not to grant the change of venue motion but to hold the trial in Decatur, where he could preside over it. As Dees saw it, if Hundley had intended to transfer the case, he would already have done so. It was then almost December, more than six months since the May 26 march. By contrast, Hundley had granted the motion to move Hines's trial about two months after his arrest.

In a final bid to persuade Hundley to move the trial (and to lay the grounds for appeal, in case it failed), we made Hundley's order transferring the Hines trial to Cullman exhibit number one at the hearing on our change of venue motion, which was held early in January 1980. The order, which characterized Morgan County as a "battleground," noted that the "present atmosphere" had so tainted the jury pool that it would have been difficult for any citizen—black or white—to remain impartial in the face of it. A jury composed of such citizens, Hundley had concluded, "could not serve in the interests of justice. Neither could it serve in the interests of itself, the State, nor the Defendant. It could not in law be called impartial."

This order became the centerpiece of our request for a change of venue, for if Tommy Lee Hines couldn't get a fair trial in Decatur, and Curtis Robinson was arrested for shooting a Klansman during a march in support of Tommy Lee Hines, it stood to reason that Curtis Robinson couldn't get a fair trial either.

By the end of the three-day hearing we had introduced some eight hundred additional exhibits into evidence in support of the motion, mostly newspaper clippings, plus TV videotapes, transcripts of radio news broadcasts, and Klan literature. Dees had, in addition, elicited some remarkable facts from the thirty-odd witnesses called to testify. A *Huntsville Times* reporter estimated he alone had written a half million words on the Hines case since May 1978; the news director for a local radio station testified the station had broadcast as many as ten thousand stories about the controversy over the same period. Perhaps the most compelling evidence, however, was the testimony of a pollster whom we had commissioned to do a survey of the attitudes of Morgan County residents in November. The polltaker, Dr. William Kimmelman, was a highly respected political scientist at the University of Alabama at Birmingham. Employing standard polling techniques, Kimmelman had administered the survey only to prospective members of the

Morgan County juror pool—those persons over eighteen years of age who were registered to vote. His results confirmed what we all had known: The pool was tainted. In the poll 80 percent of the white respondents admitted knowing about the Hines protests; 60 percent viewed Robinson as a part of them; half the white respondents blamed the marchers as well as the KKK for the May 26 confrontation; fewer than one in ten said the Klan alone was responsible. The most surprising response in the survey, however, had to do with the basic First Amendment right to protest. Nearly three out of five white residents of the county opposed the right of citizens to hold peaceful demonstrations. It was hard to see how a defendant arrested for a crime allegedly committed during a demonstration could hope to receive a fair hearing before jurors who didn't even believe in the right of citizens to conduct peaceful protest in the streets.*

When all the evidence was in, Hundley announced he had decided to delay a decision on the motion until he could review it further. Several weeks passed, and then Dees received a letter from the court. The judge had decided to take additional testimony on the motion on February 25; that was essentially all the letter said. It was unusual, to say the least, for a judge presiding over a case to initiate the taking of testimony on his own, and Dees grew suspicious. He asked Carroll to accompany him, and the two attorneys drove to Decatur for the hearing, not knowing what to expect.

They arrived at the designated courtroom and found it virtually empty. Moebes was there, as well as the judge's court reporter and a bailiff, but no one else was present: no press; no spectators; no protesters or Klan members. A minute or two later the judge entered, and as soon as he outlined his agenda, the purpose of the hearing became apparent: He had decided to respond to Dr. Kimmelman's survey by sampling public opinion on his own. The ground rules were these: Hundley would summon members of a jury pool that had assembled down the hall for an entirely different case and question them on their knowledge of the Robinson case.

---

* With the exception of Kimmelman, virtually all the other witnesses we called—reporters, public officials, and Klansmen—testified under cross-examination by Moebes that they believed Robinson could get a fair trial in Decatur. In the case of the law enforcement officers and the Klan members, this came as no surprise. As for the reporters, it shouldn't have. Many of them thought Hines had received a fair trial in Cullman.

Upon completing his questioning, he would permit attorneys for both sides to ask questions of their own.

For several hours, over Dees's protests, the scene was played out with juror after juror. Hundley asked eight or ten superficial questions seemingly designed to show the juror's lack of familiarity with Kelso or Robinson by name, then elicited an opinion from the juror on whether or not he or she believed Robinson could receive a fair trial. Dees came behind, digging, probing, searching—and excavating what usually turned out to be the juror's extensive exposure to the Hines-Robinson case. In the end about a dozen jurors were examined, and all but one, a black woman, expressed the opinion that Robinson could obtain a fair trial in Decatur. Judge Hundley seemed satisfied. In a matter of days he denied the motion to move the case.

Months passed, and still no date was set for the trial. There were only two explanations. The charitable one was that Hundley was trying to assure Robinson's right to a fair trial by waiting till the community's racial wounds completely healed (notwithstanding the fact that the need for such an extended delay would seem to lend credence to the validity of our request for a change of venue, even as it compromised one of Robinson's other rights—that to a speedy trial); the more plausible explanation to us was that Hundley, confident that Robinson would still be convicted, was trying to protect his decision to keep the trial in Decatur against any eventual appeal by waiting until the appearance of racial calm had returned to the city.

From time to time there continued to be developments in the case. In March 1980 a state appeals court overturned Tommy Lee Hines's conviction on the ground that he had been denied a fair trial in Cullman, and Governor Forrest ("Fob") James ordered him to undergo a competency exam to determine if he should be retried or institutionalized.* The same month the *Decatur Daily* obtained a copy of the FBI investigative report on the May 26 incident and published its findings. Carroll acquired a copy for us, but when it arrived, we found it almost useless since almost every name (with the notable exception of Curtis Robinson's and a few others) had been expunged. In addition, large portions of the agents' interview

* The Alabama Court of Criminal Appeals ruled that Hines was incompetent to waive his legal rights and that his confession, as a result, was invalid. Following the hearing ordered by the governor, he was adjudged incompetent and was hospitalized.

summaries had been blacked out—to protect sources, the Bureau said—rendering many other passages unintelligible. Despite these obstacles, it was clear that the report contained exculpatory material that would benefit Robinson's claim of self-defense, particularly a set of summaries of the interviews with the Decatur police and Morgan County sheriff's deputies. Carroll wrote the FBI back and requested an unexpunged copy. The request, and a subsequent appeal, were denied. This left us no choice but to sue, so in July 1980 the Law Center went to court against the FBI on Robinson's behalf. Before the suit could come to trial, however, Judge Hundley set a trial date for the Robinson case. It was to begin in Decatur on September 29, 1980.

Although set back by the FBI's lack of cooperation, Dees came up with an alternative plan to get the exculpatory evidence. During a pretrial hearing in the criminal case in early September he brought the matter of the FBI report to Hundley's attention, citing the law enforcement summaries as proof that Moebes had failed to turn over all exculpatory evidence to the defense, as the prosecution was required to do. He then asked Hundley to order Moebes to turn over the incident reports filed by each of the officers who had worked the May 26 march. But the judge wouldn't go that far. Instead he admonished Moebes to provide us with any reports containing exculpatory information. Moebes found only one that contained what he considered exculpatory evidence. It turned out to be an important one.

Back in Montgomery following the hearing, Dees convened a strategy conference during which the three of us—he, Carroll, and I—made final preparations for trial. This entailed everything from drawing up a witness list to planning motel accommodations and included going over the photos and videotapes again, for it seemed that every time we looked at them we saw something new. While Dees and I studied one set of the pictures, Carroll was examining photos in which David Kelso appeared, in order to familiarize himself with the Klansman's movements in the seconds before the shooting. Dees had asked Carroll to question Kelso at the trial, and Carroll was preparing his cross-examination.

Of the dozens of photos we had of the Bank-Lee confrontation, Kelso was clearly identifiable in three or four. His bushy beard and long, scraggly hair were fairly easy markers. Carroll, however, noticed two additional features that made identification of Kelso possible from a rear or side view: his shoes and his club, which was fashioned out of a tree limb and thus stood out among the far more common ax handles and baseball bats of the Klan mob. Using these distinguishing markers, Carroll was able to identify Kelso in a photograph that appeared to place him immediately in front of Robinson's car with his club raised.

Carroll handed us the picture. It was hard to tell at first. Only a tiny slice of the car was visible, and because the rest of the photo was obscured by the figures of several lawmen, it was difficult to say where it fit in in the sequence of events. Furthermore, because of the angle from which the picture was taken, all you could see of the Klansman in question besides his flowing sheet and hood were a beard, a club, and a pair of shoes.

As the three of us examined the photo, we noticed something peculiar. The photographer had caught "Kelso" in an unusual position, with both feet off the ground and bent forward slightly at the knees. Suddenly it dawned on us that the picture depicted Kelso just as he was being shot. The force of the bullet had lifted him off the ground.

We scrambled to get the video set up and advanced it to the attack scene. A reporter for WAFF-TV in Huntsville, doubling as his own cameraman, had shot the best footage of the incident. As Dees moved the tape forward, frame by frame, we spotted Kelso among a wave of a dozen or so Klansmen rushing up the street toward a group of demonstrators standing by the curb next to Robinson's car. The camera next caught the protesters, including Robinson, as they yielded ground. Robinson had his right hand on his pants pocket, covering his pistol. Just as the Klansmen reached Robinson's car, the picture cut off, as if the photographer, surprised by the sound of gunfire, had stopped filming and hit the deck. Although the shooting itself wasn't depicted, the crucial thing was that the video placed the wave of Klansmen at the front of Robinson's car—with Robinson's wife and five children inside—and only a few feet from Robinson himself. The entire critical sequence lasted only eight to ten seconds.

Dees ran the tape back and forth, and we watched it over and over again, periodically stopping on a given frame to compare certain scenes with the stills. In the glow of the discovery all of us were talking at once.

This was going to be the key to Robinson's defense, the evidence that had eluded us for so long. It was no guarantee of acquittal, but Dees and Carroll believed it was sufficient proof to convince any reasonable group of jurors that Robinson had acted in self-defense. Robinson, to our immense relief, had been telling the truth after all.

By the time the trial began three weeks later, autumn was breaking across the Tennessee River valley. We arrived in Decatur on the Saturday night before the Monday, September 29, 1980, starting date. Dees wanted to be there early so he could have all of Sunday to meet with our witnesses and make final preparations.

On Sunday morning we got up early and went jogging. Our run carried us from the foot of the river bridge, which the Klan had so often crossed after gathering at the pumps; through the quiet residential streets where the National Guard had marched prior to the huge June 9 rally the previous year; over to Bank Street and down the long, sloping hill to the intersection at Lee; in front of the courthouse, one of the drive-by points of the armed Klan motorcade; by City Hall, where the Klan had burned a large cross and Wilkinson had issued his threat to bring vigilante law to Decatur; around the corner from the post office, near where Hines had been arrested; past the coffee shop where the interracial couple had been threatened; and on back to the motel. For an early-morning jog it made for an evocative experience.

Over the past few months KKK activity had been declining in Decatur, and as a consequence the racial climate had cooled down considerably. The Klan was still around, as evidenced by a march it had held there only three weeks earlier, but the level of activity was nothing like what it had been in 1978 and 1979.

After showering and getting dressed, the three of us headed to the dining room for breakfast, buying a copy of the *Huntsville Times* on the way. No sooner was it opened than we noticed a big, bold headline, bannered across a full page: KLAN STRIKE FORCE UNIT TRAINS FOR A RACE WAR. The story, datelined Cullman, reported that a "select group" of KKK members from northern Alabama had formed a paramilitary unit called the Klan Special Forces (KSF) and was training for what the Klansmen believed was a coming race war. It went on to say that the training was conducted at a secluded camp once a month and involved the use of high-powered weapons like the AR-15, the semiautomatic civilian version of the U.S. military's M-16 assault rifle. The story was salted with ominous predictions and quotes by Klan leaders, such as one by Grand Dragon Roger Handley that "we're ready to wade knee deep in blood to protect Birmingham or any other Alabama city."

For a moment the three of us sat in silence, skimming the article. It was Dees's and Carroll's opinion, after finishing it, that the timing of the piece was a thinly veiled attempt by the Klan to intimidate potential jurors in the Robinson case. They based their conclusion on common sense and on the fact that the article mentioned that its author and several other reporters had been allowed to visit the secret training camp two weeks earlier. Such a lengthy publication delay had to have been more than mere coincidence. Furthermore, the KSF's "commander," Terry Joe Tucker, said in the story that ten members of the squad would be in Decatur for the opening of the trial. We had subpoenaed Tucker as a witness but knew him only as the exalted cyclops of the Cullman klavern and for the role he had played in the events of May 26. We hadn't even known about the KSF.

On Monday morning, when we arrived at court for the opening of the trial, the KSF seemed to be the prime topic of conversation among members of the press and spectators gathered outside Judge Hundley's courtroom. As it turned out, the story had run not only in the *Huntsville Times* but in the *New York Times* and, via the wire services, was being picked up by newspapers around the nation. In addition, it had been broadcast on national network television and radio and was being reported in the current issue of *Newsweek*, just hitting the newsstands. Overnight the KSF had become a national phenomenon.

As soon as Hundley's bailiff called the court to order, Dees rose and renewed our motion for a change of venue, citing the avalanche of prejudicial publicity caused by the article. Hundley would have nothing of it, however, and promptly denied it.

At the very least Dees and Carroll hoped the additional publicity on the eve of the trial would persuade Hundley to let them conduct individual voir dire, the process by which prospective jurors were interviewed singly rather than as a group. This method of jury selection was known to encourage jurors to express their opinions more candidly, and it also reduced the risk that a juror knowledgeable or prejudiced about the case would taint the whole panel by his or her answers. It was a time-consuming and painstaking process for the court, but for obvious reasons it was regarded as infinitely fairer to the defendant. Hundley denied this motion as well, and as a result, the twenty-five jurors subpoenaed in the case were questioned as a panel.

The group voir dire that followed merely validated what Dr. Kimmelman's survey had found a year earlier: It would be difficult, if not impossible, to pick a jury of twelve impartial citizens from Morgan County. Hundley made the task no easier by refusing to excuse four prospective jurors who said they knew Kelso (even one honest enough to admit he sympathized with his views) and two others who had friends in the KKK. That forced us to use our precious peremptory strikes to disqualify them ourselves. The jury we wound up with, therefore, was not a civics text model; it was simply the least objectionable one the process permitted. Like Tommy Lee Hines, Robinson was now obliged to put his fate in the hands of twelve white Alabamians, for Moebes had used one of his peremptory strikes to remove the lone black juror from the panel.

After lunch the two sides gave their opening statements. Then the state called its first witness: Marlon Owens. Owens, dressed in his police uniform, took the witness stand, and Moebes began his direct examination. The line of questioning was simple and straightforward: establishing that Owens was a veteran officer (a patrolman with fifteen years on the force), that he knew Robinson through his employment at City Hall, and that he had been assigned to work the May 26 march. After these preliminaries Moebes zeroed in on the officer's alleged encounter with Robinson during the march. Owens repeated the story contained in the incident report Dees had read in Moebes's office. This was, in its entirety, the legal basis for the attempted murder charge against Curtis Robinson, because it was the sole piece of evidence that suggested premeditation. Delivered to the jury in the clipped, unvarnished drawl of a middle-aged Southern lawman, however, it was singularly effective.

Dees began his cross-examination of Owens by insinuating that the singing of the marchers, plus the distance between the two men (Owens estimated it at 100 to 150 feet, about half the length of a football field), would have made it impossible for him to have heard Robinson yell anything. Quickly shifting gears, he tried to blindside Owens with the Paul Watson connection in an attempt to catch the officer off guard.

Q. Mr. Owens, do you know Mr. Kelso?
A. Yes, sir, I know him.
Q. Mr. Owens, didn't you inform Mr. Kelso that you could testify that Curtis went down there to shoot somebody, that he had a gun, that you would take care of this case for him?
A. No, sir.
Q. Mr. Owens, don't you work for a Klansman?
A. No, sir.
Q. I know you work for the city, but don't you work part-time for a Klansman?
A. No, sir.
Q. Mr. Owens, you don't work for Paul Watson, a Klansman?
A. I work for Paul Watson. He is not a Klansman.
Q. How long have you been working for Mr. Watson?
A. Off and on a year or year and a half.
Q. Do you know him pretty well?
A. I have been knowing him all my life.

The exchange caused a discernible stir among the black spectators; but it fell with a thud on the jury, and I suddenly wished I had done more background work on the relationship between the two men. I hadn't given Dees much to work with other than the mere fact of Owens's employment. Carroll had insisted we needed more than that, and he had argued with Dees on the eve of the trial against using the information at all. Just as Carroll had predicted, Owens's credibility seemed to have emerged from the challenge intact.

Dees wasn't through with his cross-examination, however, and his final attack was from another angle. If Robinson had displayed a gun and made the threat, had Owens attempted to stop him or arrest him for violating the gun ordinance? And by the same reasoning, had he even radioed ahead to his fellow officers at Bank and

Lee to alert them? Owens conceded that he had done neither but gave no explanation.

Under different circumstances, in a less partial setting, Dees would have scored points with these questions, but it was difficult to see that they had had any impact on this jury. When Owens stepped down from the witness stand, the first day of the trial had come to an end, and Hundley adjourned court for the night.

On Tuesday morning the trial resumed with appearances by three more Decatur policemen. The first testified he heard another officer order Robinson to surrender his gun and then observed the defendant fire it at a Klansman from what appeared to be a distance of twenty to twenty-five feet. The second said he saw Robinson turn and run up Bank Street, yelling, "Shoot the m----- f-----." The third officer testified he rushed to Kelso's aid after the Klansman was shot. During cross-examination Dees got all three to admit, at times it seemed begrudgingly, that the first shots weren't fired until the Klan had broken through the police lines and confronted the marchers, and the witness to the shooting even conceded that Robinson had been retreating when he fired the gun.

The state's final witness was Kelso, and to have heard him tell it, he was merely an innocent bystander and the KKK was simply in the street to hold a march of its own when Robinson's bullet struck him down out of nowhere. Responding to a litany of questions from Moebes, he denied hitting anyone, swinging at anyone, scuffling with anyone, chasing anyone, or beating on anyone's car.

On that note, Moebes took his seat at the counsel table, and Carroll rose to begin his cross-examination. Physically Carroll was an unprepossessing man: slightly built, of average height, with an advancing hairline and an understated chin. But these appearances were misleading. He had been a marine aviator in Vietnam and had flown numerous combat missions over the North. Easygoing by nature, he could be tough whenever the occasion called for it.

For his examination of Kelso, Carroll put on his best prosecutorial demeanor, and at one point he borrowed an old prosecution ploy and made Kelso come down from the stand to don his robe—this so as to give the jury an image of the exalted cyclops as he had appeared on May 26. To make it the more realistic, Carroll thrust a club in Kelso's hands and had him re-create a pose from one of our photographs.

Peppering him with questions, Carroll challenged the disingenuous explanation that the KKK had planned a march of its own, suggesting that the Klan had conspired to block the SCLC demonstration. Kelso denied the accusation, but Carroll's hammering interrogation produced several heated exchanges.

For many of the black spectators it was probably the first time they had heard a white authority figure express such an attitude toward the Klan, let alone do it in a Southern courtroom. At the conclusion of Kelso's testimony, shortly before noon of the second day, the state rested its case. We had reached the midway point in the trial.

At 2:00 P.M. the bailiff called court back into session, and it was time for Robinson's side of the story to be heard. We got off to a slow start, however. Paul Watson, Marlon Owens's good friend and part-time employer, was our first witness, but the jury seemed skeptical of the links Dees was trying to make between the two, even when Watson admitted that he and Owens had had breakfast together just that morning. Dees hoped the image of the early-morning rendezvous would arouse suspicion in the jurors' minds, so he declined even to ask what the men had spoken about and for dramatic effect abruptly ended the questioning. The truth is, he had probably gotten as much mileage out of Watson as there was to get. The jury seemed unwilling to entertain the notion that Owens's cozy relationship with a former Klan activist (Watson maintained he had resigned his membership, a fact we couldn't disprove) provided any grounds to question his truthfulness.

With the appearance of the next witness, Terry Tucker, the short, slender, twenty-six-year-old head of the Klan Special Forces, the tide seemed to shift in our favor. Dees caught him in several apparent lies about the twenty-sixth, and the more this happened, the more apparent it became that the young Klan leader was engaged in a cover-up of some sort. At times Dees adopted an almost mocking tone toward him, hopeful that the jury would recognize that its intelligence was being insulted by Tucker's responses. In turn, Dees hoped that this would have the effect of undermining Kelso's credibility.

Having cast a degree of doubt on the state's case, Dees now called its chief investigator to the stand, Detective Sergeant Kenneth Collier. With Collier his approach was to be altogether different. According to Robinson, the detective was as close as he had to a friend in the police department, and Dees had been impressed with the officer's professionalism and sense of fair play. Once, during a break in a hearing earlier in the case, Collier had brought it to Dees's attention that he had never observed Robinson at any of the dozens of Hines protests prior to the May 26 march. For the prosecution's chief investigator to volunteer such information, however minor it seemed, was highly unusual. Dees began his questioning of Collier gingerly, easing into the sensitive areas a little at a time. Despite Collier's genuine friendliness, he still had to regard him as a prosecution witness. As a kind of test, therefore, Dees began by asking the detective if he had seen Robinson at any previous marches. Collier said he hadn't. Reinforced by the detective's answer, Dees moved forward through his yellow pad of cryptically scribbled questions. He asked whether the Klan had appeared to be preparing for a march on May 26, as both Kelso and Tucker had insisted, and Collier disputed the claim in no uncertain terms.

At that point, the examination was about to enter a critical phase. Handing Collier a clearly identifiable photograph of Kelso, Dees asked him to study the stick Kelso was holding. He then gave him a picture of Kelso lying wounded on the ground and asked him to compare the stick at the Klan leader's feet with the one in the first photo. Collier agreed that it was the same one. Then Dees handed him the picture of the Klansman we believed to be Kelso in front of Robinson's car just as he was shot, and the following exchange occurred:

Q. Do you see a Klansman there with a raised club right in front of [Robinson's] automobile?
A. Yes, sir.
Q. Who is that?
A. David Kelso.

Detective Collier, the state's chief investigator, had placed the wounded Klansman right in front of the Robinsons' car when he could have easily dodged the question.

As of yet the jury didn't know the still photo had caught Kelso at or about the moment he had been shot, but Dees was about to try to establish that point. Before he could do it, however, he asked for a short recess to set up the video equipment. Hundley granted the request, and the jurors retired to the jury room.

Dees was visibly pumped up by Collier's testimony, and as we rolled the metal stand carrying the VCR and monitor into place, squarely in front of the jury box, he seemed to sense victory within reach.

A few minutes later the jury filed back into court, and Dees cued up the video. By the time he was ready to show it, everyone who could had gathered around the jury box to watch. It was an extraordinary sight: about thirty spectators—Klansmen and marchers and others—elbow to elbow, straining to catch a glimpse of the monitor.

The first time through, Dees played the tape at normal speed without commentary, and the only sound in the still courtroom was the dubbed voice-over of the reporter. The second time he showed it frame by frame, and with Dees standing to one side of the VCR and Collier to the other so as not to obscure the jury's line of sight, the examination of the witness continued. When it got to the critical sequence a split second before the shooting, Dees crouched down in front of the monitor and pointed out the man we believed to be Kelso. He did not name Kelso by name, however. Instead he framed the question to Collier in terms of whether the officer could tell if the Klansman holding the raised club in front of Robinson's car had a beard. It was Dees's way of containing the damage in case Collier (who had not examined the video closely before now) was unable to make the identification. If Collier said yes, Dees would then ask him to identify the Klansman by name. If he said no, Dees would glide right over the matter and into the next question, hoping the point would be lost on the jury. Collier answered in the negative, and Dees continued.

Dees then rewound the tape and showed it again but made no further attempt to get Collier to identify Kelso in the critical frame. He sought instead to establish firmly the sequence of events that led up to the shooting. Since the critical sequence ended with a policeman rushing to assist Kelso as the latter fell to the ground in the area of Robinson's car, Dees believed the jury would surmise that the figure who appeared a few frames earlier was indeed Kelso.

As Dees turned off the video equipment and moved it aside, the courtroom seemed almost to go limp. The jurors, who had been leaning forward intently in their chairs, sat back. The spectators returned to their seats in the gallery. Hundley, who had come down for a better look, took his place again on the bench.

Before finishing with Collier, Dees had one more thing he wanted to accomplish. Ever since the first stories had gone out over the wire services on May 26, the media had characterized the incident as a shoot-out. That impression had been fostered in part by the arrests of the two black parade marshals with their long guns. Through Collier, Dees proved that one of the marshals had been personally assaulted by a Klansman before retrieving his gun from the march security car (the other had been a passenger). In giving the context of the arrests, Dees hoped the jury would view the marshals' actions more sympathetically.

After the video show the rest of the trial day was anticlimactic. The final witness was a ballistics expert who had examined the shot-out right front tire of Robinson's car. In addition to confirming the fact that it had been pierced by a high-speed projectile, the engineer indicated that it had been driven on flat, as Mrs. Robinson had claimed. The fact that the car had sustained gunshot damage, of course, buttressed Robinson's assertion that he had fired on the Klansmen to protect himself and his family.

That night, while the rest of our defense team had a leisurely dinner, Dees and a juristic psychologist met with Robinson to prepare him for testifying. For several hours, in an otherwise vacant courtroom, they worked to make him feel comfortable on the witness stand and at ease with the surroundings. They role-played, Dees taking the part of the district attorney and Robinson answering the questions as he would the next day.

On the third and final day of testimony, our leadoff witness was another lawman, Lee Jeffreys. Now employed with a private security company, Jeffreys had been a sheriff's deputy on May 26, 1979, and had been assigned to work the SCLC march. Although he had filed an incident report that contained clearly exculpatory information, Moebes had not turned it over to us, and we had not learned of its existence until discovering it in the FBI report. It was the lone incident report Hundley had ordered Moebes to give us at the hearing three weeks before the trial.

It was amazing how much Jeffreys's account of the shooting differed from that of the state's single police eyewitness. Jeffreys testified that Robinson was virtually under siege when he fired his pistol and that Kelso was a distance of only six to ten feet away, rushing at him with a raised club. When Dees—over Moebes's strenuous objection—asked Jeffreys what he would have done in the same situation, Jeffreys responded, "If someone [were] advancing on me like that with me having no protection at all, I would have shot him."

Jeffreys's was powerful testimony, and it went directly to the heart of the prosecution's case. As the former deputy described it, the shooting had been a clear-cut case of self-defense. There remained only one witness to call in behalf of the defense, and that was Curtis Robinson himself.

As he took the stand and was sworn in, Robinson seemed visibly nervous. His face, usually graced with an easygoing smile, was uncharacteristically taut and expressionless, and he sat stiff and upright in the witness chair. During the early stages of his testimony he sometimes repeated the wording of Dees's questions in his own responses, as if he derived some measure of security from following in Dees's verbal footsteps. He looked all the more uncomfortable for being dressed in a business suit.

Dees set out to paint a portrait of Robinson as a model citizen of the community: native son; homeowner; family man; City Hall employee entrusted with supervisory responsibilities; holder of an honorary deputy card issued by the sheriff. The message he sought to convey to the all-white jury was: These were not the credentials of an "agitator."

One by one, Dees then confronted the questions he knew the jury would have to have answered to its satisfaction before even considering a verdict of acquittal: Owens's accusation; how the Robinsons happened to be in the march in the first place; what had led Robinson to get out of his car. After his initial case of the jitters, Robinson testified very credibly.

One of the most difficult challenges we faced was to explain why Robinson had lied to the police after his arrest. The rules of evidence, of course, didn't permit Dees to address the jury directly about black Southerners' lack of trust in white law enforcement or the reasons behind it. As a result, this information had to come out through Robinson's testimony, providing Dees with a chance to drive home an important piece of circumstantial evidence of Robinson's innocence; that he had come forward to contact the police about his involvement in the incident the very next day after it happened:

A. The next day I called the City Hall, and I asked to speak to Detective Collier. . . . So they said he wasn't in, and I told them who I were, and I told him when he come in to give me a call. So he never returned my call. So I called back, and when I reached Detective Collier, I said, "Detective Collier, I have something to tell you." I say, "Could you come out to my home?" He said, "What is this about?" I say, "I was in that—up there during that march, and I have some talk for you." He said, "Well, I can't come today." He said, "Can it hold," if I am not misquoting him, "until tomorrow," which is Monday. That also was a holiday. I said, "Well, I can come up there." And he informed me, said, "Don't come up here." Said, "Because Klans is all over the place." Say, "It will hold until tomorrow." And I said, "Okay."

Q. All right. And the next day, on Monday, did he come to your house?

A. Yes, sir.

Q. Okay. Would you tell the jury, if you would, when he got to your house what, if anything, your first conversation was with him?

A. Well, my first words to Detective Collier when he had gotten out of the car—as usual he addressed me as Goose. He said, "Hi, Goose." And I said, "Hi." I said, "I sent for you yesterday, but here you come today." I said that just for a smile. And he laughed, and I said, "Now, I want to show you this tire." I raised the trunk of my car, and he just looked in at it. And I taken him around and showed him my headlight. Then he said, "Goose, can we go inside?" And I said, "Yes, sir." I didn't say, "Yes, sir." I said, "Sure." So we goes inside, and he said, "Goose," said, "What I am going to have to do, it hurts me." He say, "I have a warrant for your arrest for shooting of the Klan." I said, "Oh, man, no." He said, "Yeah." And he said, "Goose, I haven't got a warrant to search your home." Said, "But I can get one. Do I need to?" And I said, "No." He said, "Well, where is the gun, Goose?" I said, "I don't know."

Q. You knew where it was, didn't you?
A. Yes, sir, sure did.

Over Moebes's objections, Dees proceeded to ask Robinson why he had lied about the whereabouts of the gun as well as about being yanked out of his car. Hundley permitted the inquiry—to our surprise—and Robinson admitted he had felt so wronged at being placed under arrest that he had felt obliged to do whatever he could to protect himself, even if it meant misrepresenting what had happened.

The testimony went well—so well, in fact, that Moebes pulled out all the stops during his cross-examination. Addressing Robinson by his first name, he tried repeatedly to goad him into an outburst of anger, accusing him, among other things, of "running like a rabbit" and leaving his wife and children to fend for themselves. He derided Robinson's story, bringing him down from the witness stand at one point to reenact the shooting. It was seemingly all Robinson could do to maintain his composure, but he held on. Midway through the interrogation one of Robinson's children, all five of whom had sat quietly throughout the entire trial, began to cry.

With the conclusion of Robinson's testimony the trial ended, except for closing arguments, which were made following the lunch recess. After receiving instructions on the law from Judge Hundley, the jury then retired to its deliberations at 4:00 P.M. on Wednesday. In Dees's opinion, the longer the jury was out, the better it augured for us, so we were encouraged when it had not reached a decision by 6:00 P.M., and the judge sent its members to their motel for the night.

The next morning the wait began all over again. Finally, at 3:00 P.M., the jurors sent word that they had reached a verdict.

Up until now the suspense had been unpleasant, but now it became physically uncomfortable. Everyone took a place, and silence fell over the courtroom as the bailiff handed the verdict to Judge Hundley. Hundley scanned it and then read it aloud: "We, the jury, find the defendant guilty"—there was a deep, quiet sigh of despair and an almost tangible sagging behind us among the black spectators—"as charged in the indictment, and we also recommend a sentence of probation."

Dees—barely able to control his anger—immediately asked

Hundley to poll the jury, and one by one its members rose from their seats to affirm the verdict. As they did so, Robinson's children broke into tears.

Hundley intended to pronounce sentence on Robinson without delay, and after declaring himself unbound by the jury's recommendation of probation—surplusage he called it—he sentenced Robinson to five years in prison. In the same breath, though, he suspended the sentence and gave Robinson two years' probation. After passing sentence, he put the court in recess. The trial was over.

Dees wheeled around and headed for the gallery, where Robinson's wife and children were seated, still sobbing. He knelt in front of the bench to speak to them. "When the dirty Ku Klux Klan can get by with convicting this man in court, there is no justice," he said, and several reporters scrambled to jot down his words. "Your daddy is a great man, and they're not going to do anything to him. He's not even going to have a criminal record when we get through."

A few minutes later, in a conference room elsewhere in the courthouse, Dees and the Robinsons gathered for what was supposed to be a press conference. Seated on the arm of a couch next to the entire Robinson family, under the glare of TV camera lights, Dees started off by denouncing the verdict.

"This verdict makes history in this state and this nation because it's the first time that a black man has ever been convicted of shooting a robed Klansman who advanced on him with a raised club. This is exactly what we expected would happen by having this case tried in this county. Curtis Robinson would have been acquitted in any other county out of this region and in any other state in the nation."

It wound up being an opening blast and a parting salvo rolled into one, for Dees abruptly ended the press conference and left, taking the Robinsons with him. The press corps was furious, and the next day the *Huntsville Times* called, in an editorial, for an investigation into Dees's remarks by the state bar to determine whether he had violated the canon of ethics by implicitly criticizing the jury.

The ride back to Montgomery that night was a long one, a trip of dashed hopes and second guesses. Although we had kept Robinson out of prison, we felt no joy at the outcome of the trial. A pall of defeat thick as an early-morning mist hung over the car as we headed south down Interstate 65. Not only had the Klan blocked the May 26 march with impunity, but now a jury of Morgan County citizens had ruled, in essence, that the marchers had instigated the violence. Justice, plainly, had not been done.

As we barreled down the highway, Dees kept up a constant conversation about the case, replaying it over and over, as if obsessively. Finally he said, "Let's sue the Klan."

Chapter Five

WHAT DEES had in mind was a federal lawsuit accusing the Klan of conspiring to violate the civil rights of the Decatur marchers. It was the very charge the FBI had been unable to substantiate in its five-month probe of the incident, but Dees was undaunted by the Bureau's failure. He had a hunch, bred of growing up in the rural South during the KKK's heyday, that the incident at Bank and Lee streets was the product of a well-organized Klan conspiracy, not just a spontaneous act by a few hotheads. The evidence, Dees believed, was there; the FBI had merely failed to uncover it.

Such a suit would have twin objectives: to win monetary damages on behalf of the injured marchers and to obtain an injunction barring the KKK from harassing the protesters in the future.

It was a novel idea, if not exactly a unique one. During Reconstruction, Congress had envisioned private litigation against the Klan when it created a set of civil laws to go along with the criminal statutes it had enacted to protect the rights of the newly freed slaves. The civil statutes—like the criminal ones, from which the FBI derived its jurisdiction to investigate the Decatur incident—prohibited any citizen from conspiring with another citizen to deprive a third of his or her civil rights. The main difference was that the penalties for violating the former were civil ones, monetary damages and injunctive relief, rather than incarceration. For obvious reasons, few Klan victims had ever availed themselves of this remedy.

The idea for the Decatur suit gave rise that same night to another, thoroughly original idea: the Klanwatch Project. Northern Alabama was not the only part of the South afflicted by KKK activity during the late 1970s. The Klan was growing by leaps and bounds in a number of pockets across the region, from Texas to Virginia, and even spreading to states outside the Old Confederacy. While working on the Robinson case, we had become increasingly conscious of the group's startling growth and the spiraling increase in violence associated with it. The gunning down of five anti-Klan activists in Greensboro in November 1979 and the unprovoked shooting of four black women on the streets of Chattanooga in the spring of 1980 drove the point home.

Dees, who, like many Southerners, had assumed the Klan (if not the Klan mentality) had passed into the annals of history with the 1960s, now had come to view the resurgent KKK as a real threat. In conceiving the idea of suing the KKK in Decatur, he had hit upon a way in which the Law Center's resources could best be put to use in fighting the KKK on a broader scale.

Within a week of the Robinson verdict, Dees had circulated a memorandum to the SPLC staff, outlining his proposal for establishing Klanwatch. The purpose of the new project, according to the brief memo, would be threefold: to become an information bank on the KKK for journalists and scholars; to file "selected lawsuits" against KKK groups for violating minority citizens' rights; and to provide public education. It was signed "Klanwatcher Dees."

Although the memo didn't make explicit reference to it, one of Dees's reasons for pushing the Project was the fact that there was no one else "out there" doing the work he proposed for it to do. The FBI, its intelligence-gathering apparatus pruned back as a result of the CounterIntelligence Program (COINTELPRO) scandal of the 1970s, no longer routinely monitored the Klan, and state and local law enforcement agencies in the South seemed to rank it low on their list of priorities. The one private organization keeping watch on the KKK, the Anti-Defamation League of B'nai B'rith (ADL), the Jewish service organization, was continuing to collect information on the group and sharing it with its contacts in law enforcement, as it had done—and done effectively—for decades. And from time to time it issued informative reports on the status of right-wing extremism in the country. But as valuable as the ADL program was, it did not have a litigation component. Dees saw a gap to fill.

With a sense of urgency he simultaneously set about organizing Klanwatch and drafting a complaint for the Decatur suit. For the time being, the Project would be a two-man operation—Dees and me—and would consist primarily of collecting and reading newspaper articles from across the country about KKK activity. This was done with the aid of a clipping service. As for the lawsuit, Dees used the facts on hand from the Robinson case to write a rough draft and then turned it over to Stephen Ellmann, a sharp young constitutional lawyer on the SPLC staff, to give it final shape. On November 3, 1980, the suit, *Peoples Association of Decatur, et al.* v. *the Invisible Empire, Knights of the Ku Klux Klan, et al.*, seeking one million dollars in damages, was filed in federal court in Birmingham on behalf of the marchers. Named as defendants were the Invisible Empire, Knights of the KKK; its imperial wizard, Bill Wilkinson; and about twenty individual Klan members who had participated in the conspiracy to block the May 26 march.

The novelty of civil rights demonstrators taking the KKK to court guaranteed that the suit would attract considerable publicity. *Newsweek* even termed it "historic." Unknown to us at the time, a newspaper reporter named Jerry Thompson, on an undercover assignment for the *Nashville Tennessean*, had infiltrated the Cullman klavern of the IEKKKK and was in attendance at its regular weekly meeting shortly after several members had been served with a copy of the complaint. In *My Life in the Klan*, his book about his experiences, Thompson wrote:

I had heard Klan members talk of being arrested, of past Klan violence, and even of shooting people, and it never seemed to bother them. But this lawsuit had their undivided attention—they were visibly shaken. All the Klan members in that room whom I knew had never before shown any fears even in circumstances that would make most people quake in their boots. But it was suddenly obvious that they feared a court confrontation. Despite the macho image most of them try to project publicly, they made no attempt to disguise their concern over the lawsuit.*

Unfortunately we weren't privy to Thompson's information; the book did not come out until some time later. Down in Montgomery, all we could do was wait to see if the suit had loosened some tongues.

The answer came back in less than a month. In early December Dees got a phone call from the law firm of former Alabama Governor Albert Brewer, a resident of Decatur. One of Brewer's partners had been asked by Lloyd Letson, a former Klansman, to represent him. Letson, a twenty-five-year-old laid-off pipe welder, had been arrested on May 26 for assaulting an officer and resisting arrest and slapped with a $760 fine. Letson was in bad financial straits just then, and after learning from his attorney that representation in the civil suit might eventually cost him as much as $10,000, he asked the lawyer to see what it would take to strike a deal with us. When Dees offered to drop him from the suit in return for telling us the truth about what happened on the twenty-sixth, Letson agreed. A day or two later Dees made the by now all-too-familiar drive to Decatur.

Letson was a muscular, barrel-chested young man with thick, coarse hands, a broad face, and a square jaw. His hair, a sandy brown color, was cropped close to the sides of his head and combed straight forward in the front. In the May 26 photos, dressed in blue jeans and a white T-shirt and carrying an ax handle, he looked like the typical schoolyard bully. But the experience of being dragged into court and made a defendant in a million-dollar lawsuit seemed to have softened him up, and he struck a far less defiant pose in his conversation with Dees. He was deferential, polite, and somewhat nervous.

What suspense there was surrounding the meeting was over fairly quickly. After Letson's attorney had shown the two men to a conference room where they could talk privately, Dees immediately popped the all-important question: whether the KKK had, in fact, planned prior to May 26 to block the march. Because of the restrictive way the civil rights laws were worded, it wasn't enough that the Klansmen had disrupted the protest; there had to be evidence of a conspiracy. Letson confirmed that there had been one, and with no more fanfare than that our lawsuit uncovered the plot that had eluded the FBI during its five-month investigation in 1979.

* Jerry Thompson, *My Life in the Klan.* Nashville: Rutledge Hill Press, Inc., 1988, p. 272.

From what Letson went on to say, there had been a meeting of the Decatur klavern on Thursday, May 24, two nights before the march, at which Ray Steele, the titan, had revealed the plan to interfere with the SCLC demonstration. Thirty or forty Klan members had been present, including the exalted cyclops, David Kelso. After outlining the basics of the plot, Steele had directed the Klansmen to meet at the pumps at about midmorning, Letson said, and shortly after that the meeting had ended.

Dees was excited by Letson's account, but he didn't let on. He just wished he'd had his testimony at the Robinson trial; things might have turned out differently. After finding out the particulars, he took a written statement from Letson and talked with him a while longer, steering the conversation away from the lawsuit or the conspiracy. Dees wanted to establish more friendly relations with this young man. He believed a willing witness was a more effective witness. When he found out Letson was a hunter, he invited the former Klansman to Montgomery to hunt at Rolling Hills Ranch.

As Letson warmed up to him, Dees asked him why he had joined the Klan in the first place, and Letson replied that he opposed the marches and demonstrations on behalf of Tommy Lee Hines. He believed Hines was guilty, and he viewed the efforts of Hines's supporters as an attempt to set free a convicted rapist, a black man who had been found guilty in a court of law of raping a white woman. Then he said something intriguing. "I only stayed in it a couple of months." He spoke in a thick, heavy accent that was more Appalachian dialect than Black Belt drawl. "I got out when they started running down the Jews. The Bible says the Jews is God's chosen people, Mr. Dees." The irony of his remark was completely unintended. Somewhere along the way Letson had been taught about the covenant between God and the Jews, and it had made an indelible impression on him.

With a witness like Letson in the fold, we felt much more confident about staying in court on the Decatur lawsuit. If the suit had had only allegations to stand on before, now at least there was one live witness to support it. The next step in the litigation process was for the court to schedule a hearing on the Klan's motion to dismiss the suit. Only then could the formal discovery phase of the case begin.

Early in the new year Dees brought back a former SPLC employee, a non-lawyer, to direct the Klanwatch Project. Randall Williams was a professional journalist who had done award-winning work for newspapers in Birmingham and Montgomery before joining the SPLC as a paralegal in 1976 at the age of twenty-four. Besides performing investigations for the Center's attorneys, he had written its bimonthly newsletter and assisted with various other SPLC publications. In late 1978 he had been lured back into journalism, leaving the SPLC to become editor of a fledgling regional magazine published in North Carolina.

A native of eastern Alabama, with a reddish beard and blond hair and a silky, soft Southern accent, Williams was a gifted writer and a tireless worker, and Dees wanted to put his skills to work for Klanwatch to develop the public education thrust of the Project's three-pronged program.

There was nothing modest about Dees's goals. He wanted to begin immediate publication of a monthly newsletter for journalists that would draw together reports about KKK activity from around the country; his longer-range objective—for the end of 1981—was to produce a newsmagazine-style history of the Klan for distribution to schools across the United States. These concepts gave rise, respectively, to the Klanwatch *Intelligence Report*, which was sent not only to journalists and activists (at no cost) but to the Center's supporters as well, and *The Ku Klux Klan: A History of Racism and Violence*. The magazine, published during the fall of 1981, was distributed free to the social studies department of every public high school in the nation.

During those early months of 1981 the Klanwatch office, located in one corner of the unpretentious, single-story ranch-style building that served as the Law Center headquarters, was a bustling place where the midnight oil often burned. Newspaper clippings were flowing in by the hundreds and had to be read and processed; there were files to be set up, printing deadlines to meet, numerous telephone inquiries from information-hungry reporters to answer. Besides Williams and me (and I worked on the Project only part-time because of my paralegal responsibilities), the only other staffers were a secretary and a young volunteer from Indiana. The latter, a Yale graduate named Mike Vahala, had come south to work on the Project without pay after reading a newspaper article about its formation. Although the Center received several such offers, Dees, the master of direct mail, was so moved by this young Hoosier's letter that he invited him to Montgomery and agreed to pay his living expenses. Vahala was between college and law school and had just finished serving, at the tender age of twenty-four, as the co-manager of a congressional campaign. Together we were the original Klanwatch staff.

Vahala brought strong organizational skills to the Project and quickly assumed the role of research director. One of his responsibilities in that capacity was to acquire KKK literature for our files. Klan publications, especially Klan newsletters, were rich with members' names and other useful data, such as the location of klaverns and activity reports.* This information was immensely helpful in broadening our knowledge about the KKK and in identifying Klan activists and pinpointing areas of Klan strength. The only thing was, you couldn't just walk to a newsstand and buy one of these publications off the rack or even from under the counter. But because they often served the dual purpose of membership newsletter *and* recruitment flyer, it was possible to obtain many of them through the mail or at Klan functions. To make data collection more systematic, Vahala identified the various groups that published materials and got us on their mailing lists, usually by writing a letter posing as a sympathizer and contributing a few dollars. As a result, we began to receive a steady stream of extremist literature—some of it of the vilest, most repulsive sort.† Vahala processed these publications as we did the newspaper clips, extracting every bit of usable information from them. Names went into the members' alpha card file, along with whatever biographical data were available. The location of klaverns was plotted on a United States map and color-coded according to group. Articles of particular interest were photocopied and placed in a file folder for that group, and so on. In this way we began to build up our files.

The sheer number of racist groups in existence came as some-

---

* The Klan was caught in a kind of catch-22 of its own. For recruitment purposes, as well as for the positive reinforcement of members, Klan leaders often found themselves needing to fill their newsletters with accounts of the group's activities to convey the impression of effectiveness and forward motion. But the publication of names and photos also exposed the group's activists to identification by outsiders like Klanwatch and the ADL.

† Among the most offensive flyers were a "running nigger target," with the caricaturish drawing of a black man, and a "nigger hunting license."

thing of a surprise to us. There were the three major Klan groups, but these were just the tip of the iceberg, for there was a plethora of splinter groups. North Carolina was home to several: an outfit known as the Invisible Empire, Knights of the Ku Klux Klan (unrelated to Wilkinson's group), plus the Whiteville Knights, the Carolina Knights, and the White Knights of Liberty. Elsewhere there were the Original Knights in Louisiana and Texas, the Justice Knights and the United Empire in Tennessee, the newly formed KKK of Alabama, the Independent Northern Klans in New York, the Confederation of Independent Orders, an umbrella group for "independent" Klans, the White Knights of Kentucky, the White Knights of West Virginia, the White Knights of Pennsylvania, and many, many more.

And beyond the Klan, way out on the far-right fringe of the political spectrum, were dozens of neo-Nazi organizations, from the ideological descendants of the late American Nazi leader George Lincoln Rockwell to militant anti-black, anti-Jewish extremists clothed in the garb of "survivalism" and pseudo-Christianity. The more we learned about these organizations and their followers, the more we felt obligated to monitor them as well. As the tragedy in Greensboro had illustrated so graphically, there was a growing tendency among Klansmen and neo-Nazis to cooperate and join forces. Erstwhile enemies, the two groups had begun to view themselves as allies, racial soldiers fighting a common foe. Thus, despite the parameters suggested by the name Klanwatch, which Dees chose because he liked the ring of it, we set out to keep track of the whole wide range of violent right-wing extremist groups operating in the United States.*

It was now well established that the KKK was in its first full-fledged revival since the civil rights era. Membership in all the different Klan organizations, which had reached a peak of about fifty thousand during the 1960s and subsequently had fallen to just fifteen hundred by the early 1970s, had risen to approximately twelve thousand, according to the ADL, and reports of Klan-related

* In the not so distant past Klan leaders took pains to dissociate themselves from neo-Nazis, despite the similarities between the two groups' beliefs. Nazism had a bad name with the Klan rank and file in the years after the war, owing to the fact that many Kluxers had fought in World War II or had fathers or uncles who had. For the generation of Klan recruits who joined during the 1970s and 1980s, the stigma surrounding Nazism was beginning to diminish.

violence and intimidation were up as well. This startling reversal in the KKK's decline, though nothing yet to panic about, nonetheless represented a stunning comeback for an organization previously presumed dead. But, then, such had been the long, improbable history of this infamous group.

Ever since the KKK's founding in late 1865 or early 1866 by a handful of Confederate veterans, reputedly as a social club, the story of the organization had been one of cyclical resurgences and protracted periods of dormancy. What modern KKK leaders later called the First Era of the Ku Klux Klan lasted until the early 1870s, when, having helped the forces of conservatism defeat the so-called Radical Reconstruction, the group gradually disbanded, vanishing from the Southern landscape for four decades.

It might have remained that way, except for a talented Hollywood filmmaker named D. W. Griffith. In 1915 Griffith made one of the fledgling movie industry's first feature-length motion pictures, *Birth of a Nation*, based on Thomas Dixon's novel *The Clansman*. The novel, told from a decidedly white Southern point of view, recounted the momentous events of the Civil War and Reconstruction and depicted the KKK as a noble, chivalrous organization. Griffith's adaptation brought the story vividly to life, and the film became a huge commercial success, grossing the virtually unheard-of sum, for that era, of eighteen million dollars. All the publicity prompted an Atlanta preacher turned promoter named William Joseph Simmons to search for a way to cash in on the phenomenon. Attuned to the country's fascination with fraternal organizations, and a member of several himself, Simmons decided to resurrect the KKK as a fraternal society, and on Thanksgiving Eve 1915 he led a handful of followers in a ceremonial cross burning ceremony at Stone Mountain, Georgia. The so-called Second Era of the Klan had begun. Despite the fact that its roots were firmly planted in the South, the KKK spread to the North and West and even became a predominantly non-Southern organization, the result of a backlash against the huge influx of Catholic immigrants from southern Europe settling in Northern cities around the turn of the century. This was also the KKK's high-water mark in terms of membership. More than two million Americans—perhaps twice that many—belonged to the hooded order in the early 1920s, and the KKK actually became a force in American politics. Klan efforts were credited with helping elect governors in Georgia, Alabama, California, Indiana, and Oregon, and in Texas voters sent an avowed Klansman, Earl Mayfield, to the U.S. Senate. Hundreds of local politicians all across the country owed their elections to their Klan supporters. In 1925, in a stunning show of strength, forty thousand robed Klan members marched down Pennsylvania Avenue in a huge parade in the nation's capital.*

Scandals over the group's finances and public revulsion over a series of highly publicized incidents of violence were its undoing, and by the end of the decade the KKK had entered another period of dormancy, though it never completely vanished as before.

The Third Era of the Ku Klux Klan may be traced to May 17, 1954, the date of the Supreme Court's *Brown* v. *Board of Education* decision, and this period of resurgence closely paralleled the development of the civil rights movement. It began, like the movement itself, on a tentative note, but as civil rights activists gained momentum, Klan recruitment soared, and so did Klan violence. From the mid-1950s to the mid-sixties the KKK was suspected of more than 150 bombings and hundreds of arsons and shootings across the South, in which dozens of people died and untold others were injured.

Membership crested in the mid-1960s at the highest level at any time since the flush times of the 1920s. A series of federal prosecutions and a loss of public support—the by-product of the white public's grudging acknowledgement that Jim Crow was finally dead—combined to bring an end to the Klan's reign of terror, and as the sixties drew to a close, membership once again was on the wane. This time the group's demise had an air of permanence about it. The back of organized resistance finally had been broken, and for the first time the rule of law had been established throughout the South (albeit only at the point of a federal bayonet). The existence of extralegal organizations was incompatible with the notion of government based on the primacy of the law.

Yet within less than a decade the KKK was back—if not necessarily to its previous level of strength, certainly to a level that, in the last quarter of the twentieth century, was sufficient cause for alarm.

* A fact frequently omitted from many school texts.

This latest of the Klan's periodic resurgences was vivid testimony to the undercurrent of vigilantism that still ran just beneath the surface of Southern society and evidence, furthermore, of a burgeoning white backlash against minority gains of the previous few years. But it was also to no small extent a function of personality.

Down through the years charisma and personality had played an important role in the Ku Klux Klan, from the group's first imperial wizard, the former Confederate General Nathan Bedford Forrest, to the promoter William Joseph Simmons, and on into the modern era. Since Simmons, however, many Klan leaders had been about equal parts bigot and huckster.

Coincidentally, just as the KKK was reaching its nadir in the early 1970s, a handsome, glib, college-educated young racist materialized on the scene, eager to make over its image and to lead it in yet another revival. His name was David Duke, and he was only in his mid-twenties. Duke, who had picketed a William Kunstler speech in 1970 wearing a storm trooper uniform and carrying a placard bearing the message GAS THE CHICAGO 7, had since become media-wise. By the mid-seventies, the self-styled "National Director" of the Knights of the Ku Klux Klan was plying the talk show circuit from one end of the country to the other, dressed in a three-piece suit, publicly disavowing violence, and professing a commitment to work from within the system. Hawking what he called a "new" Klan, a kind of "white person's NAACP," he eschewed racial slurs and spoke instead of his philosophical opposition to affirmative action and court-ordered school busing. Stylistically at least—even to the point of his fashionably long hair, which just covered his ears—the young Louisiana State University graduate represented a symbolic break with the past, and he was surprisingly successful in changing the Klan's image.

That was all it was, however—an image change. The reality behind the facade was still the same. Through a mail-order operation run out of his national headquarters in Metairie, Louisiana, Duke peddled Nazi literature and other hate tracts, and in private meetings with his members he reverted to the epithets and slurs of traditional Klan leaders.

Still, it would have taken a truth squad assigned to him full-time to have counteracted his public message. In interview after interview he trumpeted the birth of this "new" Klan,* suckering small-town reporters and media heavyweights unprepared for a charming, well-mannered Klan spokesman who didn't ooze with hatred and who could employ polysyllabic words in syntactically correct sentences. (Duke was so pleased with his performance on the "Tomorrow" show with Tom Snyder that he sold videocassettes of it by mail.)

For all his public relations smarts, though, Duke was not an especially effective organizer. By contrast, Bill Wilkinson was, and by out-organizing his former boss, he eventually supplanted him in the late 1970s as the leading KKK figure of the Fourth Era. Wilkinson's leadership style was a hybrid of the old and the new. He talked of a race war and made no bones about using intimidation tactics to accomplish Klan goals, but he was also a slick media manipulator and a shameless promoter. To elicit speaking invitations, he flooded colleges and universities with his flyers, and he ran a brisk concession business through his newspaper, *The Klansman*, selling everything from Klan jewelry to Klan T-shirts, Klan bumper stickers, and Klan belt buckles. (We once estimated that Wilkinson's Invisible Empire may have had annual revenues from membership dues and other sources of $100,000 or more during this period.)

In the end, Wilkinson disposed of Duke through a cleverly executed scam in 1980, duping his rival into believing he would buy the Knights' membership list for $35,000, then turning the tables on Duke and exposing him to the media. By the time the Law Center filed the Decatur suit in November of that year, Wilkinson was the number one Klansman in the country, and his Klan the fastest-

* The role of the media in the resurgence of the Klan during the 1970s was an important one. Too many reporters fell victim to the manipulative tactics of Duke and his emulators. One California Klansman handed out robes to bystanders when his own supporters failed to show for a rally, and when the reporters he had invited arrived, he compounded the duplicity by informing the journalists that each one of the dozen or so robed "members" was a representative from each of the districts in the state. The press fell for it, and the coverage that resulted made it appear that the Klan was growing rapidly in the area. By the time of the next rally, it indeed was. About thirty robed Kluxers attended, and the rally following it drew another eighty. The local media had been hoodwinked into boosting Klan membership. But while any boost the Klan received from the media was usually inadvertent, the product of poor preparation on the part of the reporter or outright manipulation by Klansmen, in a few instances it involved the witting participation of news organizations. Some newspapers accepted advertisements promoting Klan functions. The *Decatur Daily* went several steps further, running an announcement for an IEKKKK rally in its regular Calendar section, a listing of community activities, and reprinting an application form.

growing. It was also, as the Justice Department had noted in a special report on the KKK, the one most prone to violence.

In March 1981 the inaugural issue of the Klanwatch *Intelligence Report* was published, its eight letter-size pages packed with information from around the United States about incidents involving KKK members and other violent racists. In a series of "news briefs," we reported on, among other things: the grand dragon of the Michigan KKK, who had recently been sentenced to prison for conspiring with associates to murder a black man in Detroit and for firing an automatic weapon into the home of an interracial family; a cross burning in Phoenix attended by some thirty people; a Texas rally that had attracted hundreds of Klansmen and sympathizers to a coastal community not far from Houston; and a victory dinner given by a prominent Georgia racist in honor of six Klansmen and Nazis who had recently been acquitted of state murder charges in the Greensboro killings.

On the first day of spring, shortly after the newsletter was published, the body of a nineteen-year-old black youth named Michael Donald was found hanging from a small tree on a residential street in downtown Mobile. It was a gruesome crime. The murderer, or murderers, apparently had beaten Donald unconscious with a blunt instrument, slit his throat, then strung up his body in the tree, lynch-style. The battered, bloody corpse, already growing stiff with rigor mortis, was discovered dangling a few feet off the ground at dawn by a passerby, who called the police. The police in turn notified the coroner, who arrived minutes later to find the last signs of life—a trace of warmth under the armpits and in the groin—slipping out of the youth's body. The impression of a bootprint was visible on the forehead.

The murder had all the earmarks of a racial slaying, and Williams, Vahala, and I were so stricken by its enormity that we discussed going to Mobile to conduct our own investigation, particularly after local white officials had downplayed the notion that the case had racial overtones. Mobile had a long history of racial repression—as late as 1976 a black man in his twenties had been mock-lynched by a group of white policemen bent on forcing him to confess to a string of armed robberies he had had nothing to do with—and we did not want to sit by idly and let the slain youth become one more forgotten victim. Within a few days, however, the police had arrested three young white men and formally charged them with the murder. Although the trio was released several weeks later—they had been the victims of perjured testimony—we decided to defer our plans to get involved. From what we could tell, the authorities now seemed intent on solving the killing. Besides, Dees had another case he wanted to pursue.

A regular reader of the *New York Times*, Dees had run across an article in the paper about a Texas Klan group engaged in a campaign of intimidation against Vietnamese refugees who had settled on the Gulf Coast and taken up shrimping on Galveston Bay. It seemed that some white shrimpers, resentful of the refugees' prosperity and ever-increasing numbers but cloaking their prejudice in complaints about overfishing and unfair competition, had mounted a drive to run the Vietnamese-Americans out of the area and had asked the Klan for help. The leader of the Klansmen, a militant Vietnam vet named Louis Beam, had gone so far as to issue a public ultimatum in February giving the authorities ninety days to resolve the crisis—by which he meant resettle the Vietnamese—or the KKK would take matters into its own hands. To stress that the Klan meant business, Beam used the setting of a Valentine's night rally to demonstrate the "proper way" to burn a boat, a boat dubbed, not so subtly, the "USS Viet Cong." The ultimatum, widely publicized by the local media, was not lost on the Vietnamese: May 14, the deadline, happened to be the day before the opening of the 1981 shrimping season.

At the very least Beam's actions seemed to flout the federal civil rights laws. To Dees the situation smacked of something else: a possible violation of the Sherman Antitrust Act. In effect, the Klan and the fishermen were conspiring to force the Vietnamese out of the shrimping business, and Dees believed their conduct constituted an illegal restraint on trade. No one had ever filed an antitrust case against the Klan since Congress had enacted the statute in the trust-busting days of Teddy Roosevelt, and Dees relished the idea of being the first.

Before a lawsuit could be filed, of course, we had to have plaintiffs. Dees jotted down the name of the president of the Vietnamese

Fishermen's Association, Colonel Nguyen Van Nam, and called him to offer the Law Center's assistance.* Colonel Nam, a former South Vietnamese military officer, referred him to John Hayslip, a Texas City, Texas, attorney who had recently come to represent the Association, and soon Dees was on his way west to lay out his plan for suing the Texas Knights.

Arriving in Seabrook, a normally serene fishing village of some forty-five hundred people located about twenty-five miles southeast of Houston on Galveston Bay's western shore, Dees rendezvoused with Hayslip, who had offered to accompany him to meet Nam. Like Beam, Hayslip was a Vietnam vet and a gun lover, but the similarity between the pair ended there. Hayslip liked the Vietnamese people and admired them for their industry and resourcefulness. Aside from his role as their counsel he seemed genuinely concerned about their welfare. He backed the idea of the suit and expressed eagerness to assist in any way. Dees knew it was important to have him on board because as Nam's attorney, Hayslip was in a position to exert great influence over Nam's decision, and without Nam there wasn't any suit; it was as simple as that.

The two attorneys drove the short distance to Nam's house. Dees was struck by the prosperous, commercially developed appearance of the Seabrook area. Far from being the kind of impoverished, out-of-the-way place one tended to associate with Klan vigilantism, Seabrook had a thriving, modern look about it, complete with trendy restaurants and modern motels, and was only one of several such communities strung along the western shore of the bay. What made the setting all the more incongruous as a backdrop for KKK activity was that it was situated practically in the shadow of the Johnson Space Center, the headquarters of the National Aeronautics and Space Administration. Less than ten miles from where arsonists had recently set fire to several Vietnamese boats, America's top engineers and space scientists were just then preparing for the launching of the *Columbia*, the nation's first space shuttle.

Nam lived in a simple white frame house on the northern bank of Clear Creek Channel, a small stream connecting Clear Lake with Galveston Bay. The front part of the residence was a fish house,

---

* As a nonprofit law firm the SPLC was not affected by the rules governing the solicitation of clients by attorneys in private practice.

from which he ran a seafood business; the family quarters were in the rear. Directly across the Channel, as local residents called it, was another little fishing village with a sizable and growing Vietnamese population, Kemah. The two communities were linked by a steel drawbridge. The first thing Dees noticed was the presence of two or three young Vietnamese men gathered in front of the house, talking among themselves. They were a volunteer security team, standing watch as a favor to Colonel Nam, whose high profile as leader of the fishermen had increasingly made him and his family a target for intimidation.

Nam was a handsome man, forty-seven years old (twenty-two of which he had spent in the South Vietnamese military) with thick, straight black hair and dark eyes. Like other Vietnamese, he had come to the United States in 1975 after the fall of Saigon penniless but eager to start over in his adopted country. Working at various jobs and borrowing money from his family, he quickly saved enough to go into business on his own, and in 1978 he moved to Seabrook and purchased a fish house. In deference to his former military rank he was quickly recognized as a leader in the refugee community, and when trouble with the white fishermen led the immigrants to form the Vietnamese Fishermen's Association (VFA) in 1980, they turned to Nam for leadership.

For about an hour Dees and Hayslip sat in Nam's living room and talked with him about the suit, explaining the purpose of the United States' civil rights laws and what could be expected to result from such litigation. Nam was receptive, but he was clearly worried that taking legal action against the KKK might bring more trouble to the Vietnamese than they now had. Already there had been incidents of night riding and arson, cross burnings and threats at gunpoint, and many of the fishermen were ready to sell out at the first opportunity. Dees tried to assuage Nam's concerns and seemed to succeed, but he left after an hour not knowing whether the VFA leader would be able to sell his membership on the suit or whether the refugees were beyond persuasion.

Hardly a month before, in fact, Colonel Nam had announced at an emotional meeting in Seabrook between public officials and native and Vietnamese shrimpers that fully 60 percent of the Association's members, including himself, were ready to sell their boats and move on. "If you no like me to stay, yes, sir, I leave," he had said, expressing the wounded feelings of the fishermen and their families. And it was little wonder that they felt that way.

Since beginning to settle along the Texas coast about 1975, the refugees had encountered widespread hostility. Few of them spoke English, and their customs and ways were alien to the provincial South Texans. Add to the inevitable clash of cultures the fact that the state and federal governments did very little preparatory work among the host communities, and it was a perfect recipe for confrontation. As the number of refugees swelled—mushrooming from virtually zero to several thousand in the Galveston Bay area alone by the end of the decade—resentment among less tolerant whites began to approach the boiling point.

The chief complaint among the native shrimpers was that the Vietnamese overfished the waters, but they also blamed the state for exacerbating the situation by failing to enforce the laws as rigidly against the refugees as it did against the natives—an allegation for which they provided no proof—and by licensing too many refugee boats. The latter grievance was particularly specious in light of the fact that the Vietnamese had purchased their vessels secondhand (often at inflated prices) from the Texans themselves, who used the profits to buy still larger boats. While the Vietnamese were ignorant of local fishing customs, the crux of the matter was that the refugees were too numerous and industrious for the native shrimpers' liking, and their presence was altering the cultural and demographic landscape of the community.

The friction first erupted into violence in August 1979, when a dispute over the placement of crab traps led to the shooting death of an American fisherman by two Vietnamese brothers in the village of Seadrift, a hundred miles down the coast on San Antonio Bay. The night after the shooting the dead man's colleagues retaliated by firebombing several Vietnamese boats and a house trailer and beating two refugees. A curfew was imposed, and mediators from the U.S. Justice Department's Community Relations Service were brought in to restore calm. The Vietnamese brothers eventually were acquitted on the ground of self-defense, but the verdict, rendered by an all-white jury in a distant town where the case was moved on account of pretrial publicity, left native fishermen up and down the Texas coast even angrier than before.

Early in January 1981, three months before Dees's overtures to

Nam, the long-simmering resentment toward the refugees in the Seabrook-Kemah area finally boiled over. Late one night an unknown party set fire to a Vietnamese shrimp boat. Damage to the vessel was minor, but the next night arsonists struck again, this time across the Channel in Kemah. No arrests were made in either incident, and a sense of alarm swept through the refugee community.

At about the same time—coincidentally or not—the American Fishermen's Coalition, a small but vocal group of the most militant Texas shrimpers, turned up the heat in its efforts to expel the Vietnamese. On the day following the second arson 150 of them convened a meeting in Seabrook to discuss the Vietnamese "problem," and later that month a smaller delegation met with representatives of various governmental agencies to pressure the authorities into limiting the number of boats on the bay. Informed there was no statutory or regulatory authority for doing so, the shrimpers stalked out of the meeting. A day or two later their leader, a portly sometime shrimper and swimming pool installer named Gene Fisher, turned to the KKK for help.

The Klan was only too willing to oblige. Its leader, Grand Dragon Louis Beam, was obsessed with the idea that the United States was being overrun by people of color in an international conspiracy to wrest control of the country from its white majority, and he viewed the fishing dispute as potentially the opening skirmish in the fight to "reclaim" it.

For Beam, a short, intense thirty-four-year-old with dark hair and a scraggly mustache who had been a tailgunner on an army helicopter in Vietnam, this was not just an idle metaphor. In 1980 he had been arrested for lunging at Chinese Deputy Premier Deng Xiaoping in a swank Houston hotel during the Marxist leader's much publicized visit to the city, and he had been suspected by the Houston police—and even indicted, though the charges were later dropped—in the bombing of a left-wing radio station and an attack on the local Communist party headquarters during the early 1970s. On another occasion he had been charged with false imprisonment for assisting a white couple in removing their daughter from her home, which she shared with a black man, but that charge had also been dismissed.

In preparation for what he expected was an imminent and inevitable race war, Beam had his Klansmen undergoing paramilitary training twice a month in the swamplands northeast of Galveston Bay, rigorous training led, purportedly, by active-duty military personnel from nearby Fort Hood or by ex-servicemen like Beam. Membership in the group, known as the Texas Emergency Reserve (TER), was estimated by law enforcement officials to be somewhere between two hundred and five hundred.

Beam offered to put some of the American shrimpers through the Klan's training camp. "Enough of this backing up and retreating," he told several hundred supporters at the Valentine's night rally. "Enough of this lip service and no action. It's time to begin to train, it is time to begin to prepare to reclaim this country for white people. Now I want you to understand that they're not gonna give it back to us. If you want it, you're gonna have to get it the way the founding fathers got it—blood! blood! blood! The founding fathers shed their blood to give you this country, and if you want to hold on to it, you're gonna have to shed some of yours."*

Beginning that night, and for the next several days, the airwaves and the newspapers were filled with pictures of Beam setting fire to a small skiff with the words "USS Viet Cong" painted on it.

In the wake of the Klan's intervention into the fishing dispute, there was, not surprisingly, a surge in acts of intimidation against the Vietnamese and their few white friends. Marina operators who rented the refugees space to dock their boats were threatened with arson, and several businessmen who traded with the immigrants were warned of reprisals. Two more refugee boats were set on fire, and a pair of crosses were burned in the yard of a Vietnamese shrimper and near a marina locals had disparagingly nicknamed Saigon Harbor. Klan calling cards began showing up in the mailboxes of those persons who had befriended the Vietnamese. The cards, the same size and shape as ordinary business cards, bore the warning YOU HAVE BEEN PAID A SOCIAL VISIT BY THE KNIGHTS OF THE KU KLUX KLAN—DON'T MAKE THE NEXT VISIT A BUSINESS CALL. The image of a robed, hooded Klansman, mounted on a leaping horse and carrying a fiery torch, appeared adjacent to the message.

The crowning act of intimidation, however, occurred on Saturday, March 15. At midmorning an American shrimp boat loaded with

* SPLC video files.

fifteen Klansmen sailed back and forth along the Seabrook-Kemah waterfront, slowly passing the homes of many Vietnamese and skirting "Saigon Harbor." The Kluxers, clad in robes, camouflage fatigues, or black KKK T-shirts, openly brandished semiautomatic weapons and shotguns. A human effigy, hung by the neck, dangled from the vessel's rear rigging.

On its pass along the Seabrook side of the Channel, the boat pulled up behind Nam's house and stopped. At the time the only person at home was Nam's teenage sister-in-law, who was baby-sitting his infant daughter. When she saw the robes and guns of the Klansmen, she scooped up her niece and, terrified, fled from the house. The boat subsequently sailed off and headed back into the bay, where it paused about a mile offshore. The Klansmen then fired a blank round from a cannon they had brought on board, sending a concussion cascading up and down the coastline. After several hours of "patrolling" the waters, the Klansmen finally brought the menacing episode to an end and returned to port.

Such was the political climate on Galveston Bay when Dees flew to Texas in late March. After presenting his case to Nam, Dees returned home to await the verdict of the fishermen's association. Hayslip phoned with the good news a few days later: By unanimous vote, the fishermen had agreed to ask the Law Center to file suit against the KKK on their behalf.*

Dees immediately sent Williams and Vahala to Texas to gather the basic facts needed to draft the complaint. Time was limited. There were barely six weeks to go before the opening of the new shrimping season on May 15, and Dees knew that if the suit were to have any impact, it would have to be adjudicated by then. Otherwise the refugees would be faced with three equally unacceptable courses of action: to sell their boats (if they could find buyers) and get other work, to stay in port and lose money, or directly to challenge the KKK's ultimatum by going out on the bay and run a substantial risk of violence. Since it was procedurally impossible to

---

* Although the parallels between the Decatur situation and Texas were few—a different Klan was involved and a different set of victims—there was one huge similarity: the failure of the white majority to take a stand against KKK vigilantism. A serious leadership void existed at every level of society. Rather than vigorously denounce the Klan and its tactics, Texas Governor Bill Clements went so far as to impanel a commission to relocate the Vietnamese away from Galveston Bay, and the mayor of a small coastal community suggested soliciting corporate donations to help effect the relocation.

file the suit, conduct discovery, and go to trial in such a short period of time, Dees decided to include in the complaint a request for a preliminary injunction. The court had the discretion to schedule a hearing on the request, a sort of minitrial, before May 15 if it saw fit to do so.

To win such an injunction, the burden of proof was heavy: We would have to show a "substantial likelihood" that we would prevail on the merits of the lawsuit at a later, full-blown trial, that the plaintiffs would suffer an "irreparable injury" if the injunction were not granted, that the threatened injury to the plaintiffs outweighed any threatened harm to the defendants in granting the injunction, and that an injunction would not disserve the public interest. In a nutshell, it meant that we would have to do in a month what it would normally take a year or two to do.

With the assistance of Colonel Nam, two priests (one Vietnamese, the other an American), Hayslip, and officials from the Catholic relief agencies, which had helped resettle the refugees, Williams and Vahala pulled the critical facts together, and on April 16 the lawsuit, styled *Vietnamese Fishermen's Association* v. *Knights of the Ku Klux Klan, et al.*, was filed in the U.S. District Court in Houston.

By the luck of the draw, the judge assigned to hear the case was Gabrielle K. McDonald, a Carter appointee in her late thirties and the first black woman to sit on the federal bench in Texas. McDonald was known to be fairly liberal, and as an attorney in private practice she had once handled civil rights cases. As we had hoped, she quickly consented to holding a hearing on our request for a preliminary injunction and scheduled it for May 11, just four days before shrimping season opened. Expedited discovery promptly began.

If the lawsuit took some of the heat off the refugees, it became clear right away that it had merely deflected it in the direction of their attorneys. The morning after the suit was filed, a plain envelope was found on the floor outside the office of David Berg, a Houston lawyer whose firm, Berg & Zelikow, Dees had asked to associate with the case. When Berg opened it, he found a photocopy of a KKK calling card inside. On the night of the following day another one appeared in front of his home. No one could know it at the time, but this was just a harbinger of things to come.

On April 30 Dees arranged with the lawyers for Beam and Gene Fisher to take their clients' depositions. The testimony was to be taken at the offices of their attorneys, Sam Adamo and Richard Cobb. At the appointed hour Dees and a small entourage—Hayslip, Nam and three other Vietnamese, along with Vahala and Williams—arrived at the downtown Houston bank building in which the firm of Adamo & Cobb was located. As the group walked into the lobby of the ground-floor law office, Dees noticed a casually dressed young man with short blond hair seated on a couch, a camera hanging around his neck, but he thought nothing of it. Dees checked in with the secretary, who directed him to a spacious conference room down the hall where the depositions were to be taken.

In the middle of the conference room was a massive wooden table, perhaps fifteen or twenty feet long. Dees set his briefcase down beside one of the leather chairs that lined either side of the table and pulled out a legal pad on which he had outlined the questions he planned to ask the deponents. Williams, Vahala, and the Vietnamese settled into seats nearby.

Before beginning the depositions, Dees and Hayslip went back to Adamo's private office for a conference with the defendants' attorneys. While they were out of the room, the young blond man entered and, before anyone realized it, began taking photographs of the Vietnamese plaintiffs, approaching to within three feet of them. The refugees were clearly upset, but being unfamiliar with court procedure, they put up no resistance.

Williams looked up from his newspaper, however, and instantly knew something was amiss. He asked the man his name, but the man ignored him and continued to take pictures. Williams repeated himself, and the intruder mumbled something unintelligible, except for the word *soldier*, then turned and aimed the camera in Williams's direction. Williams flashed the newspaper in front of his face and asked the man to leave. When he didn't, Williams hurried from the room, still holding the paper in front of his face, to look for Dees. A few seconds later the two men returned. Finding the intruder still taking pictures, Dees ordered him out of the room, but he acted as if he hadn't heard. Seeking to avoid a physical confrontation, Dees then went and got Adamo, who prevailed upon the young photographer to stop.

Dees saw Beam's hand behind the episode, and he insisted that the man remain in the office and submit to questioning. After things had settled down, Gene Fisher, the first witness, was called in, and when Fisher's deposition came to an early end—on advice of counsel, the spokesman for the American shrimpers took the Fifth to every question—Dees summoned the photographer back to question him under oath.

Dees had him sworn in and took his deposition on the spot. His name was Russell Gregory Thatcher. None of the SPLCers recognized the name, but over the next few minutes it became apparent that it belonged in our files. Two questions into the inquiry the deposition ground to a halt, with Thatcher, who had the wide-eyed look of a zealot, refusing to give his address—"hardening the target" he called it. He explained that this was "simple military tactics and procedure." His response prompted the following exchange with Dees:

Q. It's military tactics?
A. That's simple procedure. I'm a military person.
Q. Are you a member of Mr. Beam's military organization?
A. No, I'm not.
Q. Have you ever trained at any of his military camps?
A. I refuse to answer that on the grounds it may incriminate me.
Q. Would you state the basis and detail for your grounds not to answer that question?
A. Because I'm a survivalist, and as a survivalist I minimize my contact with the enemy under certain circumstances, and some such circumstances as this right here.
Q. And who do you perceive to be your enemy here?
A. I perceive you as one of my enemies.
Q. I'm your enemy?
A. Yes.
Q. Would you state what, if anything, that I have done to make me your enemy?
A. You're involved and a tool of a system which I find oppressive to basic human rights, those human rights as founded by the Constitution—not human rights but through civil rights, and as such you're my enemy.

Thatcher was a strange young man, and his answers, not to mention his behavior and his eyes, were unsettling. Under further questioning, he testified that he was a member of the Nazi party and a "minister" in something called the Aryan Covenant Church, though he refused to divulge even where it met. He freely admitted, however, that Beam had invited him to attend the depositions.

Having established the link with Beam, Dees subsequently terminated the examination and then subpoenaed Thatcher, along with his camera and roll of film, to a pretrial hearing in the case scheduled for the next day. For good measure, he then took Williams's deposition while the incident was still fresh on the latter's mind.

Just when normality seemed about to set in, Beam, the next witness, dressed in his Klan robe and accompanied by a man in priest's vestments, appeared in the doorway. They were a bizarre sight, the grand dragon of the Texas Klan in his white KKK robe and the "priest," who was actually one of Beam's followers, in his liturgical collar and black coat. Beam took his seat in the witness chair almost exactly opposite Dees and produced a small crucifix, mounted on a stand, and placed it on the table directly in front of him. He and his spiritual counselor subsequently engaged in a prayer, in hushed tones too low for Dees or his aides to make out. After they had finished, Beam was sworn in by the court reporter.

Beam, like Fisher, declined to answer any questions, invoking the Fifth Amendment to each inquiry, even about his own identity. When Dees assured himself that Beam could not be induced to testify, he announced that he had no further questions and informed Beam and his counsel that he intended to take the matter up before Judge McDonald at the hearing the next day. Just as the abbreviated deposition was about to break up, Beam asked if he could make a statement. Richard Cobb, one of his attorneys, cautioned him not to say anything. But Dees goaded him. "Let the record show that the witness is refusing to testify—" he began.

Suddenly Beam blurted out, "Let the record show that Morris Dees [is] an anti-Christ Jew." Dees, ignoring the remark, had begun to pack his papers when Nam leaned over and warned him in a whisper that Beam was wearing a pistol beneath his robe. Dees immediately stopped what he was doing and calmly but sternly asked Adamo to determine if his client was carrying a weapon. Startled, Beam pushed back his chair from the table and began to rise. As he did, Dees noticed his robe appear to catch on what could have been the handle of the pistol. Beam glared at Dees, who had started to get up, then turned and swung around to confront Adamo. As he edged backward, the Klan leader thrust out his arm and snapped, "You don't have permission to search my body unless you've got a permit," and rushed out of the room. Moments later Adamo and Cobb and the "priest" followed.

When they returned in a few minutes, Beam had removed his robe, and there was no weapon visible on his person. But Dees had had enough. Within an hour after the end of the deposition session, he had drafted a motion for a protective order summarizing the day's strange happenings and requesting that all future testimony in the case be held in the federal courthouse in the presence of a United States marshal.

The first day of deposition taking had come to a tumultuous end. While the behavior of Beam and his followers had bordered on the farcical, the gun scare—though the weapon's existence never was proved—had been a harrowing experience, and it revived the disturbing question of just how far Beam and the KKK would go in their effort to intimidate.

On the following day, May 1, McDonald held an in-chambers hearing on our motion for protection. Security was extraordinarily tight. Marshals with hand-held metal detectors screened everyone who entered the court area. At the end of the two-hour session the judge issued a protective order requiring all future depositions to be taken in the conference room of the federal courthouse under the supervision of a U.S. marshal. She forbade outsiders from attending or interfering with the depositions and explicitly banned weapons from them. She also directed that Thatcher's film be confiscated.

Beam, who showed up outside the judge's chambers carrying a tote bag in which his robe and a Bible were stashed, tried to make light of all the commotion he and his cohorts had caused. "Of course not," he responded wryly to a reporter's question about whether or not he had worn a concealed gun to the deposition. "I had a Bible under my robe. That's enough protection."*

The protective order brought a collective sigh of relief from Dees and the rest of the litigation team. But there remained in the plaintiffs' camp a thoroughgoing wariness of Beam, despite his protestations of innocence. He was a strange man, and from what Williams

* *Houston Post*, May 2, 1981.

and Vahala had found out during the course of their investigation for the case, sifting through old newspaper clips and poring over video footage of some of his rally speeches and other activities, he was also potentially very dangerous.

The danger was twofold: that which he posed individually, on the one hand, and as the leader of a heavily armed band of militant extremists, on the other. As to the former, his unpredictable behavior at the deposition had been eloquent testimony. There was also the violent imagery that pervaded his rhetoric. In interviews with reporters he often talked fondly of the Vietnam War and bragged about his "body count." Words like *exterminate, kill,* and *annihilation* fairly tripped off his tongue. Once, referring to the day when the Klan would eventually take control in Texas, he had boasted, "We'll set up our own state here and announce to all minorities that they have 24 hours to leave. Lots of them won't believe it or won't believe us when we say we'll get rid of them, so we'll have to exterminate a lot of them the first time around."*

The larger threat, however, if not the more immediate one, revolved around Beam's apocalyptic vision of the future. Like a growing number of white supremacists, he believed in the imminent social and economic collapse of American society, and he wholeheartedly welcomed the prospect. Subscribing to the notion that the United States was a white man's country but that whites had lost control of it to racial and religious minorities, Beam viewed the chaos that inevitably would result from such a cataclysmic event as an opportunity for whites to reassert control and purge the country of what the Klan referred to as its "alien scum."

Among the most disturbing evidence of Beam's grim vision were videotapes Williams and Vahala had located of the TER's paramilitary training, which Beam had permitted a young Rice University film student to videotape. One segment depicted Beam, his voice ringing with a tinny south Texas twang, instructing his troops on the techniques of ambush, search and destroy, and the like. "When they get in that kill zone and you initiate fire—maximum damage in the shortest length of time," he could be heard telling a dozen or more camouflage fatigue-clad men sitting on the ground at his feet. "Maximum violence upon them. Everybody in there. They mustn't

* *Flint* (Michigan) *Journal,* June 19, 1980.

have a chance to do anything but one thing: die." The tapes provided vivid evidence that Beam's rhetoric was more than bluster. It also strongly suggested that the level of training TER members received might be, as Beam had claimed, in the same league with that of active-duty military.

The more we learned about Louis Ray Beam, Jr., the more we realized he was far and away the most radical, most dangerous Klansman we had encountered in our brief experience with the KKK. And what made this all the more worrisome was that he was bright and articulate, a good speaker and a skillful writer, a person of some leadership ability and true commitment. Whereas Wilkinson had long been accused of "ambulance chasing" and of mishandling Klan funds and while Duke had been accused of attempting to profiteer from his Klan position, no one had accused Beam of either. He led a manifestly unmaterialistic existence, driving an old clunker of a car and living in a trailer home with his second wife and their infant daughter. By choice he didn't even own a television, although his rationale was more ideological than ascetic: He believed the Jews owned the media.

Beam's entire existence, like that of Reverend Drummond, the Alabama Klan chaplain, and that of an increasing number of white supremacists, revolved around the conviction that the white race was ordained by God to have dominion over the earth and that world Jewry was engaged in an international conspiracy to subvert the divine plan and conquer the world for the Antichrist. Blacks, Hispanics, Vietnamese, and other racial and ethnic minorities were merely its pawns in the plot.

For Beam, the Klan's defeat in the 1960s at the hands of the federal government and the coming of racial equality (at least theoretically) was proof that whites had lost control of the United States. As a result, Beam viewed himself and his Klan colleagues as insurgents. In this respect he differed from Klan leaders of earlier times; he was fighting not to defend a way of life but to reclaim it.

As if Beam's theatrics weren't enough to cause concern among the SPLC staffers, Dees was soon faced with a challenge of a different sort. About a week before the preliminary hearing, Nam phoned him with the news that a council of elders representing the entire Vietnamese community in the Greater Houston Area had met and decided to drop the lawsuit. The council, composed of the heads of various trade associations, including the VFA, had come to the conclusion that pressing the lawsuit would only generate ill will toward the Vietnamese community in general. The organization's leaders had come to believe that the Klan spoke on behalf of the white community as a whole, and they were prepared to ask the refugee fishermen to give up the fight for the right to shrimp on Galveston Bay for the good of the Vietnamese population at large. Although Nam, who was president of the council, did not agree with the decision, he was ready to abide by it.

Dees was floored. He immediately asked Nam to assemble the council so he could appear before it and attempt to persuade its members to reverse their decision. The meeting was held in the activities hall of a small Catholic church in Houston. With a Vietnamese interpreter at his side, Dees began by explaining that the Klan did not represent the views of all whites. Then, adopting a civics class approach, he spoke to them about the Constitution and pointed out that like the millions of immigrants before them, they were entitled to the full protection of the laws. Urging them to stand their ground, he warned them that to do otherwise would invite further harassment. Then he left the room to deliberate. Just as he had hoped, they voted to reverse themselves.

But the larger issues in the lawsuit ultimately came to be overshadowed by Louis Beam's erratic behavior. More and more he seemed to perceive the case as a personal confrontation between himself and Dees, whom he apparently believed to be Jewish. During the resumption of his deposition on May 3 he sparred back and forth with him, coyly evading questions, flatly refusing to answer others, citing his Klan oath of secrecy, and periodically digressing to deliver brief speeches on this issue or that. From time to time he displayed flashes of his sardonic sense of humor. On one occasion Dees asked him if he'd ever seen a psychiatrist. "Not to my knowledge," he replied without skipping a beat. "I might add that I've had a couple of people suggest to me [who] work for various federal and state agencies that I might ought to, because they said anybody that loves America as much as [I] do must be crazy."

By the end of the deposition, however, he turned serious again and, with the permission of his attorney, launched into a rambling three- or four-minute soliloquy, much of which was directed at Dees. The transcript reads, in part:

From the outset I think that [it] should be made clear that what is happening here today is proof of the Klan's claim that this country is disintegrating and degenerating. Anytime an out of state agitator, anti-Christ Jew person is allowed to come into the state like yourself, Demon Dees, to come into the state and ferment discord between Texas people, some of whom are citizens and some of whom are guests in this state, it is proof of our claim. No anti-Christ Jew should be allowed to ask a Christian anything for [sic] a court of law. . . . So the issue is not Louis Beam opposed to the Vietnamese. I'm for the Vietnamese. It's Louis Beam versus Morris Dees, anti-Christ Jew.

On May 5 events took a chilling turn. That morning Sam Adamo and Richard Cobb, the defense attorneys, had scheduled the depositions of Colonel Nam and the three other named plaintiffs in the case. As a defendant Beam had a right to be present at the proceedings, and he chose to attend, along with one of the militant American shrimpers we had sued. Before the questioning began, Beam, who was dressed casually, took a chair against the wall opposite Dees.

Nam was the day's first witness. Promptly at 10:00 A.M. he was sworn in, and Adamo began his examination. The deposition got off to something of a rancorous start. Dees interposed a number of objections, and his challenges to Adamo's questions led to several sharp exchanges between the two lawyers.

When Dees next glanced across the table at Beam, he noticed the KKK leader holding a book in front of him, as if he were reading from it. But Beam's eyes were riveted on Dees, and he appeared to be chanting something. Puzzled by this behavior, Dees tried to read his lips. Then the SPLC lawyer's eyes fell on the title. In large type on the book's front cover was printed the word *Exorcism*.

This went on for nearly an hour. Every time Dees stole a glance at the grand dragon he was still immersed in his silent chant. Finally Beam stopped and simply stared, his eyes seemingly locked on Dees. Slowly and very distinctly he began to mouth "You die, you die, you die, you die" over and over. He continued for several more minutes, whereupon he abruptly quit, and a few moments later he left the room.

It was obvious that the judge's order had had no effect on him. For the time being, there was nothing Dees could do, and the depositions continued. After Nam, whose testimony took nearly two hours, the three other Vietnamese were deposed in fairly quick succession.

Between the testimony of the last two deponents, Vahala, who had been assisting Dees, left the deposition room to do an errand. He rode the elevator to the underground parking garage and began the short walk to his car. As he neared the vehicle, he noticed a figure standing about twenty-five feet away. It was Beam. Vahala was startled to see him, and the reaction seemed mutual. Beam edged away, paused momentarily, and then strode to the elevator, never saying a word.

Vahala felt a surge of suspicion. Only a few minutes earlier he had been a witness to Beam's death threat against Dees. Now he had come almost face-to-face with him alone in an underground garage, and from Beam's reaction it appeared that he had been caught by surprise. The first thought that came to Vahala was that Beam had planted a bomb on the car. He stooped down on his hands and knees and peered at the underside of the chassis but saw nothing unusual. Seeking to dismiss his concern, Vahala unlocked the car and settled into the driver's seat, inserted the key into the ignition, and turned it. The engine started up without incident. With a sense of relief, Vahala backed out of his parking space and exited the garage. When he returned from the errand, he parked the car in an aboveground lot across the street from the courthouse, just to be safe. Beam was nowhere in sight.

Back inside the courthouse, Vahala related the experience to Dees. Dees found it disturbing, particularly in light of the chanting episode earlier.

After the round of depositions had ended, Dees and Vahala left the courthouse for the day. It was midafternoon, a full two hours since Beam had left the premises. As the two men walked across the street from the courthouse to the parking lot, discussing the day's developments in the case, Dees realized they were being followed. Beam had materialized suddenly out of nowhere and was crossing the street some distance behind them, alone, and carrying a paper sack.

Dees advised Vahala to keep walking as if nothing were wrong. When they reached the parking lot, Vahala presented his ticket stub to the attendant. Beam was now standing on the sidewalk at the corner of the lot, watching, motionless, as the attendant brought the car up. Dees got in on the passenger's side and Vahala settled in behind the wheel. As Vahala steered toward the exit, Beam began to move down the sidewalk in their direction. He stopped a few feet short of the car, lifted the sack, and brought his right hand up to it, appearing to grasp something inside. As he did so, he crouched down, assuming a firing position.

"Mike!" Dees yelled, shocked into the realization of what Beam was about to do. "Floor it!" Vahala stomped on the accelerator, and the car bolted into the street.

As it turned out, there was no hail of bullets, no shattering of glass, no report of gunfire echoing off the Federal Building. Once again there was no way even to prove Beam had actually had a weapon in the sack. It was another of the KKK leader's bizarre pranks. But this time he had gone too far. As Vahala sped from the scene, Dees began formulating plans to ask the court for additional relief, including the assignment of federal law enforcement agents for protection, and for an order requiring a psychiatric examination for Beam.

That evening, back in their motel room, Vahala stayed up until well past midnight typing up Dees's roughed-out motion. The pleading, six pages long, set down in careful detail the frightening events that had transpired since the filing of the lawsuit: the KKK calling cards left at David Berg's law office and home; a subsequent occasion in which Berg had been followed one night by a man in a pickup truck; the alleged gun incident at Beam's deposition and the appearance of the young Nazi Russell Gregory Thatcher; the death threat chanted by Beam during the deposition of Colonel Nam; anonymous phone calls; the gun scare of earlier that afternoon. For good measure, Dees salted the motion with a sample of Beam's violent rhetoric, gleaned from the newspaper clips. Vahala finished typing the document and climbed wearily into bed.

Sometime after that, in the early-morning darkness, the phone suddenly rang, jolting both men awake. Vahala answered, but there was no response. Finally he heard a click, and the phone went dead.

It wasn't the first anonymous call the Klanwatch team had received that week, but because of the previous day's events, it seemed more menacing, especially given the hour. Dees rang the front desk to see if the operator had any clue to the caller's identity. The operator's reply, however, was of no comfort at all: He hadn't put through a call to their room. That meant that it had come from within the motel itself, perhaps from a house phone, and that whoever made it knew Dees and Vahala's room number. Someone had tailed them to their motel room.

Now both men were wide-awake, their senses on red alert. They waited for the phone to ring again, listened for the sound of someone in the hallway outside their door. Minutes passed, and nothing happened. A few more minutes dragged by. Convincing themselves that the caller had meant only to frighten them, the men went back to bed. In an hour or two daylight came.

As soon as they got up and had breakfast, they checked out of the motel and drove to the courthouse, where Dees filed the motion with the clerk's office. Subsequently he served a copy on Adamo. Later in the day came word that Judge McDonald had scheduled a hearing on the request for Friday, May 8, two interminable days away.

In the meantime, Dees decided to take additional steps to strengthen security, phoning his brother, a gun dealer in Montgomery, and asking him to send out bulletproof vests on the next flight to Houston. The vests were no deterrent, but at least they would improve the odds of surviving if anyone took a potshot at them (hence their brand name, Second Chance). Dees also asked for a .45-caliber pistol, and when it came, he began carrying it in his briefcase everywhere except to court. It was a sobering development. Naively, perhaps, nobody at the SPLC had envisioned anything like this.

The forty-eight hours leading up to the hearing on the second motion for protection were tense. No one knew what to expect from Beam in light of our challenge to his mental competency (KLAN CHIEF 'DERANGED,' LAWYER FOR VIETS CLAIMS, the headline had shouted from page one of the *Houston Chronicle*), whether he would strike out in anger or, as everyone fervently hoped, tone down his conduct—if that were possible. Beam had succeeded in terrorizing the Vietnamese and their lawyers, as he had set out to do. The question was, Was he as crazy and dangerous as he seemed or simply not as bright as we had imagined? His antics were certainly not making his lawyers' jobs any easier.

In the end there was to be no competency exam for Beam. On the morning of the hearing on the request for a broader protective order, the court announced it lacked the authority to order him to undergo a psychiatric examination, since his mental state was not at issue in the lawsuit. The court did, however, grant some relief the motion sought, prohibiting Beam from having any unauthorized contacts with anyone connected with the plaintiffs—upon penalty of criminal contempt.

That, as it worked out, marked the beginning of the end of Beam's leadership of the Texas Klan. The next night, Saturday, May 9, the KKK held a rally Beam had set up several weeks earlier. Scheduled prior to our filing of the lawsuit, it was to have been the occasion on which he delivered his long-anticipated judgment on the authorities' efforts to resolve the fishing dispute. In the wake of our intervention and of Judge McDonald's stern warning, it turned out to be a huge anticlimax. In contrast with the strong undercurrent of vigilantism that had characterized the Valentine's night rally, the atmosphere on May 9 was almost tame, and Beam's tone just short of conciliatory. In an obvious effort to save face, he claimed credit for the legislature's passage of a law restricting the number of new boats on the bay. There were no threats against the Vietnamese, no mock boat burnings, and no promises of Klan intervention during the upcoming shrimping season.

However, there was one curious development that night that meant nothing to us at the time but that took on a great deal of significance sometime later, and that was the attendance of eight or ten uniformed neo-Nazis at the rally as special guests; they were members of a little-known group called the Aryan Nations, a radical, pseudo-Christian sect based in Idaho. Beam was hooking up with the brownshirts.

Two days after the rally, on Monday, May 11, the hearing began on the preliminary injunction. In the climate created by the string of threats and Beam's outlandish conduct, the outcome was almost a foregone conclusion. After three days of often poignant testimony by the Vietnamese and the handful of whites who were their business partners and friends, Judge McDonald found in our favor, and on May 14, the day before the shrimping season opened, she issued a sweeping injunction barring the kind of intimidation campaign the defendants had been engaged in for many months.

That night the Vietnamese threw a big dinner for the SPLC legal team at a downtown Houston restaurant owned by one of the leading citizens of the refugee community. Dees, Williams, Vahala, Hayslip, and Berg were the guests of honor. On behalf of all the Vietnamese in the Houston area, Nam thanked the men for vindicating their rights. As a further token of the community's appreciation, the refugees presented each SPLC staffer with a handmade wooden wall clock, painstakingly—and exquisitely—carved in the shape of their Southeast Asian homeland.

Chapter Six

THE VIETNAMESE fishermen's case was something of a trial by fire for the Klanwatch Project, and all of us were extremely gratified with the results. Besides the sense of satisfaction we felt over the outcome, the experience proved beyond doubt our ability to react swiftly to a crisis in the making and head it off. Just as important, it demonstrated the utility of the civil lawsuit as a weapon against racial intimidation and violence.

The day after the injunction was issued, the shrimping season opened without incident, and in the ensuing weeks calm gradually returned to Galveston Bay. This is not to suggest that the suit resolved the underlying issues that spawned the crisis, but by neutralizing the vigilante element, it helped ensure that the resolution would be forged in a more equitable, democratic climate. The suit seemed to galvanize public and political support for the refugees.

In late June 1981 we learned that Beam had announced his resignation as grand dragon of the Texas Knights. His travails mounted over the next several months with the breakup of his marriage and a bitter custody battle with his wife over the couple's one-year-old daughter. The dispute exploded into the open when

Beam fled the state with the child, and his wife brought kidnapping charges against him. (The charges were later dropped.)

That summer was a busy time for the Klanwatch Project. With the coming of warm weather (traditionally the Klan's most active season), the level of public KKK activity picked up tremendously—rallies, marches, leafleting, and the like—and information flooded our office to the extent that it was all we could do to keep our heads above the tide of paperwork.

Along with the upsurge in legal activity, however, a dramatic series of arrests at about the same time gave the lie once and for all to the notion that the much hyped "new" Klan was anything else but the old KKK warmed over. One of the busts involved half a dozen Klansmen from Maryland and Delaware who had plotted to bomb the Baltimore office of the National Association for the Advancement of Colored People (NAACP); another entailed the arrest of six Kluxers in Nashville for conspiring to blow up several Jewish-owned businesses as well as a local television station that employed an outspoken Jewish talk show host. In unquestionably the most unusual incident federal authorities in Louisiana uncovered a conspiracy of nine Klansmen and Nazis to overthrow the tiny, mostly black island of Dominica in the Caribbean, from which the group had planned to run gambling and drug-peddling operations to finance the white supremacist movement on the mainland.

Meanwhile, only a matter of weeks after the injunction was issued in the Texas case, we got our first indication that our other lawsuit, the Decatur suit, was crimping Bill Wilkinson's style and hurting the Invisible Empire, Knights of the Ku Klux Klan financially. Jerry Thompson, the *Nashville Tennessean* reporter who had infiltrated the IEKKKK, reported in a copyrighted story that Wilkinson had sent a secret "Klan Action Bulletin" to his members, cautioning them to adopt a less militant profile in order to avoid arrests. "We must raise money fast or we are in trouble," Thompson quoted the communication as saying. Wilkinson warned, further, that he might have to cut back on rally appearances and other promotional activities to concentrate full-time on fund-raising. He claimed already to have spent thirty-two hundred dollars on legal fees on the suit and hinted that it ultimately could cost the Klan thousands more.

The suit was by no means the only drain on the IEKKKK treasury. Wilkinson's confrontational style, which had propelled him to national prominence and fueled the group's startling growth in the late seventies, had also led to frequent arrests of IEKKKK members for parading or soliciting without the proper permits and numerous weapons violations as well.* The legal fees apparently were beginning to mount. Wilkinson already had been forced to sell one of his most conspicuous perks, a single-engine airplane he had purchased with funds donated by a wealthy sympathizer, an aircraft he had dubbed *Klan One*. And in one of those delectable little twists of fate, one of the plane's new co-owners was none other than Dees's brother, Les. Compounding the irony was the fact that Dees and I subsequently flew to northern Alabama in the ex-*Klan One* to take the deposition of an official of the Knights of the KKK.

The occasion for the deposition was the second phase of the investigation of the Vietnamese fishermen's suit: our legal attack on the Texas Emergency Reserve, the Texas KKK's paramilitary arm. The Knights of the KKK, the national faction with which the Texas Klan was affiliated, were now based in Tuscumbia, about fifty miles west of Decatur. (With David Duke's resignation, leadership of the organization had passed to an Alabamian, Don Black.)

Although the Klan Special Forces of the IEKKKK had attracted the most media attention (beginning with the coverage it had received on the eve of the Curtis Robinson trial), the Texas Emergency Reserve now seemed to us the more potentially dangerous organization. Many of its members were Vietnam vets (unlike the KSF), and they apparently had been much more active than their Alabama counterparts. According to information we had received from an informant, scores of men, perhaps hundreds, had undergone instruction at the TER's main training facility, Camp Puller. Furthermore, the source told us the group had carried out fairly sophisticated field maneuvers, from an armed patrol for illegal immigrants along the Texas-Mexico border to a simulated response to a hypothetical civil disorder in the Houston area. With or without Louis Beam the TER seemed to pose a real threat.

The legal basis on which our challenge to the TER rested was an obscure state law rooted in the days of the Texas Republic. It said

---

* Wilkinson to some extent was a prisoner of his own rhetoric: In an effort to cast himself as a leader willing to take on the authorities on behalf of the Klan, he often promised to defy march or weapons bans. Although his defiance brought him the admiration of his followers as well as recruitment gains, it left him little choice but to make good on his threats.

essentially that other than the National Guard and the U.S. armed forces no "body of men" would be permitted to associate themselves in Texas as a military company. On the face of it the TER seemed in obvious violation.

We were joined in our effort to shut down the TER by the Texas attorney general, Mark White, a Democrat with an eye on the 1982 governor's race, and the Anti-Defamation League.

The decision in the case did not come down for more than a year, but when it ultimately did, in July 1982, it was in our favor. Judge McDonald dismissed the Klan's contention that the training was defensive in nature and ordered it disbanded.

Armed with the Texas decision, SPLC Legal Director John Carroll wrote the attorney general of Alabama, Charles Graddick, to encourage him to take enforcement action against the Klan Special Forces. Alabama had a law on its books similar to the Texas statute, and Dees and Carroll believed the ruling was applicable to the Alabama situation. Although we had no firm evidence that the KSF was even continuing to train, we thought the state should move against it nonetheless. Our rationale had as much to do with the appearance of a threat as with its reality.

It had become clear since the Robinson trial that the KSF was at least as much show as substance, part of the smoke-and-mirrors routine Klan leaders of the late seventies and early eighties used to generate publicity and promote Klan recruitment. The best information we had was that no more than a handful of Klan members (perhaps three or four dozen) had ever taken part in its exercises, and the only real "training" sessions we had been able to confirm had been on two occasions when Camp My Lai, as the group's training facility was known, was opened to journalists.

However, it was our belief that the image of a white supremacist army could have a powerfully intimidating effect on black people, particularly the very young and the very old or those living in isolated areas. It might be easy for the white majority to dismiss the Klan leaders' rhetoric of race war and armed conflict as bluster or media posturing, but for black Southerners only a decade removed from sixties-style KKK terror, perception was as important as reality. (Besides, those were real AR-15s the Kluxers had.) In the eyes of most black Alabamians, furthermore, the fact that the KSF was no longer in the headlines was by no means assurance that it was no longer functioning.

Graddick, the Alabama attorney general, declined to do anything, however, and as a result, the Law Center took the KSF to court on behalf of the Alabama NAACP, eventually winning a consent decree by which members of the KSF agreed not to engage in further paramilitary activity.

Amid our continuing courtroom battles, Klanwatch scored a major success in another forum in 1982, with the nomination of a documentary film we had commissioned, *The Klan: A Legacy of Hate in America*, for an Academy Award. The film, funded by the SPLC and researched largely by our staff, was produced by the renowned Washington, D.C., filmmaker Charles Guggenheim. Although it did not receive the Oscar (it was beaten out by *If You Love This Planet*, the Canadian antinuclear film branded as propaganda by the Reagan administration), *The Klan* won several other awards in film competitions around the country and was shown on public television stations from coast to coast.

The scorching heat of another Alabama summer had given way to those slightly milder days that pass for autumn in the Deep South when Dees decided in October 1982 to force the issue of the Decatur civil suit to a head. For reasons we hadn't been able to fathom, U.S. District Judge E. B. Haltom still had not ruled on the Klan's motion to dismiss the suit, nor had he even scheduled a hearing on it, and the case had merely been gathering dust in the clerk's office of the federal court in Birmingham for almost two years.

The delay had worked to our benefit, though. In the meantime, the IEKKKK had all but died out in northern Alabama, the result of the filing of the suit, several federal prosecutions of individual Klan members, and disillusionment among the Klan's rank and file with Bill Wilkinson, whom many Kluxers had come to regard as something of a con man. The crowning blow for the Invisible Empire in northern Alabama had been the publication by the *Nashville Tennessean* of FBI memorandums that suggested that Wilkinson was, or had been, a federal informant.

Dees sensed it was time to attack, and he petitioned the court to rule on the Klan's motion. Haltom promptly scheduled a hearing on it for October 20.

Normally the proceeding would have been a formality. It was a rare lawsuit that failed to survive the defendant's motion to dismiss. But ours was by no means a routine case. We had filed the suit outside the one-year statute of limitations, and the Klan's attorney was seeking to have it dismissed on that ground. At first glance it appeared that the law was on the KKK's side.

In a civil case the statute of limitations ordinarily begins to run from the time an offense is committed (in this instance, May 26, 1979). Under certain circumstances, however, the one-year filing period may be waived. One such circumstance is when the defendants have conspired to conceal the offense; in that event the statute of limitations clock doesn't begin to wind down until the conspiracy is first uncovered.

At the time we filed the Decatur suit, in November 1980, almost six months after the statute of limitations had run out, Dees hadn't given much thought to how to respond to this dilemma. He had been eager just to get into court. Now that the day of reckoning was at hand, he decided to counter the Klan's argument that the suit should be dismissed by playing our ace in the hole, Lloyd Letson. He would put the former Klansman on the stand to testify to the existence of the conspiracy to block the march and hope the judge would be sufficiently intrigued (or moved) to rule in our favor.

On the morning of the hearing Dees drove to Birmingham and met Letson at a motel a few blocks from the federal courthouse to go over the statement Letson had given him during their interview at former Governor Brewer's law office almost twenty-two months earlier. It was the first time the two had seen each other since Letson had visited Dees at Rolling Hills Ranch. If Letson was nervous, he hardly seemed it. Then again, Letson, a strapping, muscular country fellow, was the type who looked as if he wouldn't be cowed by anything.

Dees pored over his statement with him line by line. As he did so, it occurred to Dees at last to ask Letson whether any Klan leader had advised him to lie about the conspiracy in the event he were ever interviewed by the FBI. Letson's answer was just what Dees wanted to hear: a simple, unequivocal yes.

Dees knew he was on to something crucial. Letson identified the

Klansman as Ray Steele, the titan who had urged the members of the Decatur klavern to block the march and the person who had called the shots at the pumps and later at the Bank-Lee intersection. Steele had brought Letson to the Klan's Decatur lawyer shortly after the incident to arrange for the attorney to represent him on the charges of assaulting an officer and disorderly conduct for which the young Klansman had been arrested during the May 26 confrontation. On the way to the attorney's office the pair had stopped off at a restaurant, Letson said, and over a cup of coffee Steele had cautioned him against saying anything about the conspiracy to the attorney because he (Steele) could "get some time out of it." Steele said the same thing applied to talking to the FBI. When the FBI came to Letson's place of employment to interview him a few days afterward, he lied, just as he had been instructed.

Dees now knew we were in court to stay. Steele's actions, as Letson described them, were a clear-cut case of fraudulent concealment—in lay terms, a cover-up.

At the courthouse, on the way to the courtroom, Dees and Letson stopped by the U.S. Attorney's office to invite the prosecutor who had overseen the FBI investigation of the Decatur incident, Henry Frohsin, to attend the hearing. On the basis of the new evidence we had uncovered, Dees told Frohsin, the FBI might want to consider reopening its probe.

It was a reflection of what hard times the IEKKKK had fallen on, and ultimately of how little concern there was now in the Klan over our lawsuit, that hardly any KKK members from northern Alabama showed up for the hearing. Having emerged unscathed—and unindicted—from the FBI investigation, they apparently thought they had nothing further to worry about.

This made it easier on Letson. Had he been faced with a gallery full of his scowling compatriots, he might have been distracted by thoughts of reprisals or fear for his family. As it was, he testified with a spare matter-of-factness, repeating the story he had told Dees almost word for word to the court.

Besides implicating Steele, Letson pointed a finger at a second Klansman, a radical young racist named Bill Riccio, who had been the IEKKKK's grand chaplain, or state religious leader, on May 26, 1979.

Judge Haltom seemed keenly interested in Letson's testimony, which ended with Dees's asking Letson whether he had lied to the FBI (a federal crime for which he had not been promised immunity) and Letson's affirmative response.

The testimony couldn't have gone much better. Letson's ingenuous manner, his plainspokenness, his country airs, combined with what amounted to a confession to a federal crime, made him a compellingly credible witness. Dan Willingham, the KKK's attorney, declined even to cross-examine him.

On the strength of Letson's allegations, Haltom ruled that the Decatur lawsuit was not in violation of the statute of limitations and rejected the Klan's motion to dismiss it. His decision was a procedural green light, signaling that formal discovery in the case could finally begin.

Right after Christmas 1982 we issued formal notice to a number of the defendants in the case of our intention to take their depositions, and Dees scheduled the first ones for late January. By mutual agreement, they were to be taken at Willingham's office in Cullman.

Willingham was not the only lawyer in the case, but he was the primary one. His clients included Wilkinson, the IEKKKK organization, and several individual defendants. Other Klansmen, those who had fallen out with Wilkinson, had retained their own attorneys—and still others were representing themselves.

One of the latter was an ex-Kluxer from Huntsville named Doug Berryhill. On May 26, 1979, Berryhill had been the exalted cyclops of the Huntsville klavern, but like so many other northern Alabama Kluxers, he had since quit. When the notice of deposition arrived in his mailbox shortly before New Year's 1983, he was ready, in law enforcement parlance, to flip or roll over. To a large extent, Berryhill's motivation to come clean was the same as Letson's: money. During the Robinson case we had subpoenaed him to the change of venue hearing and caused him to miss work. The prospect of laying out money in the civil suit, either to an attorney or as damages in a civil judgment, prompted him to place a call to Dees. What must he do, he asked, to get out of the lawsuit?

Dees's reply was the same he had given Letson: Just tell the truth about what happened in Decatur on May 26. Berryhill agreed to the terms, and Dees arranged to drive to Huntsville within a few days to meet him at his home. Randall Williams went with him.

Berryhill was in his early thirties, a tall, heavyset man with light brown hair and a thick, neatly trimmed mustache. He wore a pair of metal-frame glasses. He and his wife, Carlotta, the former secretary-treasurer of the Huntsville klavern, had two children, both school-age girls. The parents worked in civilian jobs at Redstone Arsenal, a military installation located in southwest Huntsville. Randall Williams had once observed that more than a few of the Klan members we crossed paths with were basically good people, men and women who would have made good union members if the union had only gotten to them first. The Berryhills seemed like that type.

By KKK standards they were well off. They owned their own home, had two cars, a motorcycle, a color television set, and other amenities of middle-class life. Dees, a motorcycle enthusiast himself, immediately noticed the bike underneath the carport and mentioned to Berryhill that he had one for sale, and for a few minutes the men swapped biking stories. Dees was always looking for ways to relate to potential Klan witnesses.

After the ice was broken, the conversation turned to the topic of the KKK and then to the lawsuit. Like Letson, the Berryhills had learned of the plan to block the march at the regular weekly meeting of their klavern a few days beforehand. There were about thirty-five or forty Klan members in attendance that night, they said, including two unannounced guests: Ray Steele and Roger Handley, the Alabama grand dragon of the IEKKKK. It was unusual for the grand dragon to attend a meeting of the klavern, and it signaled something major in the offing.

After the meeting had gotten under way, the floor was turned over to the two men. They made an imposing appearance together, Steele, a ruddy-faced, swaggering figure who weighed at least 225 pounds and was more than six feet tall, and Handley an intense, humorless man with heavy bags under his eyes and a full, dark mustache. Both men were armed. Steele had a .45-caliber pistol in a shoulder holster, and Handley was cradling a .30-caliber rifle, a weapon that resembled a sawed-off shotgun but was legal. It was widely known as an enforcer.

Steele and Handley indicated they wanted a big turnout of Klansmen at the first anniversary march marking Hines's arrest. "We are not going to let the niggers march," Steele declared.

"We've had enough of it," Handley added in his deep drawl.

"We've put up with all we're gonna put up with, and we're gonna stop them."

From the tone of Handley's and Steele's voices, Mrs. Berryhill said, they weren't asking for participation; they were demanding it. And they even invoked the name of the imperial wizard, Bill Wilkinson, in an effort to stress the importance of making a good showing, claiming that Wilkinson had approved the idea (a claim Wilkinson has repeatedly denied).

Dees and Williams were elated. Neither had expected to uncover such startling information. In a matter of a few minutes they had obtained evidence that the conspiracy went all the way up the IEKKKK organizational ladder, up to and possibly including the imperial wizard himself. To the further amazement of both men, the Berryhills said they had never even been interviewed about the incident by the FBI.

It was still relatively early when the informal interview ended. Dees was eager to cement the ties that had been forged with the Berryhills, as he had done earlier with Letson. Toward that end he had brought a video player from Montgomery, along with a copy of the new Klanwatch documentary, both of which were still in the car. Thinking the Berryhills might be interested in it, he offered to show it to them. They seemed flattered. Someone threw out the idea of ordering pizza for dinner, since it was about that time, and Williams suggested picking up a six-pack of beer. When the pizza arrived, the former Klan members and their guests, seated on the floor of the family room, had dinner and watched *The Klan: A Legacy of Hate in America,* the Klanwatch film.

The next day, back in Montgomery, Dees looked over Williams's notes from the Berryhill interview and marked the key points. That night he phoned the couple and asked them about each item, on the pretense of making certain that the notes Williams had taken down were correct. He surreptitiously recorded the conversation. It was deceitful, but in Dees's view, it was necessary. If the Berryhills changed their mind about cooperating with us or if other Klansmen exerted pressure on them to recant, the tape would be a kind of insurance.

In order not to expose Berryhill to the Klan's attorneys, Dees decided to release him from honoring the summons requiring him to give a deposition, and when Berryhill later failed to appear at the time noted on the deposition schedule, Dees offered an excuse about his absence to cover for him.

With Letson and now Berryhill in the fold, we approached the first round of depositions eagerly, confident that we would wrap up the case in no time.

On January 25, however, two days before the depositions were to begin, Wilkinson declared the Invisible Empire bankrupt and filed a petition in the U.S. Bankruptcy Court in Louisiana seeking protection from its creditors. Under the bankruptcy law, Wilkinson had the right to demand a stay against further discovery in any lawsuits pending against the IEKKKK, and he did so. From our perspective, it appeared that he had taken the action solely to frustrate discovery in the Decatur case, and it looked initially as if he had managed to derail our investigation.

But Dees was not to be outmaneuvered so easily. To avoid a delay in the case, he filed a motion in Birmingham striking any monetary damage claims against the IEKKKK national corporation, effectively relieving it of any potential financial liability but leaving us free to continue to prosecute the case against the other individual defendants. The depositions were back on. On the morning of January 27 Dees, Williams, and I, eager to begin taking testimony, pulled up outside the Cullman office of Dan Willingham.

Cullman was a peculiar little town, with an even smaller black population than Decatur, a historical fact attributable to its location in the hardscrabble hills of north-central Alabama, where farming had always been of the subsistence variety and there had been no economic reason for slavery. Of its approximately thirteen thousand people, 99 percent were white, and even before the Hines trial drew national attention to it in 1978, it had earned a reputation far and wide for racial intolerance.

Willingham's office was located one block from Cullman's main street in a row of aging one- and two-story brick buildings, along almost the entire length of which ran a metal awning to shield patrons of the various businesses on the block from the weather.

Willingham came out to greet us and took us back to a small conference room, leading us past several of the deponents. We exchanged glances with the Klansmen, nodding perfunctorily toward them; it was clear from their sullen expressions we were not among friends. Willingham was a short, slightly built fellow with thin black hair combed loosely forward and a wispy little mustache. He seemed somewhat shy, even a bit ill at ease. The fact that both his father and uncle were Klansmen—or had been in 1979—gave him something of a personal stake in the case.

Our strategy going into the depositions was to take several of the minor defendants first—either rank-and-file Klansmen or low-level officers—in the hope that we might have a better crack at prying the truth out of them if we got to them before their leaders had a chance to learn the line of questioning Dees was pursuing. It rapidly became apparent, however, that the strategy was doomed to failure. Minor though they might have been, they were also hardcore. Not one of them would admit knowing anything about a conspiracy to block the march.

Just as we were settling into a routine, we got a sudden start from one of the deponents. The incident was all the more disquieting because we hadn't been anticipating any trouble. It happened after lunch, during the deposition of a Decatur Klansman named Dale Nelson.*

Nelson was a klokann, or Klan investigator, whose duties included doing background checks on applicants for membership. He was only thirty-one years old, but his weathered face and receding hairline made him look considerably older. From information we had collected, we knew that he was married and that he and his wife lived with his mother.

Almost from the time he entered the deposition room, I had an uneasy feeling about him. He appeared far more anxious than any other witness, and when he sat down, I noticed that his hands were shaking. He was dressed rather well, in a sport coat, slacks, and a tie—quite unusual attire for the average Klansman.

Dees began the examination as he normally did, with a few standard questions: the deponent's name, address, marital status, and so on. When he asked Nelson for his employer's name, though, the Klansman adamantly refused to respond, and after a brief conference with Willingham, the latter explained that Nelson was worried about placing his job in jeopardy. Dees, seeking to resolve the impasse without a confrontation, asked the court reporter to go

---

* In accordance with an agreement Dees made with the Klansman during the deposition I have not used his real name.

In August 1978, in Decatur, Alabama, the KKK held its biggest rally anywhere in the South since the civil rights era. Here a Klansman stands guard at the entrance to the rally site.

Bill Riccio, Ray Steele (left to right, below), and Jack Mize (left, above), three of the Klan leaders behind the Decatur conspiracy, posing for a photographer at the "pumps," shortly before the KKK blocked the SCLC march in Decatur on May 26, 1979.

Alabama Klansman Bill Riccio. His violent rhetoric frightened even some of his supporters.

The Decatur marchers as they descended the Bank Street hill on May 26.

Part of the Klan mob that attacked the Decatur demonstrators. When lawmen tried to protect the marchers, the Klansmen turned on them.

Decatur Klan leader David Kelso (center, background) shown at precisely the moment he was shot. The force of the bullet lifted him off the ground. Directly in front of Kelso is Curtis Robinson's car—a fact we were able to confirm by comparing the photograph to a video clip of the incident. Kelso's position relative to the car proved to be a crucial point in Robinson's trial.

Curtis Robinson (background) moments after shooting Kelso. Note the gun, barely visible, in Robinson's hand. Robinson's car is shown at left. One of his house slippers lies beside the left front tire.

Morris Dees delivering a blistering analysis of the Robinson verdict at a press conference. Seated in front of him are Curtis Robinson, Robinson's family, and SPLC Legal Director John Carroll.

As the KKK became more paramilitary during the 1970s and 1980s, so, too, did it become increasingly anti-Semitic.

The Klan, always big on symbolism, burned an old yellow school bus at a Decatur rally in 1979 to protest mandatory school busing.

David Duke picketing a
speech by attorney William
Kunstler at Tulane University,
1970.

Bill Wilkinson and his bodyguards. The Klansman at far left, Clarence
Brown, was convicted of a civil rights violation for harassing a
Vietnamese co-worker at a Cullman, Alabama, factory in 1980.

Photojournalist Garry Nungester covering the Selma to Montgomery Klan march in August 1979. Information Nungester provided played a major role in our early cases and may have saved Dees's life.

In all, we took depositions of more than a hundred Klansmen in the Decatur civil suit. The climate was not always hostile, however. Here, with the testimony taking behind us, a member of the May 26 mob and I share a lighter moment.

The Texas Klan went to great lengths to frighten Vietnamese shrimpers out of the Galveston Bay area in 1981. Here about a dozen robed and camouflaged Klansmen, some armed with semiautomatic weapons, are shown sailing near a marina where dozens of Vietnamese docked their boats. Note the effigy hanging from the aft rigging.

Texas Grand Dragon Louis Beam sets fire to a mock Vietnamese fishing boat at a KKK rally on Valentine's Night, 1981. Under Beam's leadership, the Texas Knights conspired to drive Vietnamese refugees out of the shrimping business on Galveston Bay.

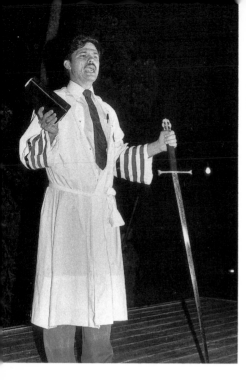

Beam, an apostle of racial hatred and violence, preaches to a Klan rally at Santa Fe, Texas, in May 1981.

Beam assuming a military stance in front of SPLC headquarters following his "visit" on September 4, 1984.

The fire that hit the SPLC in the early hours of July 28, 1983, wreaked $140,000 in damages. Klanwatch Director Randall Williams's office, seen here, suffered the worst devastation.

Dees and I conferring in the SPLC's temporary post-arson headquarters, a former women's clothing store.

The photo that cracked the SPLC arson case: a picture of Joe Garner and Tommy Downs marching with the Klan in Birmingham during the fall of 1980.

SPLC headquarters before the fire.

The "new" SPLC, in downtown Montgomery, just a stone's throw from Martin Luther King's old church.

The body of Michael Donald, moments after the murdered Mobile, Alabama, teenager was found on March 21, 1981.

Michael Donald as a youngster.

117 Herndon Avenue, where Henry Hays and several Klansmen held the party that resulted in Michael Donald's murder.

The dilapidated headquarters of Unit 900 of the United Klans of America, as the building appeared shortly before the Michael Donald civil suit went to trial in February 1987.

"Tiger" Knowles.

Henry Hays and
Bennie Hays.

A critical piece of
evidence in our
case against the
United Klans was
this drawing,
which had
appeared in the
UKA newspaper
Fiery Cross.

The headquarters of the United Klans of America outside Tuscaloosa, Alabama. The building was later turned over to Beulah Mae Donald.

After years of perseverance, the Decatur case ended on a hopeful note, with several Klansmen agreeing to take a class on civil rights. Former Klan Special Forces leader Terry Tucker (in the dark glasses) emerged from the session talking about racial "common ground."

"off the record." He explained to Nelson that it was a perfectly legitimate question and that he only wanted the information so that in case Nelson moved, we would have an alternate way of serving him with court papers. We had found this to be necessary. Klan members often picked up and moved without leaving any forwarding addresses; Willingham hadn't even been able to locate one of the Klansmen we wanted to depose even though the man was one of his own clients.

Dees's explanation failed to satisfy Nelson. For some reason, he seemed concerned that neither Williams nor I should know the information, so Dees asked us to leave the room for a moment. When we returned, Dees resumed the deposition. The very next question Dees asked was the name of the Kluxer's most recent previous employer. Once again Nelson refused to answer, and we went through the scenario a second time.

Williams and I were beginning to feel a little uneasy about all this. Nelson came across as less than stable. His responses to the questions about his employers struck both of us as slightly paranoid. But it was more than the answers themselves. It was his whole demeanor. His voice quavered, and his hands were shaking like crazy. The muscles in his face were drawn tight.

Oblivious of our concerns and apparently harboring none himself, Dees moved forward with the examination, next asking Nelson if he owned any weapons. This, too, was a routine inquiry. Weapons, and the brandishing of them, were at the heart of several acts of intimidation set out in the lawsuit, and Dees wanted to compile a list of guns owned by the Kluxers so he could portray them at the trial with a degree of specificity as the violent, vigilante force they were.

Grudgingly Nelson answered: a Smith & Wesson 9-millimeter and a .357 magnum, he said.

Though no expert on guns, I found the combination a bit unusual, and in my increasingly worried frame of mind I took it as another reason to be wary. First of all, the shotgun was the weapon of choice of the average Kluxer. Some Klansmen might also own a rifle or a .38-caliber pistol, maybe even a .45. It was noteworthy, I thought, that Nelson owned none of these but instead had two of the deadliest pistols. The 9-millimeter was an automatic, capable of rapid fire; the magnum was the hand-held cannon Clint Eastwood made famous in the Dirty Harry movies. Another element of Nelson's response that flagged my attention was the fact that he had purchased both weapons relatively recently.

As Dees turned the questioning toward Nelson's Klan membership, it became increasingly clear that the witness considered the questioning invasive. Once, when asked the name of his klavern leader, Nelson turned to Willingham and snapped, "Do I have to answer that?" Willingham conferred with him in a whisper, and Nelson subsequently provided the name. His responses were clipped and unadorned, occasionally tinged with sarcasm.

Then Dees asked why he had joined the KKK, and the answer set off alarm bells in my head:

Q. For what reason did you join the Klan?
A. Well, I guess for what it stood for.
Q. What was that?
A. The white movement.
Q. What white movement are you talking about?
A. The white movement against racism, race mixing, and this sort of thing.

The expression "the white movement" was one only true believers used. It was the etymological currency of the ideologue, the theoretician, the polemicist. One picked it up from reading and studying radical white supremacist literature, and it betrayed the user as a radical. The average redneck wouldn't have known what it meant.

As soon as the expression rolled off Nelson's lips, I thought: *He's got a gun on, and any minute he's going to pull it out and start shooting.*

I jotted down, "Ask him if he's got a gun on," and handed the note to Williams to pass to Dees. Williams read it and looked at me with concern. He, too, had noticed how unstable Nelson seemed, and it was clear he shared my fear. He calmly took the note, written on a small piece of self-adhesive paper, and affixed it to the edge of the table near Dees's arm.

Dees apparently didn't observe it right away. He had proceeded to his next question. Meanwhile, Nelson was getting more agitated by the minute; the breaking point seemed close at hand.

Dees asked a question about the oath of secrecy the Klan administers to new recruits.

"Now that one, I won't answer," Nelson announced flatly.

With each question he seemed to feel more threatened, more closed in. Willingham counseled him, and reluctantly he provided the answer; but he appeared to be retreating into a psychological corner. I wondered what would happen when he felt the wall against his back.

Immersed in his interrogation of the witness, Dees pressed on, as if inexorably pursuing a prey.

Williams and I were now leaning forward, our eyes trained on Nelson, watching intently for the first sign of a sudden movement, poised and ready to turn the table on top of the Klansman if he came up firing.

Finally Dees noticed the note. He removed it from the table's edge, held it in his hand, and posed the question in a much less prosecutorial voice than before. "Do you have a weapon on you here today?"

The muscles in my legs and arms tensed up. I knew if Nelson were going to go off the deep end, it would be now.

"Yes, sir," he said, "I sure do."

The room was totally still, except for the court reporter's fingers dancing silently over her transcription machine. Even Willingham seemed mesmerized by the colloquy.

"What kind of weapon do you have on you today?" Dees asked slowly and deliberately.

"The three-fifty-seven."

"Have you got a license for that in this county?"

"I sure do. It is required in my line of work."

"Well," Dees said, "just keep it where it is, and everything will be all right." With that the tension seemed to dissipate suddenly. It was as if getting all the facts on the table somehow defused the situation. Nelson's demeanor changed, and he seemed to relax. Dees quickly wound up the deposition, and afterward we took a short break.

Over dinner that night we discussed the day's events and came to the conclusion that we couldn't hope to crack open the conspiracy merely through the deposition process. Out of the six deponents Dees had questioned we had learned virtually nothing of importance, not even any new identifications. The three of us agreed we had to identify additional participants of the hundred-member Klan mob involved in the May 26 incident and hope that we could shake another Berryhill or Letson out of the bunch. The problem was, how?

It occurred to me then that the time was right to play the McGlocklin card. Bill McGlocklin was a former IEKKKK leader from Decatur who had been among the top two or three ranking Klansmen in the state before resigning in a dispute with other Klan officials in mid-1979. He had left on bad terms, and the rumor was that some of his former Klan friends had set him up on a gun charge on which he had been arrested shortly before he quit. Wittingly or not, he had been one of Garry Nungester's best sources. During the Robinson investigation I repeatedly had asked Nungester about setting up a face-to-face meeting with him for me because McGlocklin was well connected and had remained on the periphery of the Klan world. But Nungester, who could be very protective of his sources, had always cautioned against the idea for fear that it would jeopardize his own relationship with McGlocklin. Several years had now passed, and McGlocklin's value as a source had diminished in the wake of the IEKKKK's decline in the area, so the time seemed right to make contact. I suggested we call him directly and simply ask him if he would meet with us.

Dees took to the idea immediately. While Williams and I took care of the bill, he called McGlocklin from a pay phone just inside the restaurant. McGlocklin agreed to see us that night.

A self-employed mechanic, McGlocklin lived in a small, modest house in a neighborhood of small, modest houses on the south side of Decatur. Although we'd never met, he greeted us at the door like long-lost friends and waved us in, joking at our being about at such a late hour. Once inside, we followed him through the house back to the kitchen, where, he observed, we would be able to spread out the pictures we had brought.

Dees explained that all we wanted him to do was to identify any Klansmen he recognized in the photographs. McGlocklin, an easygoing, good-natured fellow of about forty, readily agreed, and thus began the most singular interview any of us had yet conducted with a Klansman. For more than an hour this high-ranking former IEKKKK leader thumbed through our photos, putting names to more than a half dozen faces and providing us with leads on still a dozen more Kluxers: nicknames, hometowns, hangouts, and other inside information. Between identifications, he kept us entertained with illuminating anecdotes about behind-the-scenes Klan affairs, such as how after a well-attended rally in Decatur, a top Klan official reportedly made off with a large garbage can filled with cash donations from the crowd.

We never knew precisely what McGlocklin's motivation for helping us was. Whatever it was, he quickly reconsidered the decision to do so. He met with us only once more before politely but firmly declining to help any further. He had talked with the "boys," he informed Williams and me one day, and they didn't think he ought to be providing assistance; somebody, apparently, was worried that we were making progress.

From time to time we saw him as our investigation progressed during the spring and summer of 1983, and once he accompanied a Klan buddy to a deposition. At the conclusion of the deposition we found a Klan calling card in the waiting room where he had been sitting. We never saw or heard from him again.

Chapter Seven

Upon arriving back at the Law Center the day after our interview with McGlocklin, Dees found the following letter on his desk. It had been sent by certified mail.

January 21, 1983

Morris S. Dees, Jr.
THE POVERTY LAW CENTER
P.O. Box 548
Montgomery, AL 36195

Mr. Dees

It has been brought to my attention that you are still travelling the country practicing perfidy.

In your unceasing efforts to undermine the Constitutional laws of this once great nation you have followed in the steps of other evil perverters of the same tribe.

I personally feel that this behaviour should no longer be allowed to go unchecked.

I have myself seen you in the courtroom. You can lie to, deceive, and manipulate colored girls with great advantage. (Considering who's being treated in this manner it's no great accomplishment.) However, I feel certain that this is the limit of your maleficent abilities and that if you were called upon to face other than a descendant of the hottentots of Africa, you would prove yourself a coward.

In order to substantiate this supposition (your inate [sic] jewish cowardness) it is necessary for empirical observations to be made.

I therefore challenge you to a dual [sic] to the death. You against me. No federal judges, no federal marshals, no F.B.I. agents, not anyone except yourself and I.

We go to the woods (your state or mine) and settle once and for all the enmity that exists between us. Two go in—one comes out.

As the challenged you may choose whatever weapon you desire, guns, knife, etc., it matters not to me.

You have 30 days from receipt of this certified challenge to inform me of the place, time and weapon to be used.

If you are the base, despicable, low-down, vile poltroon I think you are—you will of course decline, in which case my original supposition will have been proven correct, and your lack of character verified.

If on the other hand you agree to meet me, you will raise immeasurably the esteem others hold you in. Imagine: Acquaintances, associates, supporters, friends, family—your mother—think of her, why I can just see her now, her heart just bursting with pride as you, for the first time in your life, exhibit the qualities of a man and march off to the field of honor. (Every mother has a right to be proud of her son once.) You will be worse than a coward if you deny her this most basic of rights. Think of her.

In closing, let me make it clear that I believe you so base a coward that you will be too timid to even place a pen in hand and answer this letter, for I know a craven anti-Christ jew when I have seen him. Here's your chance to prove me wrong.

For a White America,
(signed)
Louis R. Beam, Jr.

The letter was typed on the stationery of the Aryan Nations, the Idaho-based neo-Nazi group that was beginning to attract the most radical racists in the country to its heavily wooded compound on the edge of the Coeur d'Alene National Forest. From what we knew, Beam had taken refuge there in 1981 after fleeing Texas with his infant daughter. Apparently he was still there—and still smarting over the Vietnamese case even after nearly two years.

If the episode hadn't been a little unnerving (in light of the earlier threats), it would have seemed comical, for the letter was vintage Beam: clever, articulate, and dripping with sardonic humor. Whatever his ultimate purpose in sending it, it served as a not-so-subtle reminder that he was still nursing a grudge, and it left the lingering impression that we had yet to see the last of him.

In the meantime, we forged ahead with the Decatur investigation. Our effort to gather additional leads prompted me to pay a visit to one of our few contacts in the law enforcement community.

It was a fact of life in 1983 that the SPLC had few friends among Southern law enforcement officers. The Law Center had not endeared itself among the old guard, especially in Alabama, by suing the all-white Alabama State Troopers during the early 1970s and forcing the agency to integrate. A decade later the case was still in the courts, alienating a new generation of white recruits, whose careers had been ensnared in our efforts to break up the old-boy network that regulated promotions and assignments within the troopers' ranks. But that wasn't all. The Center had sued the Montgomery Police Department on sex discrimination charges and funded suits against other police agencies for everything from framing an innocent man for a murder charge to staging a mock lynching. What was just as bad, in the view of many law enforcement officials, was our vigorous opposition to the death penalty, which the vast majority of police favored. (During the 1970s the SPLC had been in the forefront nationally of the fight against capital punishment.) As a result, the Law Center had earned the reputation of being unsympathetic to the interests of law enforcement.

One of the handful of officers with whom we were on good terms was an official of the Alabama Bureau of Investigation (ABI), an arm of the state troopers. By coincidence the officer, Lieutenant John Hendrix, happened to be the custodian of several hundred ABI photographs taken at various KKK demonstrations around the state since 1978. One day not long after the first round of depositions I telephoned Lieutenant Hendrix to see if he would allow me to take a look at the mug shots of the IEKKKK members arrested in

Montgomery in 1979. Hendrix agreed, and by the end of the session I had managed to identify and obtain addresses for three or four Klansmen previously unknown to us.

With these new leads, plus the ones from McGlocklin, Randall Williams and I launched our first investigative field trip to Decatur. Our ultimate purpose was to locate more witnesses to the conspiracy. This meant tracking down the Klansmen we already had identified and identifying as many other members of the May 26 mob as possible. We found the going more difficult than we had expected, however. In a number of cases the person we were looking for had moved without leaving a forwarding address. In short, we discovered that the job of identifying, locating, and interviewing witnesses was a time-consuming affair, with many more failures than successes. The two interviews we managed to conduct on the first full day of work produced nothing. The following day we had more luck, obtaining a statement corroborating the Berryhills from a former Klansman who had only been a teenager at the time he participated in the May 26 attack.

We then flew to the Mississippi Gulf Coast to follow up on one of McGlocklin's more intriguing leads: The former head of the Mississippi IEKKKK (who claimed to have been an ex-Philadelphia, Pennsylvania, police officer) had broken with Wilkinson in a nasty dispute and might be willing to give us help in identifying members of the Mississippi Klan who, it was rumored, might have been in Decatur on May 26. Although we were unable to track him down on that occasion, the trip illustrated the fact that we were willing to spare no expense to get to the bottom of the Decatur conspiracy. Unfortunately it also showed how disorganized our first efforts at field investigation were and what a scattershot approach we were taking. After our fruitless—and costly—journey to the Magnolia State, we returned to Montgomery with the realization that we had to draw up a more logical plan of attack.

As the second round of depositions approached, Dees got a phone call from yet another defendant in the case. This time it was Roger Handley, the former Alabama grand dragon of the IEKKKK.* It came on a Saturday night, around midnight, at Dees's home.

* Early in 1982, after the *Tennessean* had published its stories about Bill Wilkinson's FBI ties, Handley had quit the IEKKKK and started his own Klan faction. At the time of his resignation he had been second-in-command to Wilkinson in the national hierarchy.

Handley immediately launched into a discussion of the lawsuit. Dees broke in and told him it would be improper for him to talk about the case outside the presence of Handley's attorney. But Handley insisted, bellowing out in a deep, raspy drawl, "Hell, Morris, what do you want? What do you want from us?"

He sounded drunk. This was not the first time he had called under the obvious influence of alcohol. Again Dees tried to cut off the conversation, but Handley didn't want to take no for an answer.

"I'll tell you what we want," Dees said at last. "I want to know whether Bill Wilkinson called you up and told you to get your men down there to block the blacks on May twenty-sixth."

"Oh, so you want Wilkinson's neck on the chop block?" Handley asked.

"Well, Roger, it's either his or yours," Dees replied.

Handley did not take the bait, and the conversation ended on that note. Dees's attempt to flip Handley to obtain direct evidence against Wilkinson had failed, at least for the time being; but he had succeeded in planting the idea, and he hoped it would eventually bear fruit. It was obvious merely from the fact that Handley had called that he was worried about where our investigation was headed.

Over the next month or so we took the depositions of another dozen defendants, almost all the key figures known to us at the time, including Handley, Steele, and Riccio. As had been the case earlier, no one owned up to having knowledge of a conspiracy.

Handley, who came in limping on a cane and proclaiming his innocence, testified he had been at the beach some 350 miles south of Decatur on May 26, 1979, with his wife and another couple. On the surface it seemed like an airtight alibi, but nothing he said actually contradicted what his chief accusers, the Berryhills, had told us. The Huntsville klavern meeting at which they placed him had occurred several days prior to the twenty-sixth, just like the one in Decatur.

Handley's alibi—which we had already gotten wind of from a source—was significant in one respect: It represented a classic illustration of how the KKK often functioned. Down through the years it had been standard operating procedure for high-ranking Klansmen to plot or encourage violent acts, prime the rank-and-file members to carry them out, and then make themselves scarce when the crime occurred so that, like Handley, they could claim to have clean hands if anything went awry.

For their part, the rank-and-file members we questioned during that round of depositions insisted that they simply had been trying to stage a march of their own when the trouble erupted. They did their best to sell the idea that the outbreak of violence had been a spontaneous event, the inevitable result of two opposing groups that got within clashing distance. The only problem was, the Kluxers couldn't get their stories straight. Some said the KKK had intended to march in front of the SCLC; some said behind. Others suggested the plan had been for the Klan to fall in beside the blacks as the demonstrators marched past the Bank-Lee intersection—or simply to observe. We must have heard every lie in the book.

Other Klansmen were busy elevating the memory lapse to an art form. Perhaps the most notorious was Derane O'Neil Godfrey, a custom van painter in his twenties who lived in a Birmingham suburb. Godfrey adopted what we came to dub the paint sniffer defense. The slender, casually dressed young airbrush artist, sporting a mustache and blow-dried hair, had difficulty remembering just about anything, from the name of a past employer to the explanation of how he even managed to be in Decatur on May 26.

Q. Who told you to go [to the pumps]?
A. I don't recall who told me. I heard it somewhere, you know.
Q. You just heard somewhere about it?
A. Yeah.
Q. How far is that park from your house?
A. Oh, let's see. I really don't know. Maybe 60, 70 miles maybe.
Q. You have got no idea who told you to go there?
A. No. . . .
Q. Did you know anybody that you were going to see there?
A. Maybe one person I knew that was going to be there, one or two maybe.
Q. Who was that?
A. Let's see. I can't remember the names.
Q. You can't recall any names?
A. No.
Q. Were they the ones that told you to come?
A. I don't remember if it was them or not.

Q. Did you expect there was going to be a boat show up there or a carnival or something? What I'm trying to get at is, did you decide to go 60 miles to a park in Decatur on Saturday morning not knowing anyone? . . .

A. Someone told me that it was going to be a meeting there, you know, not with the blacks but there was going to be another meeting.

Q. Did they tell you there was going to be a Ku Klux Klan meeting there?

A. I don't recall. . . .

Q. So when you got to the park you didn't know there was going to be any Klansmen there, you just drove up to the park?

A. I thought it might be some Klan there, yeah.

Q. Why did you think it might be some Klansmen there?

A. Well, I think I knew some Klansmen.

Q. Who did you know that was in the Klan?

A. I don't recall the people.

Q. You can't recall any names?

A. No, I sure can't. . . .

Q. Did you know Billy Riccio before you went up there?

A. I sure didn't.

Q. Have you communicated with him since?

A. I've talked with Bill, yeah.

Q. Have you talked to him recently by telephone?

A. No. I can't recall. No, not recently.

Q. Has he called you in the last thirty days on the telephone?

A. I can't recall if he has or not.

Q. Have you called him within the last thirty days?

A. I can't recall.

Q. Has he called you in the last ten days?

A. I can't recall that. I don't know if he called me or not or if I have called him.

Q. You just don't remember?

A. I just don't remember. I breathe a lot of paint and I've breathed a lot of toxic paint in the last year.

Q. Does that affect your memory?

A. Yes, it does.

Q. I see. Are you under any kind of medical care right now for this memory problem?

A. No. . . .
Q. Have you declared for any unemployment compensation because of your physical disability?
A. No. I don't have a physical disability. I just said that I breathe a
lot of paint and I'm a painter just like millions of other
painters and this paint that I use is toxic and it does make you
dingy, you might say.

Godfrey's responses about his purpose for having an ax handle at
the Bank-Lee intersection were equally preposterous:

Q. Did it have a blade on the end of it?
A. No, no blade.
Q. Did you have an ax you were going to put it in?
A. Oh, no. No. I just—I had the ax handle.
Q. Well, what was it for?
A. Well, I originally, you know, when I first bought it I bought the
ax, you know, to buy a blade for it but not for anything to do
with what we are talking about.
Q. So you were going to buy an ax handle and then go buy a
blade and put it in it?
A. Not that day, no. I had just carried the ax handle in my car. I
just had it in my car. I have no intention of buying an ax blade,
no, not that day.
Q. But when you first—
A. Oh, when I first bought it, yeah, I was going to buy an ax
blade for chopping wood.
Q. You were going to get a blade later?
A. Yeah.
Q. To chop wood?
A. Yeah.
Q. But you didn't have enough money to get the ax and the blade
all at one time?
A. Right.

The flippant nature of Godfrey's responses reminded me of
something I had read in the FBI report prior to the Robinson trial.
During an interview with one of the Bureau's special agents investigating the incident, one Kluxer explained the KKK's presence in

Decatur on the twenty-sixth by saying that the Klansmen had intended to "have a little church service at Lee and Bank streets and that it just happened to be at a time that blacks were coming down the street." Then the Klansman paused, laughed, and said he realized the agents were too smart to believe that.

Williams, Dees, and I were already powerfully motivated to get to the bottom of the Decatur conspiracy, but the saucy attitude of Godfrey and some of his compatriots provided us with additional incentive.

Despite the adversarial nature of the proceedings, the atmosphere surrounding these depositions was relatively civil, particularly compared with the Texas case. Dees went out of his way to keep things amicable, with both opposing counsel and members of the Klan. Not only did he genuinely dislike personal conflict and animosity, but he also believed it was in his clients' best interest for him to keep the lines of communication open with the Klan's attorneys. Beyond that, he figured that the better the Klansmen knew him, the less likely they would be to want to harm him. As a result, he made an effort to be personable to all but the most hostile deponents, and he made a point of emphasizing his rural Southern roots.

I first saw Dees employ this approach when we were working on a death penalty trial in Georgia in December 1978, several months before we became involved in anti-Klan work. During a recess I noticed him talking to a spectator seated on a bench in the back of the courtroom. They carried on what seemed like a cordial conversation for several minutes. Then Dees walked over and asked me if I knew the man. I didn't. "That's old J. B. Stoner," he said. Though I didn't know the face, I recognized the name. Stoner was a lawyer and the head of the National States Rights party, a white supremacist group based in Marietta, Georgia. Shortly before we saw him he had been indicted for the 1958 bombing of a black church in Birmingham. He was free pending a ruling on his attempt to fight extradition. He eventually lost the fight, and was tried and convicted.

It was in the same vein that Dees challenged Terry Tucker, the Klan Special Forces official, and Bill Riccio, the IEKKKK grand chaplain, to a friendly game of billiards during a break in the depositions. Startled, they accepted the invitation, and the five of us—Randall Williams and myself included—walked down the street to a dingy little pool hall a few doors away from Willingham's office and cued up. Dees was an avid pool player, though not terribly good at it. But neither were Tucker and Riccio. We played for about a half hour, needling each other about missed shots and relating more like drinking buddies than adversaries in litigation, and when the time came for the depositions to resume, we returned our cue sticks to the rack, strolled back to Willingham's office, and continued the proceedings.

Riccio was one of the Kluxers we were wariest of. From all appearances, he was a hard-core Klansman in the Beam mold, a rousing speaker who, though then only in his mid-twenties, had already been in the KKK for nearly a decade. Both Lloyd Letson and Doug Berryhill had fingered him as one of the key leaders behind the May 26 conspiracy.

Like Beam's, Riccio's rhetoric was often chilling, evidencing a pathological hatred (or fear) of minorities. In the August 30, 1981, edition of the Sunday newspaper supplement *Parade*, he was quoted as telling writer Roy Blount, "Some other Klan groups don't have a real clear creed. They say niggers are all right just as long as they stay in their place. But we say either they go back to Africa or they can be fertilizer on our farms." And about Jews: "The Jewish problem must be settled, a final solution. I'm not going to hang up my robe until the last Jew is deported to Palestine or executed."

Our file on Riccio was brimming with similar quotations. His diatribes against "ape niggers," "white niggers," and Jews had become a common refrain at KKK rallies across northern Alabama during the late 1970s and early 1980s. One particularly telling example was this observation about the Atlanta child killings: "Well, some people might think my opinion is kinda morbid. I don't think I better say. I'll say *this*: Little niggers grow up to be big niggers. And that's twenty of 'em we won't have to kill later."

There was something exceptionally disturbing about this intensely dedicated young Klansman. You could see it in the wild look in his eyes whenever he donned his Klan robe or began talking about race. Jerry Thompson, the undercover reporter, had noticed it during his stint in the Alabama IEKKKK in 1980, describing him in *My Life in the Klan* as "not only menacing but also downright frightening" and reporting that Riccio had once threatened to kill any Klan member who testified against him.*

Riccio was not your typical Klan thug, however. A skilled auto mechanic and former Bible college student, he was intelligent and well spoken—but deeply troubled. In a brush with the law in 1981 he had been arrested for animal cruelty for shooting a neighbor's dog with a bow and arrow. What made the incident even more bizarre was Riccio's explanation: He said that the animal had attacked his own dog—but the neighbor's pet was a dachshund, and Riccio's was a German shepherd. In 1981 federal prosecutors successfully used the incident, and a separate weapons violation, to have Riccio's probation revoked on a ten-year sentence he had previously been given for possessing a sawed-off shotgun.

Despite his contempt for us and for what we were doing, he seemed to warm up to us just a little bit after the game of pool, displaying an affable side that hardly seemed capable of coexistence with his darker self. Like Handley and Steele before him, he denied being privy to a conspiracy to block the march, however, and his deposition added nothing to our knowledge of events surrounding the Decatur incident.

Back in Montgomery, having completed the second round of depositions, Williams and I sat down to figure out a new investigative game plan. Up to that point we had learned the identities of approximately thirty-five or forty Klansmen of the one hundred or so present at Bank and Lee streets. Of these forty we had deposed only fifteen or twenty; the other half we either did not have addresses for or had not yet tried to locate. That left about sixty Klansmen of the hundred still unidentified.

With the idea of putting our leads in the most usable form, we typed the name of each Klansman we knew but had yet to locate on a separate sheet of paper, added to it whatever we had in the way of an address or hometown or other leads (if any), and put the material in a loose-leaf notebook.

Next we examined the photographs—again—and singled out the key players, those Klansmen who had actually attacked the police or the marchers or who stood out for some other reason as prominent witnesses. Of the sixty Kluxers whose identities we didn't

* Op. cit., p. 269.

yet know, the twenty-five or thirty who fell into this category became our priority IDs.

To make it easier for us to refer to the priority IDs in discussions between ourselves, Williams and I gave them nicknames based on their appearances. Thus there was Bristlehead, whose hair stood on end like the bristles of a wire brush; Sha Na Na, a Kluxer in a white T-shirt with bulging biceps and a pair of dark glasses; Lisp, who looked as if he spoke with one; Porter Wagoner, after the country music singer; Houndstooth Collar, who wore a shirt (only the collar of which was visible) in the pattern of Bear Bryant's trademark hat; Stripes, the wearer of a striped T-shirt; Mayor Folmar No. 1 and Mayor Folmar No. 2, both of whom resembled Emory Folmar, the mayor of Montgomery; Shooter, who had a pistol in his hand in one photograph; Cowboy Hat; Potbelly; Polo Shirt; Irish Cap; Paisley; and a host of others.

Fortunately, because of information we had obtained from Nungester and McGlocklin, we had a general idea of where to start our search. The Klansmen whom we were looking for, they both told us, most likely came from klaverns in Birmingham, Cullman, Huntsville, Hartselle, Athens, the "Quad Cities" (Tuscumbia, Muscle Shoals, Florence, Sheffield), and, of course, Decatur. Still, it was an awfully big haystack, as big as northern Alabama, from Birmingham to the Tennessee border, from Mississippi in the west all the way to Georgia.

Once we got organized, we headed up north for a second round of field investigation, starting in Decatur. The going, as before, was exceedingly tough. Getting identifications turned out to be only half the problem, and too often the easier half. The hard part was physically locating the person. Many of the Klansmen we sought were shiftless, moving from one address to another, leaving no forwarding instructions at the post office or any other easily discernible tracks. And many of the addresses we *did* have were out of date.

In the course of pursuing every available lead, we went down our share of rabbit trails. On one occasion I spent several hours tracking down a car that had been seen at the pumps on May 26, only to discover that its owner was a black man. Apparently he had parked his car near the KKK's staging area during a fishing outing on the river. Another time I managed to get an identification of a Klansman in our photos from the man's former employer. When I subsequently located the "Klansman" in question, he politely insisted that it was not his image in the photograph at all, and he was right. His boss had been mistaken. But the victim of the misidentification took it well, marveling at his resemblance to the Kluxer.

Despite the obstacles and setbacks, we pressed on. One Friday afternoon, as I was headed back to Montgomery, enjoying the classical music station I frequently tuned in to while on the road, I decided to look up one of the Kluxers I had identified from the Montgomery arrest pictures sometime earlier. He was a young Klansman of about thirty named Tom Reid,* and the only information we had on him was that he lived in a little coal town in the hills of rural Jefferson County, northwest of Birmingham.

By the time I arrived in the small town of Adamsville, it was about seven o'clock. My first step was to call the information operator for Reid's number and address. I was informed there was no such listing. Past experience told me that didn't mean the address I had for him was no longer valid—chances were he didn't own a telephone—so I drove to his house. There I found that like so many of his counterparts, he had moved since 1979, and his neighbors claimed not to know where he had gone. The only lead I uncovered was that his parents were thought to live in a nearby community.

Although tempted to give up (darkness was coming on), I drove to the adjacent town, found another street-side phone, and dialed the parents' number. Reid's mother answered. I introduced myself as an investigator (I didn't say for whom) and explained that I needed to talk to her son about an incident he had been involved in several years earlier. Clearly concerned, she asked what it was about. I equivocated, apologizing that I couldn't be any more specific. She told me her son had asked her not to give out his phone number, but when I pressed her, she agreed to relay the message as soon as we hung up and told me to call back in a few minutes for his reply. When I called back, Mrs. Reid said that her son had agreed to meet me at her house the next morning. He had been beaten up by some fellow Kluxers one time over a dispute about the klavern treasury, and apparently he thought that was what I wanted to see him about.

The next day I rose early and headed to Reid's parents' residence,

* Not his real name.

arriving in plenty of time to reconnoiter the situation from a distance. The Reids lived in a mobile home in the country set back a little bit from the main road. I drove by it, parked on the side of the road, took my microcassette tape recorder and a blank tape out of my briefcase, and strapped the recorder to my calf beneath my trousers, clipping the microphone underneath my shirt.

I had decided to record my interview with Reid surreptitiously (as was perfectly legal). In the event he said something important, I wanted it preserved, and I was uncertain that I could persuade him to sign a statement. I was also concerned about his recanting. In addition, I wanted to protect myself from any subsequent accusations of improprieties.

After checking to see that everything was working, I drove the few hundred yards back to the Reids' residence. I was more than usually nervous, aware that if the recorder malfunctioned and started to squawk I would have to make a hasty exit. I turned the recorder on before getting out of the car.

The Reids met me at the door, and it wasn't until I was inside that I realized their son had not yet arrived. I didn't like the idea of Reid coming in behind me; there was always the possibility he might bring a carload of his Klan buddies, and the whole thing could be a setup. Also, I was worried about the batteries in my recorder running down. After a few minutes I excused myself, went to the bathroom, and shut the recorder off. Reid arrived, alone, shortly after I came out.

As soon as I heard his car door slam, I activated the recorder through my pants leg. A few seconds later he opened the door and entered, speaking to his parents affectionately and glancing in my direction. It was as if he had walked right out of the May 26 photos: I would have recognized him anywhere.

"I'm a private investigator from Montgomery," I said as I rose to introduce myself, "and I'm working for some attorneys down there who have filed a civil lawsuit against the Klan."

"About?" Reid asked, his voice trailing off.

"Decatur."

"Decatur. Oh, goddamn," he said. "Well, I'll tell you something. I'll tell you what you want to know. The Klan started it. Now I can guaran-damn-tee you that."

And then he proceeded to spill his guts: the conspiracy, the cover-up, names, dates, places, a raft of new identifications, and additional evidence, albeit hearsay, against Wilkinson. He seemed to hold nothing back; it was as if he had been waiting to get the burden off his chest. We talked so long I had to excuse myself and go out to the car to flip the cassette.

The balance of the interview took place at the kitchen table, with Reid on one side and me at the adjacent corner only an arm's length away. While we talked, I tried to make certain the mike, which was concealed underneath the pocket of my shirt, was facing directly toward him at all times. I wanted to catch every word he said. Whenever he sat back, I hunched forward. If he turned, I turned with him. When he said something good, I asked him to repeat it. As the interview progressed, I felt such a rush of exhilaration I found it hard to maintain the tough cop persona I tried to project in my dealings with Klan members.

Reid's account of the conspiracy had a familiar ring to it. Two or three nights prior to May 26 the titan over the Birmingham district, a man named Jack Mize, had come to the regular weekly meeting of the Adamsville klavern and informed Reid and the fifteen or so other members in attendance about the plot to block the demonstration. "We ain't gonna let the niggers march," Reid quoted Mize as saying.

Mize didn't specify the details of the plot, but he encouraged the Klansmen gathered together that night to answer the call of the Decatur klavern, adding that "Bill [Wilkinson] wanted us all down there."

Early on the morning of the twenty-sixth, Reid said, a handful of members from the Adamsville klavern rendezvoused at Mize's house, and the group drove in a caravan to Decatur and went directly to the pumps. There, and again at the corner of Bank and Lee streets, Reid heard Steele instruct the assembled Klansmen to block the path of the demonstrators. "We've come down here to stop them from marching, and goddammit, that's what we're gonna do," Steele declared.

A few days after the attack, Reid said, the Adamsville klavern held another meeting, and Mize was on hand again. There was an air of accomplishment all around, and Mize announced with satisfaction, "We done what we said we was going to do. We did not let them march."

When I had asked every question I could think of, I thanked Reid for his truthfulness and took my leave. It had been an extraordinary interview. Once back in the safety of the car, I reached down and rewound the tape to check the quality of the recording. Every allegation was audible.

The evidence Reid had provided practically blew the lid off the conspiracy, establishing that it was of a statewide nature. Now we had proof of participation by a third klavern (Huntsville and Decatur being the others) and strong allegations against yet another top-ranking IEKKKK official, Jack Mize. The investigation was really coming together.

Over the course of several months Williams and I talked to hundreds of additional northern Alabama citizens as we sought to identify and track down Klan members who we had reason to believe knew something about the May 26 incident. Sometimes it took twenty or twenty-five separate contacts to locate one Klansman, and in the end he might refuse to talk to us. In such a case we simply subpoenaed him to a deposition. As we combed the countryside, we showed our photos to postal carriers, law enforcement officers, car dealers, factory officials, neighbors and former neighbors, gas station attendants, and (so it seemed) nearly every little country store in the northern third of the state.

Some of our success, however, was attributable to sheer luck. One afternoon I was driving through Decatur, flipping through the stations on the radio, when I locked onto one station just in time to hear the announcer say, "And the winner of today's floral bouquet is Chris Christian."

Immediately I perked up. That was the name of a Klansman we were looking for. Although I was skeptical that the contest winner and the Klansman were one and the same, I decided to check it out. I located the radio station a few blocks away and asked to speak to the disc jockey. Swallowing the cock-and-bull story I told him about why I wanted the information, he repeated the name and address of the florist's for me and said that Christian was to pick up his bouquet before 5:00 P.M. It was then about 3:30.

Immediately I drove across town and found a parking space in front of the shop. For the next few minutes people came and went, but none of them resembled the lanky, long-haired Klansman pictured in our 1979 photos. Then, about half an hour later, a large red sedan pulled up, and a tall, heavyset man in his late twenties, accompanied by a woman who appeared to be twice his age, got out of the car. The man bore a strong resemblance to Christian, but I couldn't be positive. He was a good twenty or thirty pounds heavier; furthermore, he had on a cowboy hat and sunglasses and was now sporting a beard. If I hadn't known better I might have mistaken him for Hank Williams, Jr., the neo-redneck country singer who made his home in Cullman.

As I watched, they went into the shop, then emerged several minutes later with some flowers. As they made their way to their car I wondered whether I should follow them or not. It was still only a few minutes past four, plenty of time for the real Chris Christian to show up if I was wrong. After a moment's indecision I went with my instincts and turned on the ignition. As I backed away from the florist's, I watched in dismay, however, as the red sedan went around the corner and turned into a parking lot in front of the hospital across the street. From there the couple got out and carried the flowers inside. I, on the other hand, found a parking space from which I could watch both the florist's and the hospital.

A few minutes later the couple returned. Now I was faced with a real dilemma, for I was much less convinced than before that the man was Christian. The resemblance was strong, but events seemed to suggest otherwise—the possibility certainly existed that the gentleman I believed to be Christian was simply someone with a loved-one in the hospital. Still, when the red sedan pulled out of the parking lot, my gut reaction was to follow, so I went with it. With no experience in tailing cars, I nearly lost sight of the red sedan more than once in heavy traffic. Finally I observed it turning right onto the Beltline, a bypass on the southern outskirts of Decatur, and a short distance later it turned again into a shopping center. Parking a few rows away, I got out and followed the couple into a discount department store. In an attempt to make a positive ID, I wandered over to where they were browsing. As nonchalantly as possible I glanced over at the man and was persuaded it was Christian after all. As the pair went through the checkout, I hovered over a candy display near an adjacent cash register, timing my entrance into the line so that I could exit the store a few steps behind them. They were totally oblivious of my presence. When they eased back onto the Beltline from the parking lot, I slipped in behind them, and we continued for another mile before they finally turned down a road that led into the country south of town.

The road was winding and slightly hilly, and I found myself constantly speeding up or slowing down to remain at a safe, inconspicuous distance. It seemed we drove for miles, but finally I saw the car turn onto a gravelly driveway and glide up to an attractive ranch-style house. I continued several hundred yards farther and stopped at a residence at the bottom of a hill where a middle-aged woman was working in her yard. I told her I was a friend of Christian's and that I had lost my way to his house.

"You didn't miss it by much," she said. "It's the one up there on the right. He lives with his mother and stepfather."

Returning to the car, I drove slowly back up the road, took down the box number, and noted the mileage on my odometer so I could measure the distance back to town. A few weeks after the episode we subpoenaed Christian to a deposition. Although he confessed to having intentionally blocked the march, he refused to implicate any Klan officials. We never got to use him as a witness in any court proceeding, however; within the year he was dead—a suicide.

Whenever I was doing fieldwork in the Decatur area, I was in the habit of driving through the parking lot of the Waffle House, a onetime Klan hangout on the southern edge of town. McGlocklin had told us that the gray-haired, middle-aged man in our pictures we had nicknamed White Power Stick (for a club with those words written on it that he had been photographed holding) was a regular patron. He could often be found at the restaurant having a cup of coffee in the evening after work, McGlocklin said. That, a car description, and the fact that the man may have been a construction worker were the only things we had to go on.

Nearly every evening I glided through the lot, scouting for the vehicle. From time to time I went inside when I didn't have anything else to do, and I spent my share of time there, sitting and waiting, always on the lookout. But he never appeared.

Then one Saturday afternoon, on what I had come to think of as my Waffle House patrol, I took yet another spin through the parking lot. The car fitting McGlocklin's description was nowhere to be seen, but when I looked inside, I noticed a man who resembled

"Stick" seated at the counter with his back to the window. Trying to ID someone you've never met from a four-year-old photograph is not necessarily easy, so I went inside and took a seat at the counter a couple of chairs down from him. After ordering a Coke, I glanced his way, and I knew we had our man. There was no mistaking his face. But the job was only half finished. Now I had to find out his name.

It was late in the afternoon, a warm spring day, and the restaurant was practically empty. "Stick" was bending the waitress's ear about something. I waited for an opening and eased my way into the conversation. In a matter of minutes the waitress had returned to her chores, and "Stick" and I were shooting the breeze like old buddies. For nearly a half hour we kept this up. I gave him a line about being a free-lance writer working on a story about environmental pollution in northern Alabama. That prompted him to say he was a construction worker, convincing me beyond any doubt that he was our man. I eventually wound the conversation down and told him I had to leave.

"It sure has been a pleasure talking to you," I said in all truthfulness. "If you're ever down my way, look me up. My name's Bill Stanton."

"I'll do that," he said. "I've got some family down below Montgomery, and I go down there once in a while. I'm Robert Borden."

We shook on it, and I turned and walked out the door. There were only one or two vehicles in the parking lot, and as I drove through it on my way back out to the street, I jotted down their license plate numbers. When I ran them through the state Motor Vehicle Division the following week, one came back registered to Robert Borden, giving his home address.*

As time went on, we became fairly seasoned investigators, skillful practitioners of the art of insinuation, deftly wielding the bluff and the threat to encourage witnesses to cooperate with us. Each new piece of evidence became at once a building block in our case and a lever with which to move it forward, a device to make recalcitrant Klansmen think we knew more than we actually did. The idea was

* Borden claimed later that he had not been involved in the May 26 incident and had only gone down to the Bank-Lee intersection to find his father, a Klan sympathizer pushing eighty.

to frighten them into believing that everyone else was coming clean with us, that the conspiracy of silence upon which the KKK has historically depended had been broken in this instance and was crumbling fast.

Sometimes it worked. In other cases the mere shock of an investigator's showing up on the doorstep four years after the fact was enough to persuade some people, like Tom Reid, to cooperate.

Each situation had to be handled differently, of course. In general, we operated according to the three cardinal rules of private investigation:

1. Act with authority, and people will believe you have it.
2. Say no more than necessary about the nature of your business.
3. Occasionally it may be necessary to represent yourself as someone you are not.

The third rule, as we practiced it, involved a minimum of deceit. It amounted to little more than my posing as Chris Christian's friend for the purpose of verifying where he lived or using a ploy to manipulate Robert Borden into introducing himself. We never strayed across the border into illegality—representing ourselves as law enforcement officers, for example—nor did we promise any witness anything more than a fair shake in return for his or her cooperation.

For the most part we managed to conduct the investigation according to the first two rules. By donning coats and ties (we weren't used to wearing them around the office, which was a pretty casual place) and adopting a tight-lipped, no-small-talk approach to our interviews, we strove to project an air of authority. And after Williams applied for and received a license to operate a private investigative business from the Montgomery Police Department, we obtained very professional-looking identification cards and badges, which we often displayed by way of introduction.

The PI idea grew out of the difficulty we sometimes had in securing cooperation from certain police officials. (Before Williams obtained the license, more than one officer we approached for assistance insisted first on calling the Montgomery PD to verify our identities.) As it turned out, it served us well in all phases of the investigation. Not only did the license seem to confer legitimacy on us in the eyes of law enforcement, but it also smoothed the way for our appeals to private citizens for assistance. The combination of dress, manner, and professional-looking identification seemed to have a compelling effect on potential witnesses. Admittedly we also took advantage of the natural friendliness and helpfulness that most Southerners possess in abundant supply.

As an inside joke we dubbed ourselves 3-11 Investigations. The name was a play on KKK (*K* being the eleventh letter of the alphabet). Williams even designed a business card for us, enumerating our areas of expertise and featuring the slogan "When the butler didn't do it."

As the end of June 1983 approached, the Decatur case began to attract national publicity, largely as a consequence of a motion we had filed several weeks earlier to have Bill Wilkinson cited for contempt of court. We sought the citation for his failure to turn over to us certain documents we had requested through the discovery process, documents that Judge Haltom had earlier ruled we were entitled to. Although the information embodied in our request pertained to a variety of matters, the crux of the dispute was over our effort to obtain the names of Wilkinson's Alabama and Mississippi members, which we needed for the purpose of locating and interviewing all the individuals who potentially had knowledge of the conspiracy and cover-up.

In a typical lawsuit against a typical corporate defendant, the documents would have routinely changed hands; but Wilkinson asserted that the request violated the Klan members' rights to privacy and free association, and he indicated his willingness to go to jail rather than comply with the judge's order. The confrontation had the makings of a constitutional showdown. Judge Haltom scheduled a hearing for June 30 to resolve the question.

The situation was not without irony. On the one side was the Southern Poverty Law Center, a civil rights organization whose head attorney had been an avid defender of the First Amendment for twenty years, now attempting to compel the Ku Klux Klan to reveal the identities of its members. For its part, the Klan, a group notorious for flouting the law, was seeking refuge behind a famous 1958 Supreme Court ruling in which the Court quashed an attempt by the Alabama attorney general to obtain the membership list of the state's NAACP chapter.

Simply stated, the legal issue in the Decatur dispute boiled down to this: Did the plaintiffs' need for the names outweigh the defendants' rights to privacy and free association?

It was a thorny question, to be sure, one wherein the lofty sentiments of the First Amendment seemed to meet the real world. Under the U.S. Constitution it was just as legal to be a member of the KKK as it was to belong to the Masons or any other secret society (or, for that matter, the NAACP or the Republican party). In the neutral eyes of the law the Klan was a legitimate group, and its members had the right to organize to pursue common goals, no matter how repugnant the beliefs that motivated them. It was the KKK's position that in view of this fact, it would be an abridgment of the rights of those who had joined the organization in anonymity to force it to reveal their names, particularly in light of society's need to protect the rights of citizens whose beliefs fall outside the mainstream.

Our intention in seeking the names was not to violate the Klansmen's rights or to establish a bad legal precedent, which might later be used against left-wing or civil rights groups. However, the courts had made clear over the years that the freedoms guaranteed in the First Amendment were not absolute (the prohibition against crying "fire" in a crowded theater being perhaps the best-known example) and that in circumstances in which the rights of opposing parties conflicted, as in the Decatur lawsuit, the interests of the parties had to be weighed to determine whose rights were paramount. To make such determinations, the courts had created what they called balancing tests.

In the case at hand, the Klan members' rights to privacy and free association would have to be weighed against such factors as the importance of the information sought to the task of proving the allegations set forth in the complaint as well as whether all reasonable means for obtaining the information had been exhausted. An additional factor that would be given weight was the matter of the public interest.

Courts had long considered the public interest in cases in which the rights of competing parties conflicted over issues of constitutional significance. All things being equal, if one side to a dispute could demonstrate that its position would serve to promote the commonweal, it might tip the court to rule in its favor.

Here we believed that the law was clearly on our side. The Reconstruction Congress had passed the Ku Klux Klan Acts under which the Decatur suit was filed expressly to protect the rights of the newly freed slaves. In bringing the lawsuit, our clients, the marchers, were in effect promoting a long-standing public policy by seeking to enforce these laws.

Finally there was the matter of legal precedent. In 1928 the U.S. Supreme Court had upheld a New York State law requiring the KKK to file a list of its members, basing its decision in part on the group's history of violence and lawlessness. Thirty years later, applying the same logic to a different set of facts, the Court had refused to require the Alabama NAACP to hand over its membership precisely because there was no evidence the group was then or had ever engaged in illegal activity.

On the day of the hearing we arrived at the Federal Courthouse in Birmingham, convinced we were in a no-lose situation. Judge Haltom, after all, had already ordered Wilkinson to turn over the names. The purpose of the hearing was merely to allow Wilkinson to explain why he hadn't done so and to show cause why he shouldn't be held in contempt. The way we viewed it, our side came up a winner either way: If Wilkinson chose to give us the information, we got what we needed and Wilkinson was finished as a Klan leader. If he refused to obey the court's order, he was headed for jail.

The normally garrulous, wisecracking imperial wizard appeared downcast as he took his seat with Dan Willingham, his attorney, at the counsel table. Ironically, the courtroom was the same one in which Lloyd Letson had first broken his silence about the conspiracy more than eighteen months earlier. As had been the case then, there were only a few Klansmen among the spectators, not even enough to fill up one section of the gallery. Directly behind Wilkinson, outside the bar, sat his wife Barbara, who doubled as the office manager at national headquarters, and one of Wilkinson's two sons. To judge by the looks on their faces, they, like Wilkinson himself, seemed to be expecting the worst.

On our side of the aisle the mood was considerably more upbeat. A handful of the marchers had come down to the hearing from Decatur, and they seemed to take satisfaction at the prospect of the once high-flying imperial wizard getting his comeuppance.

Three hours of testimony and arguments later, however, the hearing came to an anticlimactic end when Judge Haltom abruptly announced he had to leave to preside over a previously scheduled trial. Before adjourning, he announced that the proceedings would be in recess for three weeks. It was a reprieve of sorts for Wilkinson, and in a parting remark the judge advised him to spend the interim reconsidering his position.

For those of us working on the case at the SPLC the continuance seemed like an interminable delay. And to our dismay, when the hearing reconvened on July 21, it ended on the same anticlimactic note, with the judge deciding to take the whole matter under advisement before issuing his ruling. It was obvious—and understandable—that he wanted time to reflect upon all the evidence before taking the drastic step of depriving Wilkinson of his freedom.

Soon after the July 21 hearing, an official from the Justice Department contacted us about obtaining whatever evidence we had of criminal wrongdoing arising out of the Decatur incident. It was the first direct confirmation we had gotten that the feds had reopened their inquiry into the case.

For some time we had known that the evidence we were uncovering was possibly of a criminal nature. The allegations against Steele, Handley, Riccio, and Mize, if true, constituted crimes, not just violations of civil law. But the ramifications had not fully sunk in— at least so far as Williams and I were concerned—and we greeted with ambivalence the news that the feds wanted us to hand over our evidence. While we were pleased to hear that the criminal inquiry had been reopened, we nonetheless looked on the feds as interlopers horning in on our case—and after we had done all the hard work. It was a selfish, shortsighted reaction perhaps—particularly in light of the fact that the civil rights community had been lambasting the Reagan administration for retrenchment on civil rights enforcement—but we were highly skeptical of the feds' motives, and we were afraid, too, that our role in the case would be obscured. However, Dees assured us there would be plenty of credit to go around—"We'll see to that," he said—and informed us he had agreed to a meeting with two Department of Justice (DOJ) attorneys at FBI headquarters in Birmingham on July 27.

Williams and I remained skeptical, though, and by the day of the meeting we had concocted a plan of action. We told Dees we would accompany him to Birmingham and hear the feds out, and if we liked them, we would agree to cooperate. There was one proviso: that we not identify any of our sources until the three of us had had a chance to evaluate the outcome of the meeting.

Methodically, meticulously, we edited our informants' statements with a felt-tipped black marker, deleting any references to names, locations, or other information that might provide clues to their identities. To be on the safe side, we photocopied these redacted statements (to use the feds' term) so no one could hold them up to a light to read through the blacked-out portions. Then we gathered together the statements, the photographs, and other key evidence we planned to take with us to illustrate our presentation. Late on the morning of July 27 we set out for Birmingham as scheduled.

The meeting had not gone far before Williams and I were won over by the two DOJ lawyers, Dan Rinzel and Craig Shaffer. It was apparent they shared our desire to see justice done in the case. In the end we spent the better part of two hours laying out our knowl-edge of the conspiracy for them and answering their questions, even though Rinzel stressed that the relationship between us would have to be a "one-way street." They would be happy to receive any evidence we could provide them, but they were prohibited by fed-eral law from reciprocating. By the end of the meeting a good rapport had been forged among us, and Williams and I had agreed to turn over unedited copies of our materials.

The Decatur investigation had entered a new phase, and on the way back to Montgomery the three of us speculated about this dramatic turn of events. How many Klansmen would the feds indict—and when? What effect would the criminal case have on the civil case? How long would Judge Haltom wait before ruling on the contempt motion? Knowing that our modest little civil suit had set the massive federal prosecutorial machine in motion gave us a heady feeling.

Eight miles outside Montgomery we crested the last wave of hills that roll across central Alabama just north of the capital, and the gleaming white buildings of the state office complex came into view, as if out of nowhere, against the horizon. Descending the long, sloping incline, we crossed the rich black bottomlands of the Ala-bama River—huge, flat fields planted wall to wall in cotton—and swept across the bridge into town. Less than five minutes later we pulled up in front of the Law Center. It was the end of a typically sultry summer day in southern Alabama. Ducking inside just long enough to drop off our briefcases, we emerged from the office and went our separate ways into the muggy evening air, buoyed by the fact that things were finally beginning to jell.

Chapter Eight

LATER THAT night—somewhere around 4:00 A.M.—came word from the Montgomery Fire Department that the Law Center was on fire.

A dispatcher rousted Dees out of bed with the news, and from there it spread rapidly along the organizational grapevine, so that when I arrived at the scene at about five-thirty, a small crowd of SPLCers already had set up a grim watch in front of the building. The flames had been extinguished; but none of our people had yet been allowed to enter to assess the damage, and the whole area was cordoned off with bright yellow ribbon. Two or three fire trucks remained parked out front, along with a police car or two, and a maze of hose was strewn across the lawn. Fire fighters were coming and going, tending to the business of cleanup, while investigators sifted through the rubble inside for clues to the origins of the blaze.

Huddled on the sidewalk in the first light of morning, we looked on in a state of shock, compounded by anger and fear. None of us had to be told we were the victims of arson, and our gut feelings were confirmed when the investigators reported to Dees they had discovered evidence that a liquid accelerant of some sort had been poured or sprayed throughout the building before it had been set on fire.

The good news (there was some) was that the fire had consumed the accelerant and all the available oxygen within the building in a brief inferno without ever really igniting the building itself. By the time the fire fighters arrived, the blaze had almost burned itself out, starved for air; damage thus was far less than it otherwise might have been. Had the perpetrator or perpetrators only knocked out a few windows, the officials told us, the Law Center would have most likely burned to the ground, and everything in it, including any evidence, would have gone up in smoke. As it was, the only additional evidence the investigators had been able to locate was a glass pane from the window through which the arsonist or arsonists had gained entry at the back of the office, and a pair of gloves.

After completing their probe of the crime scene, the officials finally let us go inside, and what we found was an absolute mess. Soot was everywhere, from one end of the labyrinthine office to the other. It covered the walls, ceiling, furniture, file cabinets, computers, maps, telephones, and doorknobs. The entire building was cloaked in a fine dusting of black ash, which smudged at the slightest touch. It had penetrated closed file cabinets and even closed file folders within the cabinets. The air was heavy with its stale, grimy odor.

With the exception of the carpet, which had been doused with accelerant throughout the entire office and which bore the snaking, charred path of the flames, fire damage was much more localized. It appeared that the arsonists had concentrated their efforts on the Klanwatch wing and the legal files outside the attorneys' offices. In a common area adjacent to the latter, several file cabinet drawers containing case files had been pulled out and drenched with the accelerant—believed to be a petroleum-based liquid—before being ignited. A number of these files had burned.

On the Klanwatch side, Randall Williams's office bore the brunt of the attack. Virtually everything in it was destroyed, including a collection of his personal books and papers. The heat had been so intense it had partially melted the venetian blinds on the windows and seared the paint off the walls. His leather briefcase, however, containing the Decatur photographs we had so casually laid aside after returning from the Birmingham trip twelve hours earlier, was sitting on the floor in a corner of the room, miraculously unscathed.

The main Klanwatch office, which housed nearly all of the Project's newspaper and investigative files (in fireproof file cabinets) had sustained only smoke damage. All in all we had been exceedingly fortunate. From an evidentiary standpoint nothing irreplaceable had been lost. Statements of witnesses, photographs, interview notes, audio and videotapes all were safe. With the exception of Williams's personal effects, damage was confined to furnishings and equipment.

It was apparent from the first walk-through of the building, however, that we would have to relocate to temporary quarters while repairs were undertaken. Determined to deprive the arsonists of any satisfaction, Dees told the reporters who had already begun to gather at the scene that the fire would disrupt the SPLC's operations only minimally, and he vowed to be back in business within a day or two. In the meantime, he arranged to have a professional photographer come in before the cleanup began and photograph the destruction wreaked by the fire. In his role as chief fund-raiser for the Center, Dees was already thinking about using the arson attack as a vehicle to raise money to build a new, safer, more modern headquarters downtown.

Having set these various balls in motion, he turned his attention to what he considered the most important task of all that morning: catching the arsonists. He had no intention of sitting by and ceding the responsibility for solving the case to the authorities; he viewed the arson as a personal attack as well as an assault against the organization.

Moreover, Dees didn't trust the Montgomery Police Department (or the Fire Department, for that matter) to conduct a vigorous investigation. Aside from the standard law enforcement grievances about him—his reputation as a "radical," the perception of him as anti-cop—Dees had another strike against him at the Montgomery PD. It was the source of great umbrage there, and it was known as Todd Road. Todd Road was a street (a dirt road, to be more precise) in one of Montgomery's poorest black neighborhoods. Earlier that year it had been the site of a serious racial incident involving two undercover officers and out-of-state black mourners in town for the funeral of a family member. Many facts concerning the incident were in dispute, but the upshot was that the two plainclothes officers had been injured (one severely) after they had burst into the house where the mourners were staying and had been subsequently assaulted (one, in fact, was shot). Several of the mourners, who claimed they did not know the intruders were police officers, had been arrested and thrown in jail. When it became clear that Montgomery blacks were having trouble raising the defendants' hefty bond, Dees entered the picture, personally putting up a five-hundred-thousand-dollar property bond to obtain their release. As a result, Dees's relations with the police, never good, were worse just then than usual.

There were any number of people who logically could have been considered suspects in the arson. Dees and the SPLC had a sizable, and growing, list of enemies. Beam topped the list of obvious candidates, especially in light of his January duel-to-the-death letter. And there were dozens of IEKKKK members from northern Alabama who had a motive for burning down the Law Center in retaliation for the Decatur suit. But as Dees turned over all the possibilities in his mind during his predawn drive to town, he became convinced that the culprit behind the arson was another, far less notorious KKK figure: a Montgomery-area Klan leader by the name of Joe Garner.

Joe Michael Garner was a balding, self-important little man in his late thirties who spoke with a slight lisp and had a penchant for Shakespearian malapropisms. Although active in KKK affairs for years, he had opted to keep a low public profile about his membership in the group. Married and the father of a young daughter, he made his living by managing a pair of convenience stores, one in town and the other—more of a country store—located in the community of Snowdoun, eight miles to the south.

Like many Klansmen, Garner was a high school dropout, but he had completed the course of work for a general equivalency degree while in the army, and by the standards of most Klan members he was fairly prosperous. He had an attractive, modest house on the southern outskirts of Montgomery, owned two vehicles, and had achieved a measure of respect as, of all things, the head of the Snowdoun Volunteer Fire Department.

Though neither a scintillating speaker nor an especially effective organizer, Garner was energetic and eager, and in the post-David

Duke Knights of the KKK that often counted for more than talent or ability. In August 1981 he had pulled together a Klan "Unity Rally" in Montgomery for the purpose of fostering harmony among the various Klan factions operating in the Southeast; he had even served as the event's emcee. He had also helped bail the group's grand wizard, Don Black, out of jail after Black was arrested for violating the U.S. Neutrality Act for conspiring to overthrow the government of Dominica. Gradually Garner had achieved status as one of the Knights' leaders, eventually landing a seat on the Grand Council, the organization's national governing body.

Our first encounter of any significance with him had been in 1982, when he ran for sheriff of Montgomery County. From the outset he never stood a chance since he was going up against an incumbent who had held the office for more than two decades. After he won the lightly contested Republican nomination, however, we blew the whistle on him, with the help of a Montgomery newspaper, and he went down to an overwhelming defeat in the general election.*

It was not that run-in, though, that Dees had in mind when he settled on Garner as the number one suspect in the SPLC arson. Only about six weeks prior to the fire we had tangled with him again, this time about an even more serious matter.

Late in the spring of 1983 Dees had received a call that Garner allegedly had been harassing the family of a young white student who was socializing with a black female classmate. Garner had reportedly visited the youth's father and allegedly had "advised" him to make his son terminate the relationship. Subsequently the white family had been the victims of vandalism and harassment.

After Dees had shared this information with Williams and me, we urged him to let us begin an investigation and file suit if the allegations were borne out. Dees was lukewarm to the idea, and he had proposed instead that we take Garner's deposition about the incident and in that way put him on notice that we were aware of it. Then Dees appeared to have second thoughts about doing even that much. In the past he had expressed concern that we risked

* Despite having been informed of Garner's Klan affiliation before the primary election, the Montgomery County Republican party took no action to keep him off the ballot or even to disavow his candidacy.

retaliation by stirring up trouble with local Klan members, and his enthusiasm seemed to wane as he recalled his earlier misgivings.

But Williams and I had persisted, and Dees had finally agreed. On June 10, 1983, we took Garner's deposition in the conference room at the Law Center. To no one's surprise, Garner denied threatening the family and claimed to have no knowledge of the vandalism, and in that sense the deposition was a washout. But despite Garner's failure to admit to the harassment, Williams and I were satisfied that the exercise had served its purpose of putting him on notice.

A short time later Dees learned that Garner had left the deposition meeting seething about the way he supposedly had been treated. According to Dees's source, Garner felt that Dees had shown him a lack of respect.

On Dees's way into town the morning of the fire he recalled the whole episode. It by no means amounted to probable cause; but it was sufficient to constitute a credible motive, and Dees believed we should turn our investigative focus in Garner's direction. Before the morning was out, he informed agents from the Bureau of Alcohol, Tobacco, and Firearms about his suspicions and encouraged them to do likewise.*

Dees was consumed by the desire to solve the case and impatient to get started on it as soon as possible. He sent me out to comb the neighborhood around the Law Center to find out if any of our neighbors had seen anything suspicious. When this turned up nothing, he dispatched me down to Snowdoun to interview Bobby Taylor, the source of his previous information on Garner. Taylor, a sports car mechanic, lived and worked directly across the highway from Garner's Snowdoun store. From their earlier conversations Dees knew that the store was the sometime home to a young man named Tommy Downs, who would be a prime suspect if Garner were indeed behind the arson. Downs was a troubled youth of about twenty, and Garner had taken him under his wing. Garner provided him with a place to stay in a small, windowless storeroom in the back of the building, in return for which Downs helped Garner run both

* The Bureau of Alcohol, Tobacco, and Firearms (BATF) was the federal agency charged with investigating arson. Dees trusted the BATF agents because federal officers tended to be less susceptible to provincialism and the influences of local politics.

the Snowdoun store and the one in town, as well as doing other odd jobs for him.

By the time I got to Taylor's shop, he had already heard about the fire, and the thought that Garner and Downs might be behind it had already occurred to him. Taylor was wary of Garner, whom he knew to have a mean streak, and he had observed firsthand the influence Garner exercised over Downs and other young men like him. Despite his hunch, however, he had neither seen nor heard anything to suggest Downs's involvement. For good measure, he gave me the names of several other Snowdoun citizens whom Garner had alienated and promised to contact us if he observed anything suspicious.

Because it was already late in the day, I returned to the Law Center to fill Dees in on what I'd learned. There I found the cleanup operation in full swing. Temporary quarters had been lined up, and the movers were due to appear the next morning to begin relocating us. Estimates of the damages from the fire were running in the hundred-thousand-dollar range. (The final bill exceeded that figure by nearly half again as much.)

It was apparent even that afternoon that the Center had entered a new phase in its existence. Things would never be the same again. In the span of only a few minutes the arson had become a watershed event in the life of the SPLC. Ironically, we now shared something with our clients, a sense of victimization, and for the first time we felt physically vulnerable in our own community. For the whites on our staff, the phenomenon of racially motivated violence and KKK intimidation, which heretofore had been something that always happened to someone else, now took on a very personal and immediate connotation.

That night I got a phone call at home from Garry Nungester, our resident consultant on the Klan. He had been trying to reach me at the office for most of the day before he finally heard about the fire.

I described the day's events and asked him if any suspects came to mind. When I sounded him out about Garner, he was dubious. On the few occasions he had heard Garner mention Dees's name, it had always been with a healthy dose of respect. Garner had gone so far as to warn other Klansmen that Dees was someone the Klan shouldn't "mess with"—unless, he said, it wanted trouble.

*   *   *

Forty-eight hours after the fire the SPLC was back in business, its temporary headquarters a former clothing store on the Southern Bypass, a major east-west traffic artery lined with fast-food restaurants, filling stations, and shopping plazas. Our new office was set in one such small plaza behind a facade of tinted plate glass windows. The interior was a single, vast open room—perhaps 150 feet by 50 feet—which we rapidly carved up into smaller work spaces for our respective departments by erecting a system of portable dividers. It wasn't home, but it would have to do for the time being.

The BATF agents, who had taken charge of the official investigation, had forwarded the windowpane, the gloves, and a trace sample of the accelerant to their regional laboratory in Atlanta for analysis. The windowpane was of particular interest because it had on it a piece of duct tape that the arsonist had employed to keep the glass from shattering during the removal of the pane from the sill, and the agents were hopeful their lab colleagues would be able to lift a fingerprint from it. Their expectation was that the arsonist had taken his gloves off to loosen and pull the tape from the roll. Other than that, the agents were taking a sit-back-and-wait approach. It had been their experience that amateur arsonists (as opposed to organized crime professionals) invariably were overcome by the temptation to brag about their exploits once the heat was off. Accordingly, the officers had primed their network of street informants and other contacts, and they told us they hoped these clandestine ears of theirs would pick up something within a week or two.

Although Dees respected the commitment and expertise of the BATF agents, he was not a very patient man just then. Word had already gotten back to us that the police suspected Dees of setting the fire himself for publicity purposes, and the fire chief was preparing to have him polygraphed. Dees was livid; he became convinced that the situation called for something more to be done. Against the advice of the BATF officials, he posted a twenty-five-thousand-dollar reward with Law Center funds for information leading to the arrest and conviction of the person or persons responsible for the fire.

Two developments during this time reassured us that we were on the right track. Within a few days of the fire Bobby Taylor phoned Dees to tell him Tommy Downs had inadvertently left a sprayer in his shop that reeked of gasoline. Taylor poured out a small sample of the liquid and set it aside; later he turned it over to the BATF for comparison. The other development was our verification of Tommy Downs's membership in the Klan and subsequent acquisition of his original membership certificate.

His suspicions now all but confirmed, Dees grew increasingly restive as each day passed, and by the end of the first week or so he had begun to consider launching an undercover operation against Garner and Downs. The scheme would entail planting someone close to Downs and letting him work his way into the young man's confidence. The goal would be to elicit a confession or, at the least, to gain some other incriminating evidence that would help break the case.

It would not be easy. Downs would be instinctively suspicious of any strangers, and Garner would undoubtedly be trying to keep an eye on him. What's more, we didn't know any of Downs's hangouts, so simply arranging the initial contact presented a problem in itself. But the first and most important matter of business was finding the person with the savvy to do it.

For this, Dees turned to an old high school buddy, James Killough, a hard-drinking, chain-smoking, street-smart friend of his who had been with the mob that attacked the Freedom Riders when they had arrived in Montgomery on their trip through the South in the spring of 1961. Although Killough had gone down to the bus station to join in the assault, he later told Dees he had been repelled by the wantonness of the attack on the defenseless protesters, and he related how he had punched out a fellow member of the mob who was about to bash one of the riders in the head.

Dees broached the idea to Killough, who agreed to do it, with the understanding that he would collect the reward if he succeeded in busting the case. Subsequently Dees talked to Bobby Taylor about his helping with the scheme. The plan was for Taylor to hire Tommy Downs to do some construction work on his business and to tell him he had employed a foreman (Killough) to head the job.

It didn't take long for Killough to ingratiate himself; the construction setting was perfectly suited for it. Over a period of days Killough began to weave the topic of race into his conversation with

Downs, recounting some fabricated slight at the hands of a black person or engaging in a harangue about interracial marriages or some other racially inflammatory subject. Eventually he brought up Dees's name, cursing him for his role in promoting civil rights, and then quickly turned the conversation away. This went on for a week or two.

Then one night Killough took Tommy Downs out for a night of drinking. After a few rounds he abruptly confronted the young Klansman about the SPLC fire. Downs admitted he had set it and implicated Garner. "Did I do right?" he asked.

Dropping the front, Killough persuaded Downs to accompany him to a pay phone to call Dees, so they drove to a twenty-four-hour restaurant down the street from the bar. It was past midnight. But when Killough got Dees on the line, Downs balked at talking to him and handed the phone back to Killough.

In his eagerness to obtain Downs's confession, Killough had jumped the gun. According to the scenario Dees had laid out, he was supposed to try to manipulate Downs into a confession only after he had been fitted with a body mike.

Now that the trap was sprung, Dees realized this might be the only chance we would ever have of obtaining direct evidence against Garner. He knew he had to act, and swiftly, to salvage the undercover operation. Instructing Killough to bring Downs home with him, Dees promised to meet him there as soon as possible. When he arrived half an hour later, Killough was pacing back and forth on his lawn in the dim light of a streetlamp, dragging hard on a cigarette. Downs was back in Snowdoun at a friend's house, where he had insisted on being taken. It looked as if the scheme, which had been going so smoothly, would end in disaster.

Killough, however, clung to the hope that Downs would talk if a face-to-face meeting with Dees could be arranged, and he suggested that they drive to Snowdoun. It was now early in the morning.

While Dees waited in his car on the highway, Killough continued alone to the house. He returned a few minutes later without Downs, having been told that Downs had already left. Killough didn't believe it and suggested they wait out of sight. Sure enough, a half hour later headlights suddenly materialized along the lane. The car turned onto the highway and headed in the direction of the Snowdoun store. Dees and Killough let the vehicle pass and then followed at a distance. Eventually it turned in behind the store.

Killough proposed summoning a law enforcement officer, whose mere presence, he believed, would persuade Downs to talk. Dees knew a confession obtained under such circumstances would probably be inadmissible, but Killough's suggestion prompted another idea: to call up his friend Jimmy Evans, the district attorney, and ask him to issue a grand jury subpoena for Downs and his brother, Bodie, who sometimes stayed with him. Dees left Killough behind to watch the store while he drove back to town to a pay phone and called Evans, who agreed to do it.

While Dees returned to Snowdoun to take up his watch with Killough, a member of Evans's staff went to the home of the grand jury foreman and obtained his authorization to issue the summonses. The whole process took a few hours, and when the authorities finally arrived at Garner's store, dawn had broken.

From their hidden vantage post across the road, Dees and Killough observed as the officials knocked on the storeroom door where the Downs brothers were holed up. No one answered. They knocked a second time and identified themselves, but the door remained shut so they left. But one officer returned after a few minutes and casually knocked at the door again. To his surprise (and Dees's and Killough's), Bodie Downs opened it, and the deputy served the subpoenas.

At their appearance before the grand jury later that morning, however, both Downses denied any knowledge of the SPLC arson, and Tommy, furthermore, denied having admitted anything to Killough. A grand all-night attempt to salvage the undercover operation had failed.

Dees still had one more card to play, however. Within a day or two he obtained civil subpoenas for Garner, the Downses, and another young man we had identified as one of Tommy Downs's best friends, Charles Bailey, and scheduled their depositions. The face-to-face confrontation ended on the same note: To a man, the deponents denied any connection to the fire.

Williams and I had never seen Dees more frustrated. For months after that the item "Get Joe Garner" headed the notations on his "To Do" list, the personal daily agenda he kept on a legal pad on his desk—as if he needed the reminder. But with the collapse of the

Killough project, there seemed little else we could do about it but wait for the results of the tests the BATF lab experts were performing on the physical evidence.

That was not to say we were wanting for work on other fronts, however. In fact, once the Killough phase of the arson investigation began, we immediately picked up the Decatur case where we had left off the night of the fire and in nearly no time were back to full throttle.

Chapter Nine

THE POST-ARSON phase of the Decatur investigation was largely a mop-up operation. Methodically we crisscrossed the northern tier of Alabama counties, interviewing Klan members and taking depositions, until we had collected more than enough evidence to win the lawsuit. In the process we flipped witnesses right and left: a relative of Steele's who had lied to us during the Curtis Robinson phase of the case but who, faced with the prospect of losing his mobile home and his pickup truck in the suit, came clean and agreed to give evidence against his kinsman; a Huntsville Klanswoman who broke her silence about the conspiracy despite threats from her husband; a former member of the Klan Special Forces who revealed the Cullman klavern's role in the plot. Remarkably, none of these witnesses had ever been contacted by the FBI.

In the wake of one of our forays, an envelope full of three-by-five cards arrived in the mail—anonymously—with the names of thirty or forty Klan members from northern Alabama, proof that the veil of silence had come down. Klavern by klavern we continued to unravel the conspiracy, forwarding on to the Justice Department each new piece of evidence.

By the fall of 1983, when Dees decided we should gear down our investigation, we had interviewed several hundred Klan members, taken the depositions of about 125, identified 70 of the 100 members of the May 26 mob, obtained direct evidence against four of the highest-ranking IEKKKK leaders in Alabama—Handley, Steele, Riccio, and Mize—and pinpointed the location of ten klaverns to which most of the conspirators belonged.*

In a little less than a year we had logged about ten thousand miles in case-related travel, paid at least three thousand dollars in witness fees, run up close to seventy-five hundred dollars in food and lodging expenses, and spent the equivalent of approximately one-third of the calendar year 1983 on the road.

Now, more than four years after the crime (for we now had the evidence to employ that word with confidence), we were at last ready to go to trial. But there would be no trial anytime soon. The re-opened federal probe had blossomed into a full-fledged grand jury investigation, and because criminal cases take precedence over civil suits, it had effectively shoved our case to the back burner.

One of our last activities before winding up discovery that fall was to take the deposition of Bill Wilkinson, who was still free pending Judge Haltom's long-awaited ruling on our motion to hold him in contempt. (It had begun to appear that Judge Haltom had put off a decision in the contempt matter in the hope that the criminal inquiry would render the issue moot.) We had delayed deposing Wilkinson until the last moment to give ourselves time to collect as much evidence as possible against him, so that we wouldn't have to take his testimony more than once. Although the deposition itself was anti-climactic—Wilkinson denied anything to do with a conspiracy and proved to be a bland witness—the events leading up to it were not.

Because Wilkinson was no longer represented by Dan Willingham and had not hired a new attorney, we realized we would have to subpoena the imperial wizard directly. The matter of how to get the subpoena into his hands, however, posed something of a dilemma and led to our version of a sting operation. The problem was Wilkinson's inaccessibility. Beyond the fact that he was often surrounded by gun-happy bodyguards, he was constantly traveling and thus something of a moving target. Out of this quandary

---

* The klaverns were: Decatur, Huntsville, Athens, Cullman, Center Point, Wylam, Adamsville, Muscle Shoals, Hartselle, and Moulton.

Randall Williams came up with the idea of trying to serve Wilkinson with the subpoena during one of his public appearances, one at which there would be plenty of police on hand.

The scheme hinged on a ruse. The subpoena, folded down to a fraction of its normal size, would be concealed in a wad of cash in the amount of the standard federal witness fee of thirty dollars, plus mileage, and would be hand delivered by one of our law clerks posing as a sympathizer offering a contribution.

As it happened, the leaders of the Roanoke klavern in eastern Alabama had scheduled a march and rally in their community at about that time and had invited Wilkinson to speak, so we decided to try to nail him there. On the day of the rally Williams, the law clerk, and I drove over to Roanoke in plenty of time to scout out the situation before the march, which was scheduled for midafternoon.

After walking the length of the parade route, we concluded it would not be wise to attempt to serve the document before or during the march. The pre-march staging area was on a side street, where access to Wilkinson would be restricted, while any effort to hand him the subpoena during the march itself might be construed by the police or fellow Klansmen as an attempt to disrupt it and might lead to a brawl or worse. The logical thing to do, we decided, was to wait until after Wilkinson had finished making a short speech at the conclusion of the demonstration and then to approach him as if to make a donation.

Finally the march got under way, with close to a hundred participants parading up main street in full regalia. The sidewalks were filled with Saturday shoppers and the curious (many of them black), attendance enhanced by the fact that this was the first KKK march through the community in many years.

In a departure from the usual, the Klansmen walked in absolute silence, refraining from the chants of "What do we want?/White power!" that had been a regular feature of every other Klan function I had ever observed. The only noise audible was the rhythmic sound of shoe soles smacking the street and the sweep of robes against pants legs.

The parade route was only a few blocks long, and the marchers covered it in a matter of minutes. When they arrived at the courthouse, they broke out of formation and gathered around a makeshift podium that had been set up on the front lawn. There Wilkinson gave a brief stump speech and promoted the rally coming up later that evening. Stationed across the street, Williams and I followed the progress of events, keeping our eyes on our law clerk, who had worked his way well into the crowd of spectators standing behind the robed Klansmen, and watching for anything out of the ordinary. As Wilkinson finished his remarks, we held our breaths. For a moment he disappeared from view as he came down from the podium to mingle with his supporters. About that time our clerk plunged into the sea of white robes surrounding Wilkinson and also disappeared. Less than a minute later he emerged and walked briskly toward us, wearing a poker face. As soon as he reached us, however, he broke into a big smile and said everything had gone off without a hitch. He had slapped the donation in Wilkinson's hand, informed him of service, and gotten away before Wilkinson or the Klansmen around him could figure out what happened. No one had laid a hand on him.

When Wilkinson appeared for the deposition, he complained mildly about the way we had subpoenaed him, but I got the impression he was almost amused by it. The way things worked out, however, our efforts to get him into the deposition room went for nothing, for little came of his testimony. He categorically denied being part of the conspiracy or cover-up, maintaining that he had been at a rally in Augusta, Georgia, three hundred miles away, on the date in question. Subsequently we visited Augusta to investigate his alibi and discovered that it checked out. There was a photograph of him in the May 27, 1979, edition of the *Augusta Chronicle*, leading the cross burning ceremony at the previous night's rally. Williams and I didn't accept that as concrete proof of his innocence, of course; KKK history demonstrated that some Klan leaders would go to great lengths to establish an alibi. Besides, during the course of our investigation we had located three Klansmen who told us (though not under oath) that they had actually seen Wilkinson at a Klan meeting in Decatur the afternoon of May 26, shortly after the shooting. There was also the claim of the Berryhills (who had since backtracked on it, once they had been called on to testify) that Handley and Steele had told the Huntsville klavern that Wilkinson had sanctioned the plot to block the march, plus an unproven allegation by Tom Reid, in a subsequent interview, that Wilkinson had, in essence, told him to lie to the FBI if questioned about the conspiracy. But after we failed to punch a hole in Wilkinson's alibi, Dees decided not to sink any more time or resources into pursuing that angle of the case. Wilkinson's Klan was crumbling, and Dees had other fish to fry.

The effect of the decision, however, was to let Wilkinson off the hook entirely in regard to the Decatur incident, because the feds apparently had already eliminated him as a target of the criminal investigation. The news that they had done so, coming, as it did, at the outset of the grand jury probe, resulted in quite a jolt to us, especially Williams and me. One morning not long after the grand jury had been impaneled, we opened the newspaper and were startled to find a bold, five-column headline proclaiming KLAN LEADER SAYS POLYGRAPH TEST REMOVES HIM FROM SUSPICION.

The story said that Wilkinson had taken the test to refute allegations that he was involved in the May 26 conspiracy. Although federal officials would only confirm that the exam had been administered, the article quoted Wilkinson as saying an assistant prosecutor in the Birmingham U.S. Attorney's office had informed him that prior to the polygraph he had been a target of the investigation into conspiracy and obstruction of justice charges but that he no longer was. Wilkinson said he interpreted that to mean he had passed.

What immediately aroused our suspicion about all this was the timing. Why had the feds given Wilkinson a lie detector test so early in their investigation? It stood to reason that the exam could not have been as thorough then as it might have been several months down the road, by which time the grand jury might have turned up additional evidence against him. It appeared to us as outsiders that Wilkinson had been given special treatment, and it raised the question of whether someone—namely, the FBI—was trying to protect him. For years the rumor that Wilkinson was an FBI informant had been rampant in the Klan world. Rivals had used the charge against him in recruitment battles. In 1981 the *Tennessean* had published conclusive evidence in the form of internal FBI memorandums obtained under the Freedom of Information Act. The first memo, marked "urgent" and "confidential," had been transmitted from the special agent in charge of the New Orleans FBI office to the director of the Bureau on March 28, 1975, less than a year after Wilkinson had first joined the Klan. It noted that he had been interviewed more than once and had "indicated a willingness to furnish information to [the] Bureau." The second memo, written several months later and reprinted in the *Tennessean* on August 31, 1981, was even more illuminating:

> This informant [Wilkinson] is not willing to testify in open court or before administrative hearing boards. He has no plans to write any books or articles or publicize his activities.
>
> New Orleans feels assured that this source will not take any action to embarrass the Bureau as he has always indicated a strong desire that his contact with the Bureau not come to the attention of his colleagues or anyone else and has sought assurances that this contact not be revealed in any way.

The documents, which must have slipped past the FOIA censor by mistake, certainly implied that a close relationship between Wilkinson and the Bureau had once existed. Had the FBI administered the polygraph to get him off the hook?

It was impossible to know for sure. There was no question, however, that if Wilkinson had been an informant for the FBI during the late 1970s and early 1980s while he was raising race-relations hell from one end of the United States to the other, it was in the Bureau's interest to see him removed as a target of the Decatur investigation. During the COINTELPRO scandals of the 1970s, the Bureau had come under sharp congressional criticism for its handling of Klan informants. One sure way of preventing any embarrassing revelations about Wilkinson—if there were any—was for him to undergo a polygraph early in the grand jury investigation, designed to deflect attention away from the imperial wizard by "proving" his innocence. On the other hand Wilkinson may have been totally innocent with respect to the Decatur conspiracy and cover-up, and the timing of the polygraph examination may have been nothing more than coincidence. Certainly the evidence we gathered was inconclusive as to his alleged involvement.

The year 1983 turned out to be a watershed for Klanwatch and the SPLC. There was the fire, of course, which nearly destroyed our headquarters and gave us a sense of what it was like to be victims of hate violence; by the end of the year, however, we had returned to our renovated Hull Street office, where we would stay until a new, more secure building downtown could be constructed.

But it was a noteworthy year for other reasons, primarily for our success in cracking the Decatur conspiracy. The act of uncovering evidence of criminal wrongdoing awakened us to the possibility that our suits might have an additional application: to expose criminal activity to which law enforcement agencies were either indifferent or oblivious and thereby force them to become more vigilant about the serious problem of hate crime in the United States. This realization added another dimension to our work. Although it did not fundamentally alter our approach to litigation—we did not suddenly begin to look at potential suits in terms of how many indictments we thought we could rack up—it prompted us to become more aware of our responsibilities in this area and to cultivate better ties with law enforcement generally.

There was definitely room for improvement in the performance of law enforcement—and not just at the local level. More than one assistant U.S. Attorney in more than one Southern U.S. Attorney's office had confided to us that he was dismayed at the lack of commitment to the prosecution of civil rights cases he had encountered in some quarters of the federal law enforcement bureaucracy, from the field offices of the FBI to the top echelons of his boss's staff. Certainly the Decatur investigation—in which the FBI agents assigned to the case apparently just went through the motions—lent credence to the charges.

The year 1983 ended, however, without indictments in either the Decatur or SPLC arson cases. Insofar as the Decatur case was concerned, this was not particularly disconcerting. We knew it was only a matter of time until the grand jury handed up indictments. The evidence was there, and it was unequivocal. As for the arson investigation, though, our unease grew with each passing week. The federal inquiry seemed to have hit a brick wall. The strategy of sitting back and waiting for Garner or Downs to slip up and confess within earshot of an informant had failed to produce results, partly as a consequence of Dees's decision to offer the reward (as well as the Killough escapade). It looked as if Garner and the Klan might have the last laugh after all.

*　　*　　*

One spring day in April 1984 I happened to be in Decatur taking care of some investigative loose ends when I decided to pay a courtesy call on Ken Collier, the Decatur policeman who had testified for us during the Curtis Robinson trial. Collier now held the rank of captain, and his star was on the rise in the department. Over the years we had remained in touch, and periodically I stopped by to chat with him when I was in town.

Although on this particular day I was bearing the news that Curtis Robinson's appeal had been rejected by a federal court, signifying the end of the case, that wasn't the main reason I had dropped by to see him. I was eager to sound him out about the ongoing federal investigation. The new year was a quarter gone, and indictments had yet to be handed up. The grand jury had now been sitting for more than eight months. We were at last becoming concerned at what was turning into an inordinate-seeming delay. Time was running out. The statute of limitations for criminal violations under the federal civil rights laws was five years, and May 26 would mark the fifth anniversary of the Decatur incident. In other words, there were less than two months before prosecution in the case would be barred forever.

My decision to stop by proved to be propitious. The first thing Collier told me was that it looked as if the indictments were "off." Incredulous, I asked him what he was talking about, and he said he had heard through the grapevine that the Justice Department had decided not to seek them after all.

I was floored. After all the work and energy we'd spent digging up witnesses, cajoling them, leaning on them, holding their hands, and promising them they had nothing to fear for testifying truthfully, after all the lies we'd had to wade through, after all the injustices of the Tommy Lee Hines case, that there might not be any indictments at all was too much.

I left Collier and went to phone Dees at once with the news. When I returned to Montgomery a day or two later, I learned that he had already launched a behind-the-scenes campaign to pressure the feds to bring the indictments. His first move had been to call Dan Rinzel, the head of the criminal section of the Civil Rights Division at the Department of Justice. Rinzel was cordial, as he had been in all our limited dealings with him, but he shook off Dees's efforts to learn whether Collier was right or not. Dees subsequently called a reporter for the *New York Times* who covered the Justice Department and happened to be a friend of a former SPLC attorney. The reporter jumped on the story right away. When he phoned Rinzel for his side of it, Rinzel denied there were problems, saying the investigation was still on track.

With the statute of limitations about to expire, however, Dees decided not to take chances. He asked Williams and me to draft a memorandum setting out the crucial evidence in the case and to attach informant statements and depositions to make the memo more compelling. It was his intention to deliver the document to Morris Abrams, a member of the U.S. Commission on Civil Rights. Abrams was a fellow Southerner, a Georgian, and Dees knew him from the 1976 Carter presidential campaign. If push came to shove, Dees was prepared to ask Abrams to exert pressure of his own, and, if necessary, to go public with the evidence prior to the deadline. In the meantime, in our effort to pull out every possible stop, Williams and I drew up a list of influential reporters and ran off extra copies of the same document for them.

What we didn't know at the time was that there was a colossal struggle going on in the Justice Department over whether to seek indictments in the case. Craig Shaffer, the line attorney, and his boss, Rinzel, were utterly committed to the prosecution and eager to indict. But Frank Donaldson, the U.S. Attorney in Birmingham, was doing his utmost to derail the case. Donaldson, a former law school professor, viewed the violations under investigation as too insignificant to warrant prosecution and believed that the indictments would only stir up the Klan in Alabama. In the middle of this tug-of-war, being pulled in both directions, was William Bradford Reynolds, the much maligned head of the Reagan Justice Department's Civil Rights Division, whose approval was necessary to bring the case. Donaldson was lobbying Reynolds furiously to withhold it.

Donaldson, we were to find out later, had opposed reopening the Decatur criminal investigation in the first place. After the Letson hearing in October 1982, Dees had forwarded a copy of the ex-Klansman's testimony to Assistant U.S. Attorney Henry Frohsin, who had overseen the original FBI investigation in 1979, to call Frohsin's attention to the new evidence. Frohsin, a veteran Klan prosecutor and the chief assistant in the office since the mid-1970s, routinely informed his boss, Donaldson, that he, in turn, was going to send the material to Rinzel at the Civil Rights Division, which has final authority over all civil rights cases brought by the federal government. But Donaldson had directed Frohsin not to do it, indicating that he didn't want to see the case reopened. Frohsin protested and forwarded the statement to Rinzel anyway.

On the strength of Letson's testimony the department, of course, had reopened the case. But despite the fact that Frohsin was the most experienced Klan prosecutor in the Birmingham U.S. Attorney's office and had put more Klansmen in the federal penitentiary than any prosecutor in Alabama history, Donaldson refused to permit him to assist Shaffer and Rinzel on the case. Now, with the statute of limitations deadline looming, Donaldson was making a final effort to block the indictments.

The irony of the situation was immense: The Reagan Justice Department was being stymied by one of its own appointees, who was threatening further to refuse to provide any assistance to the Washington prosecutors if they went against his wishes and obtained indictments.

In the wake of our lobbying blitz, the wait began anew. Days passed, and eventually several weeks. One of the IEKKKK leaders who had once publicly conceded the fact that he expected to be indicted called a Birmingham reporter as time ran out and gloated, "I think it's about over, don't you?"

But Shaffer and Rinzel prevailed, and on May 17, 1984, nine days before the statute of limitations would have run out, nine IEKKKK members were indicted on various civil rights charges arising out of the Decatur incident. These included Roger Handley, the former grand dragon; Ray Steele, the Decatur titan; and Bill Riccio, the grand chaplain. The remaining six defendants were David Lee Kelso, the Decatur exalted cyclops wounded by Curtis Robinson; Ricky Lynn Creekmore, a nighthawk of the Muscle Shoals klavern; William Johnny Mason, a titan from Muscle Shoals; Lenwood Lewis

White, a kleagle from Muscle Shoals; Terry Joe Tucker, the Cullman exalted cyclops and former Klan Special Forces commander; and Derane O'Neil Godfrey, the paint-sniffing Klansman from Gardendale. A tenth Klansman, Jack Ray Mize, the titan from Birmingham, pleaded guilty. Moreover, eighteen other Kluxers, all members of the May 26 mob, were named as unindicted co-conspirators. In all, it was one of the largest prosecutions of KKK leaders on federal civil rights violations the Justice Department had ever undertaken.

JUSTICE IN THE NICK OF TIME was how a witty headline writer for the *New York Times* put it, and the characterization was hardly hyperbole. Between the Klan attack on the marchers and the handing up of the indictments by the grand jury 1,818 days had passed. All that stood between the Klansmen and permanent immunity from prosecution were nine measly days.

Within a few days of the grand jury's action, Nungester called to say he had heard from one of his Klan sources that six of the nine were on the verge of following Jack Mize's lead and pleading guilty to the charges.

Unfortunately that was before the assignment of Judge William M. Acker, Jr., to preside over the criminal trial. Acker was a right-winger in his mid-forties named to the bench by Ronald Reagan in 1982, and his selection as the presiding judge (by the same random method that had seen Judge Gabrielle McDonald chosen to hear the Vietnamese fishermen's suit) transformed what should have been an open-and-shut case into a long, drawn-out court battle. Almost before we knew it, we were drawn into the fray.

In pretrial motions the attorneys for the Klansmen accused us of violating their clients' rights and sought to portray the Kluxers as victims of a politically motivated prosecution. In short order, Dees, Williams, and I found ourselves subpoenaed to a hearing Judge Acker had called to take testimony on whether he should throw out the evidence we had supplied the government.

The thrust of the defendants' arguments against us centered on two main allegations: first, that we had abused the civil process by filing the lawsuit solely for the purpose of trying to obtain criminal indictments and, second, that we had acted in collusion with the Justice Department, in essence, operating as the DOJ's "alter ego."* The defense attorneys argued that our failure to give the Klansmen Miranda warnings and otherwise to advise them of their rights tainted the discovery process and made the exclusion of the evidence necessary.

It was fair to say the fate of the case hinged on Acker's decision.

At the hearing in early July, first Dan Rinzel and then I took the stand to deny the accusations of improper conduct. (Dees was at the Democratic National Convention.) Under intense questioning, Rinzel recalled the standoffish attitude we had exhibited toward Craig Shaffer and himself at our first meeting in July 1983 and pointed out that the statements we had turned over to them had been partially blocked out.

For my part, I recounted how we had greeted the news that the Justice Department had reopened its investigation with a mixture of pride and concern—pride that we had scooped the FBI and concern that the feds were trying to horn in on our case to swipe the credit for cracking it. In addition, I mentioned the reasons we had filed the lawsuit in the first place: our desire to see justice done and to right the wrongs committed against Curtis Robinson and the Decatur black community. Finally, as a gesture of good faith, we produced for the court our correspondence and phone records to demonstrate the limited nature of our contacts with the DOJ.

It was all too clear, however, that the judge didn't believe Rinzel's testimony or mine. His hostile attitude toward Craig Shaffer and the government, combined with remarks, bordering on the snide, that he directed toward me and the SPLC in general, foreshadowed his decision a couple of weeks later. On July 27, 1984, he issued a scathing twenty-eight-page ruling, suppressing much of the evidence we had turned over to the Justice Department and attacking both the DOJ and the SPLC.

* Had such a relationship existed—that is to say, had we coordinated our investigation with the government's and acted as its agents—we would have been bound by the rules of criminal, not civil, procedure and been obligated to "Mirandize" witnesses and otherwise comport ourselves as law enforcement officers. However, we never asked for or received assistance from the feds at any time, other than during the Robinson case, when we sued the FBI to get an unredacted copy of its Decatur investigation report—a measure that hardly smacked of collusion.

Taking care to disavow any sympathy for the KKK "as an organization," he concluded the opinion by equating the Law Center with the Klan:

> This court agrees with the general understanding that the Klan is a vigilante group which undoubtedly from time to time violates the constitutional rights of citizens. However, one vigilante group does not justify the creation and operation of a counter-vigilante group in violation of the constitutional rights of the first group. The basic distinction in this case between the Klan and the Center is that the Klan members were and are unsophisticated, impecunious and ignorant of legal procedures, whereas the lawyers and investigators at the Center are quite sophisticated, socially acceptable and well financed. To tolerate a rape of the rights of the members of the Klan would be a recognition that some sort of double standard exists for the application of constitutional protections. A member of the Southern Christian Leadership Conference surely has every right to expect the federal courts to uphold and to protect his civil rights. A member of the Ku Klux Klan has every right to expect the same.

We found the ruling both infuriating and demoralizing. It was riddled with factual and legal errors, which led Dees to compose a point-by-point refutation that he forwarded to Judge Acker and Judge Haltom, the judge in the Decatur civil suit. But there was little else we could do about it. The case, not to mention our professional reputation, was in the hands of the Justice Department's appellate section. Later that summer the department appealed the decision to the U.S. Court of Appeals for the Eleventh Circuit in Atlanta. The celebrating we had done at the news of the indictments on May 17 now seemed grossly premature.

Chapter Ten

HAVING SET ourselves up as a clearinghouse for information on the KKK, we were forever getting inquiries from journalists, or so it seemed. Most of these were by phone, but occasionally a reporter would visit our office for a firsthand look at our operations. Rarely, however, was this done without prior arrangement.

It struck me as unusual, therefore, when our receptionist buzzed me on the intercom a few weeks after the Decatur indictments and informed me that a television crew was in the lobby seeking an interview with Dees, who was not in the office that afternoon and had not been expecting any visitors. The receptionist said that she had told the group that Dees was not in and that they then had asked to speak to Randall Williams. When apprised that he, too, was away from the office, they had asked to speak to anyone in Klanwatch. I told her I would be right there.

As I walked along the carpeted mazelike hallway from the Klanwatch offices toward the front of the building, I was puzzled and a little annoyed. It was the day after Labor Day, and I was trying to make headway against the mound of paperwork that had amassed on my desk during the final weeks of summer. The last thing I wanted was an interruption.

Entering the lobby, I came face-to-face with Louis Beam and two other men, and suddenly my heart was in my throat. My first thought was that Beam had gone off the deep end and was there to kill us. Then I noticed that none of the three had weapons—at least any that could be seen. Beam, who was dressed in a gray pin-striped business suit, observed recognition in my eyes and remarked tartly, "I see by the look on your face you know who I am," or something very similar. He repeated his earlier request to interview Dees. As he did so, I glanced to the other side of the lobby and saw that the "cameraman" was videotaping the episode. When I looked back at Beam, I noticed a tiny microphone clipped to his tie. The third member of the "crew" I recognized as Thom Arthur Robb, the national chaplain of the Knights of the KKK.

Not knowing exactly what to do, I walked briskly around the corner to the secretarial pool to tell someone to call the police, but neither of the secretaries was there. From the lobby I could hear Beam making derogatory remarks about Dees and the SPLC—not in a strident voice but as if he were narrating a documentary.

I rushed past the secretaries' station and into new Legal Director Dennis Balske's office and asked him to make the call. Then I returned to the lobby and found Beam still engaged in a running commentary about Dees and the Law Center. The camera was still rolling.

In as firm a voice as I could muster, I instructed the men to leave at once. Beam repeated the question, Mike Wallace–like—"You want us to leave?" or words to that effect—and turned around and walked out, taking his camera crew with him. But he didn't leave the property entirely; he merely retreated to the sidewalk, where he did a stand-up shot in front of the building. The three looked fairly professional. I could see how the receptionist, not knowing Beam, might have thought they were legitimate.

As they continued to film, I realized I should try to get a picture of them while they were still on SPLC property, so I ducked inside and asked someone to get my camera from my office. When Beam saw me with it, he immediately assumed a military stance, clasping his hands behind his back and spreading his feet apart. The cameraman subsequently appeared to turn his camera on me, and we stood there for a moment photographing each other. Then the three turned and headed up the street to a red Lincoln town car. As his two companions got in, Beam wheeled around to face me, his hand on the right front passenger door. "Sir," he snapped, in a loud, emphatic voice, "we will no longer be intimidated! We are bringing the war to you!" With a straight face he turned to his companion behind the wheel, said sharply, "Gentlemen, start your engines," and climbed into the car. As the vehicle pulled away, I hurried toward it and jotted down the license plate number. Then they were gone.

Shaken, I dashed back inside and phoned Glen Kibler, the Bureau of Alcohol, Tobacco, and Firearms agent in charge of the arson investigation, and informed him about the incident. He, in turn, contacted the city police to request that patrol units be advised to be on the lookout for the automobile. Within a few minutes Dees called in, and I recounted the incident to him. He subsequently began to make a few phone calls, and as the evening wore on, we pieced together more information about the affair. By late that night we had determined that Beam was in the process of making some sort of "documentary" on Dees and the SPLC for propaganda purposes. From what we learned, the trio had been observed videotaping at Dees's ranch and at an abortion clinic owned by his wife. What's more, they had been seen in the presence of Joe Garner.

Sometime around midnight the police finally located the automobile leaving a bar on the eastern side of Montgomery. When they pulled it over on suspicion of drunken driving (the car was weaving from one lane to another), Beam and his companions were not in it. We subsequently found out that they had already returned it to the airport rental agency from which they had obtained it and had apparently left town by plane.

The experience left the whole SPLC staff shaken. Although the arson had made us more cognizant of our security concerns, we had become somewhat complacent with the passage of time; the thought that anyone would be brazen enough just to walk into the office like that had never even occurred to us. In the wake of Beam's visit, everything changed. The following morning the SPLC's days as a walk-in storefront law firm ended. Reluctantly we instituted sweeping new security measures, including the installation of a remote-controlled electronic door lock system operated from the receptionist's desk. Admittance to the building was restricted to only those individuals with appointments. A sign-in log was established for all nonemployees, so that we would have a record of all visitors, even service personnel and friends of the SPLC staff.

The changes were not wrought without difficult adjustments, and even some bruised feelings, from the printer's rep who for years had dropped by periodically to socialize and now found himself obliged to sign the visitors' log to the staff attorney who didn't see why his black clients had to make appointments. For an organization that had thrived on informality, that viewed its jeans and running shoes style as an integral expression of its identity, the changes necessitated by the security considerations did not come easily.

Within two weeks Nungester phoned with deeply disturbing news. A radical Klansman he had recently met at a right-wing gathering in Tennessee had tried to solicit information about Dees's personal habits for what Nungester believed was going to be an attempt on Dees's life: information about Dees's schedule; the make and description of his automobile; the route he drove to work; his favorite bars and hangouts.* According to Nungester, the Klansman was then living in northern Alabama, but the plot did not seem to have any direct connection to the Decatur case. Rather, from what he could surmise, it appeared to be related to some shadowy new organization composed of the most radical right-wing extremists from across the country, extremists who Nungester believed were plotting nothing less than to start the race war that Beam and other Klan leaders had been predicting for years.

Nungester's information was so startling, so farfetched that it was hard to comprehend—especially in view of the fact that Klan activity was once again on the wane—yet we couldn't ignore it. Nungester had proved a highly reliable source in the past, and he had excellent contacts. Since our first encounter with him during the Curtis Robinson case, he had continued to burrow his way deeper and deeper into the KKK and from there into other right-wing extremist organizations, and he had gained the confidence of some of the most radical white supremacists in the country.

Nungester's phone call was followed in short order by one from the FBI, which advised us that it had received intelligence informa-

* The Kluxer was believed by Nungester to be a major connection in a cocaine ring and reportedly plowed the profits from his sales back into the white supremacy movement.

tion about a plot on Dees's life. Although Dees was unable to pry any further details from the agent who delivered the warning, the warning itself served as a kind of confirmation that Nungester was on to something. In the wake of the Beam incident and Nungester's phone call, Dees was clearly worried, and despite his efforts to put the best face on the situation for the rest of the staff, anxiety spread throughout the SPLC.

On the basis of the threats, and after consultations with federal law enforcement officials and members of the Center's board of directors, we hired a private security company to provide protection for us. A twenty-four-hour bodyguard was assigned to Dees, and an armed, uniformed guard was posted outside the front door of the Center. But the precautions didn't stop there. Upon the recommendation of the security firm, we bought shotguns and placed them in strategic locations around the office—the closet adjacent to the secretarial pool and back in our department—and Williams and I, who were deemed to be most at risk after Dees, were issued .38-caliber pistols and advised to carry them with us at all times. A counterterrorism expert with the security company, Danny Welch, was brought in to teach the three of us the elementary rules of evasive driving and other tips to fend off kidnap attempts since subsequent reports from Nungester had indicated that the plot might involve an abduction. Additional lighting was installed around the office and at Dees's home, and bushes and shrubs were pruned back around both structures to eliminate obvious sanctuaries. So-called panic buttons, like those used by bank tellers, were placed at the receptionist's desk and in Klanwatch, giving us a direct electronic link to the police in case of an emergency. Once again we began wearing our bulletproof vests for court appearances or, on occasion, while conducting field investigations. The bill for these precautions, including others too sensitive to mention here, ran to several hundred thousand dollars over the course of the next few months.

Week after week the situation appeared to grow more grave. Logging on to Aryan Liberty Net, a new nationwide computer bulletin board organized by Beam for the purpose of electronically linking right-wing extremists around the country, we discovered an unattributed message about Dees that ended: "According to the word of our God, Morris Dees has earned two (2) death sentences. '. . . Thy will be done in [sic] earth as it is in heaven. . . .' "

In the first of two intrusions at Rolling Hills Ranch, armed men in camouflage fatigues were spotted by Dees's bodyguards within a couple of hundred yards of his house one night, and a camouflage groundcloth—apparently misplaced or discarded—was recovered from a pasture in front of the residence. Meanwhile, the Montgomery office of the FBI advised us that a second death threat against Dees had been uncovered. It seemed all hell was breaking loose, and the worst thing about it was that we possessed precious little information about who was behind the threats or even whom to tell our security people to be on the lookout for.

The first name that came to mind, quite naturally (in view of our earlier encounters with him), was Louis Beam. In his new role as ambassador-at-large for Aryan Nations, the increasingly influential neo-Nazi group, Beam had emerged as one of the top two or three racist leaders in the country, and by all indications he was more radical than ever. In a self-published collection of his writings called *Essays of a Klansman* he had embraced assassination as a tool for dealing with civil rights activists and "race traitors." He had even gone so far as to devise an assassination point scale system rating the enemies of the white race by category (that is, federal judges, politicians, media figures, civil rights activists, and so on).

But these were just words on his part (and supposition on ours); nothing, certainly, to go to court with. The fact was we had no proof of who was actually behind the threats.

Amid the turmoil caused by the threats we attempted to carry on with our litigation, for several suits, including one we had filed against a militant North Carolina Klan group, were then in the critical discovery stage. The decision to go forward, however, inevitably led to some harrowing experiences.

In November 1984 Dees, Williams, and a staff attorney traveled to North Carolina to take some depositions in the suit there. At the time the state was the primary hot spot in the country for KKK activity, and the most active of the Klan organizations operating within its borders was the Carolina Knights of the KKK (CKKKK), led by a former U.S. Army officer by the unlikely name of Glenn Miller. Miller, a former member of the National Socialist Party, had been among the Klansmen and Nazis involved in the Greensboro incident in 1979, in which five anti-Klan protesters were shot to death. We had filed suit against the CKKKK on behalf of a black prison guard who had been harassed by several of its members for seeking to become the first black sergeant at the local correctional institution where he was employed.

On the eve of the trip we learned from Nungester that the Klansman collecting information on Dees had plans to be in North Carolina at the same time and that Beam and Bill Riccio, the radical young Kluxer under indictment in the Decatur case, would also be there. We didn't know if the visits were connected, although we were aware of growing ties between Miller and Beam—but the coincidence alone was enough to send shivers through our staff.

Despite the possibility of trouble, Dees was disinclined to cancel the trip, and the three SPLC staffers and their bodyguards flew to Raleigh as planned. Once on the ground, they proceeded in two cars equipped with special police radios to a downtown hotel, where they registered under aliases.

When they arrived at the Wake County Courthouse the next morning, they found a contingent of militant camouflage fatigue-clad CKKKK members waiting for them, bent, apparently, on confrontation. Although the Klansmen initially mistook the bodyguards for FBI agents, they soon learned that they were not, and as the realization dawned on them they became verbally and physically aggressive toward the SPLCers, uttering veiled threats and attempting to bait them with inflammatory remarks. More than once the Klansmen formed a kind of gauntlet in the hallway through which the SPLC entourage had to pass or took flash photographs at close range to intimidate them. On these occasions the bodyguards did their best to wedge a path through the Kluxers, managing to do so only with great difficulty. It was a volatile situation, and Don Terry, the head of the SPLC security detail and a retired lawman himself, appealed to the sheriff for assistance. The sheriff, who was black, refused to become involved, however. The consequences of his decision not to intervene soon became evident.

On the afternoon of the first day Williams emerged from the deposition room to attend to some business and was approached by a member of the CKKKK group holding a camera. When he got close to Williams, he swung the camera up and prepared to take a picture. Williams threw his hands up in the air to conceal his face and, in so doing, hit the camera, which in turn struck the photographer, who complained that he had been assaulted. Williams reported the incident to Dees and went on about his work; but the CKKKK sympathizer marched off to the sheriff's office and swore out a warrant, and the next morning Williams was arrested on a misdemeanor assault charge. He was booked and then released on his own recognizance. (He was acquitted three weeks later.)

Interpreting the sheriff's inaction as weakness, the CKKKK members stepped up their harassment—to the point that Don Terry urged Dees to terminate the depositions immediately and return to Alabama. Terry, a former captain with the Montgomery Police Department, was so worried that the Klansmen might provoke an incident before the SPLC party could leave the courthouse that he came up with a plan for the group to exit the building surreptitiously. During a midafternoon recess Dees and the others left the deposition room on the pretext of taking a break and never returned, beating a hasty exit down a stairwell and leaving the Klansmen upstairs waiting to resume. Once clear of the courthouse, the group rushed to the airport and took the first plane back to Montgomery.

It was not long after the Raleigh episode that we learned that Nungester had been right: A radical new racist group had been formed with the avowed purpose of fomenting a white supremacist revolution in the United States, and Dees was on its hit list. The group was called the Order, and it was comprised of several dozen racists and anti-Semites drawn from the entire spectrum of right-wing extremist organizations: the KKK, the Aryan Nations, the Posse Comitatus, and the Christian Identity "churches."*

Led by Robert Mathews, a former activist in another neo-Nazi group, the National Alliance, the Order had launched its revolution with a series of carefully executed bank and armored car robberies on the West Coast, designed to bankroll the group's activities, in late 1983 and early 1984. The holdups had been wildly successful, netting the racist bandits more than four million dollars in cash. With the proceeds Mathews hired a paramilitary instructor, bought land in Idaho on which to train a guerrilla army, and purchased guns and other equipment to outfit it. Then he set about recruiting

* These "churches" were little more than gatherings of white supremacists under a veneer of religion. Adherents of Christian Identity take the dogma of Aryan superiority to the extreme; they believe that northern Europeans and their American descendants are the true Israelites, the true chosen people, and that Jews are impostors. In recent years Christian Identity has gained increasing popularity among right-wing groups.

additional soldiers. He was following the blueprint for a white supremacist revolution set out in *The Turner Diaries*, a racist novel penned by the National Alliance's chairman, William Pierce, a former Oregon State University physics professor.

One of the measures employed by the racists in *The Turner Diaries* is assassination, and that was where Dees and the SPLC fitted in. In the book the murder of prominent establishment figures, minority leaders, and civil rights activists served to destabilize the political system and help bring about war between the races—a bloody confrontation that, in the book at least, the white supremacists would eventually win.

By the time Nungester first picked up on the conspiracy in the fall of 1984, an Order hit squad had already successfully carried out its first assassination against an outspoken Denver radio announcer named Alan Berg. Berg, who was Jewish, had hosted a talk show on KOA radio and for years had engaged in a running verbal battle with right-wing listeners in his audience. A hit squad of Order members, including Mathews, had gunned Berg down in June 1984 outside his home one night, as the controversial radio personality, holding a bagful of groceries, stepped out of his car.

Dees, it turned out, was to have been next. Sometime before the trip to Raleigh, Mathews flew to Birmingham to gather as much intelligence as possible on Dees, and the Order leader may have been stalking him in North Carolina during the depositions. Whether Mathews actually intended to carry out an assassination attempt there was not clear, but a few weeks later he confided to a federal informant that such an attempt was imminent. The informant, Thomas Martinez, was a friend of Mathews from their days together in the National Alliance. Unknown to Mathews, however, Martinez was now working for the feds as part of a deal to avoid a prison sentence for passing counterfeit currency.

Late in November 1984, just three weeks after the North Carolina depositions, Martinez flew to Portland, Oregon, to meet with Mathews, ostensibly to go underground with the racist group. In fact, Martinez's real purpose was to lead the FBI to Mathews so that the Order leader could be captured. Martinez did his part; but the attempt to apprehend Mathews ran into problems, and the Order founder escaped in a shoot-out at a Portland motel with several FBI agents. Two weeks later, however, Mathews was killed in a firefight with more than a hundred FBI SWAT team members on an island in Puget Sound, Washington. In the ensuing months Mathews's followers were tracked down and arrested by the feds, prosecuted as a group, and sent to prison.

It was only after Mathews's death that we learned how close a call it had been. But despite his demise, we kept our guard extremely high for the next several months, and things never returned to the way they had been before. The days of the walk-in SPLC office were over forever.

Although the Order died with Mathews, or shortly thereafter, the idea of a white supremacist revolution did not, and the rise of the revolutionary racist group marked a turning point in the history of white supremacy in the United States. It had now become clear that at the same time that the Klan was once again on the fade, certain elements within the racist movement were growing more radical, even to the point of taking up arms against the federal government.*

At the height of the death threats scare, there were two important developments related to other SPLC cases. The first was Bill Wilkinson's resignation. Wilkinson, whose Klan had been losing more members than it had been taking in for several years, went quietly, announcing his decision to quit at a rally outside Atlanta. His departure meant that the two men responsible for resurrecting the KKK during the 1970s—the other one, of course, being David Duke—were gone from the scene. As a practical matter, Wilkinson's resignation had no impact on the Decatur suit; as soon as we learned the name and address of his successor, James Blair, we substituted his name for Wilkinson's in the litigation.

The other news was a major break in the SPLC arson probe. Leafing through our photo files, we stumbled across a picture of Joe Garner and Tommy Downs in Klan robes, a discovery that made liars out of them both and ultimately led to the resolution of the case. The photograph had been taken by Garry Nungester as the

---

* The irony of this happening during the Reagan years was evident, yet to people like Mathews and his followers, Reagan was merely the figurehead of a government dominated by Jews and minorities, what white supremacists increasingly referred to as the Zionist Occupied Government (ZOG). Just before his death Mathews drafted a dramatic declaration of war against "ZOG."

two paraded through the streets of Birmingham in 1980 during a KKK demonstration. It had been in our files all along, and the discovery of it was an accident.

The significance of the picture lay in the fact that Dees had questioned the two men about their Klan membership during the depositions we had taken of them immediately after the fire. They had denied ever joining the KKK, and Downs had gone so far as to say he had never even participated in any Klan functions.

Because both Dees and the court reporter had forgotten to administer the oath to Downs until midway during the deposition, Dees believed Downs would have to be induced to lie again to make a perjury charge stick, so he came up with a plan to present to Jimmy Evans, the Montgomery County district attorney, to summon the young Klansman to a grand jury. The idea was for Evans to subpoena Downs and question him about whether he had ever belonged to the KKK or engaged in any KKK activities, just as Dees had done earlier. If Downs took the bait, Evans would have an airtight perjury charge against him, which could then be used to hold over his head to extract a confession and implicate Garner.

Evans agreed to lay the trap, and in a matter of days Downs was summoned before the Montgomery County grand jury. Everything went according to script, and when he emerged from testifying, Evans confronted him with the photo, informing him that he faced five years in prison for lying under oath. Just as we had hoped, Downs immediately caved in, confessed to the arson, and implicated both Garner and Downs's close friend, Charles "Dink" Bailey, as well.

Getting Garner did not prove so easy since Alabama conspiracy law demanded more than the word of one conspirator against another to obtain a conviction. It required corroborating evidence, such as the gasoline sprayer that Downs said Garner had given him prior to setting the fire or, alternatively, the statement of a nonconspirator to whom Garner had confessed his role in the crime. But Garner and Downs already had disposed of the sprayer and the little other physical evidence there had been. Lacking the latter, the Montgomery County District Attorney's office, the Montgomery County Sheriff's Department, and the Alabama Bureau of Investigation launched a major investigation of Garner. The probe uncovered more than enough evidence to wrap up the arson case, and it led to the discovery of a host of other crimes committed by Garner and his cohorts, including a previously unknown plot to bomb a civil rights protest and the armed robbery of a dice game.

The crucial piece of evidence in the arson case came from one of Garner's convenience store employees, Sherry Rhodes, the wife of one of his Klan buddies. Garner had made a number of incriminating statements to Rhodes about his involvement in the fire. Rhodes, who was an exceedingly devoted employee of Garner's, did not give up the information easily. The only way the authorities won her cooperation was by obtaining leverage over her: evidence that her husband, Buster, had participated with Garner and other Klan members in a scheme to steal and stockpile explosives for future use against a civil rights demonstration. With her husband facing almost certain conviction, Sherry Rhodes struck a deal to provide the information against Garner. In return, the authorities agreed to accept a guilty plea from Buster Rhodes and to recommend a lighter sentence against him.

When the dust finally settled from the investigation, Garner, Downs, and Bailey had entered guilty pleas in the SPLC arson and the theft of the explosives, and, furthermore, Garner and Downs had acknowledged burning a cross on the lawn of a black Montgomery County commissioner in early 1983. Garner was sentenced to fifteen years on the various charges, Downs and Bailey to thirty months.

Meanwhile, the North Carolina case ended on a successful note in January 1985. In a deft piece of investigative work leading up to its resolution, Randall Williams extracted a confession from one of the key figures involved in the harassment of the prison guard by carrying the Klansman to a cemetery not far from his home and suggesting—in so many words—that he would pay for his actions in either this life or the next. The Klansman, Jerry Michael Lewis, broke down and admitted his role in the harassment and implicated two fellow CKKKK members. Lewis eventually pleaded guilty to a federal civil rights violation. His plea, in turn, indirectly led to the conviction of another Klansman on a perjury charge.

A second phase of the case, our legal attack on the CKKKK's paramilitary operations, had an even more bizarre conclusion. Like the Texas Knights under Louis Beam, the CKKKK under Glenn Miller had a formidable militia, despite the fact that the North Carolina legislature had outlawed paramilitary activity. Dees, as he had done in the Vietnamese fishermen's case, had piggybacked a complaint against the CKKKK's paramilitary operations onto the harassment charge, and the issue appeared headed for trial in 1985. However, during a break in a round of depositions in early January of that year, Dees struck a deal with Miller to settle the case out of court. The terms of the settlement called for no monetary damages or sanctions against the CKKKK but rather included a pledge on Miller's part not to operate a paramilitary army. It was, frankly, something of a face-saving agreement for both sides. Because of the tense security situation, we had been unable to conduct the kind of thorough field investigation we were accustomed to doing, and as a result, we didn't have as strong a case as we would have liked. Dees was looking for a suitable way to settle the case, and when Miller agreed to the self-imposed ban, Dees took it. Miller, on the other hand, was eager to get us off his back.

On January 17 the court held a settlement hearing to make the agreement official. Over the objections of our security people, Dees traveled to Raleigh alone, and when he arrived at the courthouse, he discovered that Miller was also there by himself. When the hearing adjourned—the judge approved the terms of settlement—Dees, acting on an impulse, asked Miller to give him a ride to the airport to catch his flight back to Montgomery. The move was typically Dees: aggressive, flamboyant, with a dash of recklessness. But there was also a purpose behind it—Dees wanted the chance to interact with Miller one-on-one. He suspected that Miller was heavily involved with the Order and might be privy to any future plots to assassinate him.

Surprisingly Miller agreed to give him a lift. On the way to the Klansman's car Dees kept an eye out to make certain that they were not being followed, and after he got into the vehicle, he glanced around for weapons, opening the glove compartment and poking around. But all he saw in his hasty inspection were stacks of the CKKKK's monthly newsletter, the *Confederate Leader,* on the backseat.

The two men kept a running conversation all the way to the airport. Miller harangued Dees about Jewish conspiracies and Ar-

yan superiority. Dees countered by pointing out that Miller, with his
dark brown hair and brown eyes, hardly resembled the Aryan ideal
and asserted that the strength of the United States was in its ethnic
diversity.

At the end of the half-hour ride Miller pulled off the highway,
turned into the airport complex, and proceeded to the terminal. As
he brought the car to a stop next to the curb, he turned to Dees and
said, "You know, Morris, there're some people who're trying to kill
you. You be careful."

Chapter Eleven

NEWS OF the arrests of two Mobile Klansmen in the Michael Donald murder had come midway during the Decatur investigation, in 1983. Although it probably shouldn't have come as a surprise to us, it did nonetheless. That, more than a decade after the end of the civil rights era, Ku Klux Klansmen would abduct a black teenager off the street at random, club him into unconsciousness, and choke him to death, then string his body in a tree, lynch-style, on a downtown residential street was shocking. There was no other word for it. All the more so because the KKK in Mobile was numerically weak; comparatively speaking, Mobile didn't have a Klan problem.

From the outset I couldn't help but think that we had failed to monitor the Donald case closely enough. An organization that undertook to "keep watch" on the Ku Klux Klan should have made more of an effort to investigate the death of a young black man whose corpse was found dangling from a tree. We hadn't even gone to Mobile to interview anyone. Notwithstanding that we had been preoccupied in March 1981 with other matters—getting the Project organized and undertaking the Texas case—it was still, in retrospect, a glaring oversight on our part.

Ever since hearing of the arrests, Dees had wanted to sue. He didn't know whom specifically (beyond the murderers, that is) or even on what basis (save that any suit would have to be undertaken on behalf of the slain youth's estate, through a parent or sibling); but he knew there was a lawsuit there, and he was bent on bringing it. It was, after all, the single most horrific act of KKK violence since the 1960s.

Although the arrests were made on June 16, 1983, the day nineteen-year-old James Llewellyn ("Tiger") Knowles came forward to plead guilty in federal court to a felony civil rights violation in the case, few additional facts about the killing—the kinds of details Dees wanted to know before proceeding—emerged in the weeks and months that followed. Many unanswered questions remained. Were there any other accomplices, or was the murder simply the work of two demented individuals? If other Klansmen were implicated, were any of them higher-ups? Was the Klan organization involved in any way? Who were the prosecution's witnesses? How had the case been cracked?

The slowness with which these key facts came to light was due primarily to two factors—the decision of the second defendant, Henry Francis Hays, to plead innocent and the transfer of jurisdiction over Hays from the federal to the state courts at the request of the Mobile County district attorney, Chris Galanos. Galanos, a progressive young Democrat elected to office in 1979 with the support of the county's large black population, was eager to bring Hays up on a capital murder charge.

The Justice Department had complied with Galanos's request, dismissing the federal civil rights indictment and handing Hays over to Mobile County. It had done so partly out of a long-standing commitment to encourage Southern authorities to prosecute cases of racial violence and partly out of a willingness to defer to the court of primary jurisdiction. But the decision meant that the case would have to be presented to a state grand jury, and that would translate into a delay of a few weeks. As things worked out, it wasn't until early December 1983, about the time we were completing work on the Decatur investigation, that the trial began. Only then, on the occasion of the prosecution's laying out the circumstances of the murder for the jury, did Dees get the answers he was looking for.

Eager to learn what the state had in the way of evidence, Dees decided to attend the trial in person. The day before it began, he and I departed Montgomery for the three-hour drive down Interstate 65 to Mobile, in the far southwestern corner of the state.

Nearly three centuries old, Mobile is the oldest continuously inhabited community in Alabama. Genteel, rich in history and culture, it is the state's only major seaport, situated on the western shore of a large bay that empties into the Gulf of Mexico.

Mobile—parts of it, at least—is a beautiful old city with magnificent antebellum houses, expansive squares and public spaces, and lots of wrought iron. In some respects it resembles its more celebrated cousin New Orleans. Massive two-hundred-year-old live oaks line many of its streets, shielding its residents from the subtropical sun that beats down relentlessly during the city's habitually long, muggy summers and lending a graceful charm to lawns and parks. Every spring the entire town is awash with color from tens of thousands of red, pink, and white azalea bushes; hence its nickname, the Azalea City.

Perhaps more than in any other major Southern city, however, the Old South mentality has thrived in Mobile, from the annual spring pilgrimage of homes glorifying the antebellum way of life to the reluctance of the white community to acknowledge the contributions of black people to Mobile society.

But the existence of the Old South frame of mind has often manifested itself in far more insidious ways, frequently taking the form of opposition to the most minimal black gains. Because of intransigent white attitudes, it was not until 1985 that the first black Mobilian was elected to the municipal commission, the city's governing body, and then only after protracted litigation that led to the expansion of the Federal Voting Rights Act. Before that, despite constituting a third or more of Mobile's two-hundred-thousand population, blacks were without an elective voice in the affairs of the city, the victims of an election plan that had helped make it virtually impossible for minority candidates to win.

By far the most powerful symbol of official white repression however, was the Glenn Diamond incident, an incredible mock lynching in 1976 that eerily foreshadowed the Michael Donald murder. Nearly five years to the day before Donald was slain, and only a half mile away from the tree on which his body was found, Diamond, a young black Mobile resident in his twenties, was stopped by the Mobile police on a robbery stakeout near a fast-food restaurant. The officers, all of them white, were members of a special detail called the 600 Squad, charged with fighting urban armed robberies. In an attempt to force Diamond to confess to a string of unsolved crimes that he had had nothing to do with, they placed a noose around his neck, threw it over a tree limb, and hoisted him up so that his feet barely touched the ground. Diamond refused to confess, however, and later he sued the police department over the incident. Although assault charges were filed against several of the officers, the two who went to trial were acquitted by all-white juries, and the charges against the others were subsequently dropped. All eventually returned to the force. Nevertheless, the city declined to contest the civil suit, settling out of court for more than forty thousand dollars.

As Dees and I traveled to Mobile that night in early December, we had no way of knowing whether Tiger Knowles and Henry Hays had been inspired by the example of the Mobile police to hang the lifeless body of young Donald in a tree or whether they had arrived at the macabre idea on their own. That was just one question among many we hoped to answer.

The trial began the next morning in the courtroom of Judge Braxton L. Kittrell, Jr., at the Mobile County Courthouse. Outside the courtroom security was tight in recognition of the emotionally charged nature of the case. A metal detector had been set up to screen spectators for weapons, and several armed sheriff's deputies stood guard in the vicinity of the entrance. We inched our way through the line with dozens of other spectators and made our way inside. The gallery, though small, was not quite filled to capacity—a surprise considering the fact that the murder had so inflamed racial tensions in the city.

Most of the morning session of the first day was taken up with preliminary matters, including jury selection. After lunch, with a panel of eleven whites and one black having been seated to hear the case, testimony finally began. The first witness was the passerby who had discovered the body; next up was the first police officer to arrive at the scene. It was not until the second day of the trial that Tiger Knowles, the state's star witness, took the stand.

Though only twenty, Knowles looked and acted considerably older than his years, a fact that had helped account for his election at the age of seventeen to the office of province klaliff, the second-ranking post in the Mobile district of the UKA (United Klans of America), which covered the southern half of the state. Knowles was a short, burly young man with a mustache and long sideburns that flared beneath his earlobes. His hair, parted neatly on the left side of his head, was dark brown, made darker by an overly generous application of oil. He was casually attired in jeans and a beige sports shirt. Looking self-assured and relatively at ease, the former Klan leader took his seat in the wooden witness box next to the judge's bench.

Less than twenty-five feet away from him sat Henry Hays, the former kligrapp, or secretary, of the Mobile klavern, staring stoically from the counsel table. In contrast, Hays looked younger than twenty-nine, his hair freshly cut and brushed stylishly across his forehead. He wore pinkish slacks and a matching two-tone vest with a white short-sleeve shirt.

Knowles recounted the details of the grisly slaying with a startling lack of emotion, displaying no remorse at all. After an hour or two of his sometimes graphic testimony, though, a clearer, more distinct picture of the crime began to emerge:

In essence, Michael Donald had been the victim of a random revenge killing carried out in retaliation for the failure of a predominantly black Mobile jury to convict a black man accused of shooting to death a white police officer.

During the week of March 16, 1981, five days before Donald was abducted and murdered, the trial of Josephus Anderson had begun in Mobile County Circuit Court. Anderson, a transient, was charged with killing Officer Eugene Ballard after a bank robbery. Ironically, neither the accused nor the victim was from Mobile—the case had been moved from Birmingham on a change of venue motion—but because of the racial dynamics involved in the case and the fact that eleven of the twelve members of the Anderson jury were black, the trial caught the eyes of Knowles and Hays. The two young Klansmen resolved that if the jury should turn Anderson loose, as they believed it would, they would retaliate by taking the life of a black person and hanging the victim's body in a tree. In Knowles's words, this would "show Klan strength in Alabama."

During the course of the Anderson trial they passed the idea by Hays's father, Bennie Jack Hays. The elder Hays, a convicted cattle rustler from Missouri, was the southern Alabama titan for the United Klans of America and the highest-ranking UKA official south of Montgomery. Bennie Jack Hays gave his approval to the conspiracy—but with a stipulation. Since the plan was for the Kluxers to hang the body of their victim in a tree on Herndon Avenue, where Henry Hays and his wife lived in a house belonging to his father, and since Bennie Hays was trying to sell some other property he owned on the same block, the elder Hays warned the two not to do anything until the sale went through.

On the assumption that the deal would be consummated, however, Knowles and Hays went forward with their plans, laying the groundwork for the murder. In what was apparently an attempt to set up a cover for the pair, Hays decided to invite several friends over to his house for a night of drinking and cardplaying on the evening the verdict was to be returned. One, Frank Cox, the exalted cyclops, was instructed by Knowles to build a cross and bring it to the party. The cross would play a crucial role in the plot. It was to be burned at the Mobile County Courthouse the night of the murder and would constitute the KKK's "signature," providing a subtle but unmistakable symbolic link among the slaying, the Anderson trial, and the KKK.

On Friday, March 20, the defense in the Anderson trial rested, and the case went to the jury. Coincidentally, that afternoon Bennie Hays and a local real estate broker signed the papers closing the sale of the Herndon Avenue property. With the transaction final, Knowles and Hays put their plot into motion.

As evening approached, Knowles and the other guests began to show up at Hays's house at 117 Herndon Avenue: Frank Cox, the exalted cyclops of Unit 900, one of two Mobile-area UKA klaverns;* Teddy Kyzar, a klexter, or guard; and several of Bennie Hays's tenants, with whom Henry was friends. Denise Hays, Henry's wife, was also on hand. Hays apparently wanted a mix of Klansmen and "aliens," as non-Klansmen were called, the better to camouflage the real purpose of the gathering.

When Cox arrived, he unloaded the cross and placed it underneath a shed in the back of a vacant house owned by Bennie Hays two doors down from 117. Inside 117 the party was getting under way.

---

* The other, Unit 1000, was the klavern to which Knowles belonged. (Unit numbers were arbitrarily chosen and did not reflect the total number of chartered klaverns.)

After a little while Hays, Knowles, and Cox (who was Hays's brother-in-law) slipped out of the house together in Hays's red Buick and drove to Cox's mother's house in Theodore, a small community ten or fifteen miles southwest of downtown Mobile. Cox borrowed a rope from her, telling her that Knowles's mother's car had broken down on the interstate and the rope was needed to tow it. Next they went to another Klansman's house and obtained a pistol before returning to Herndon Avenue to await news of the verdict. On the way back to Hays's house, Knowles began to tie a hangman's noose. With Cox's cigarette lighter he frayed the ends of the rope, seeing to it that the knot had the required thirteen loops in it. Once back at 117 Herndon, the three rejoined the party.

At 10:00 P.M. the late news came on television, and with it the report that a mistrial had been declared in the Anderson case as a result of the jury's inability to reach a verdict; the jury had dead-locked. To Knowles and Hays, it hardly mattered that Anderson would not go free, that he would remain in custody while awaiting retrial; the jury had failed to convict a black man who was guilty in their eyes of killing a white man. Within minutes of the broadcast the pair left the party, this time alone. They drove off in Hays's car into the darkness, headed for a nearby black neighborhood. For some time they cruised the half-deserted streets, looking for a suitable victim. At one point they spotted an old man at a pay phone but rejected him on the ground that he was standing too far from the curb. After a few minutes more they happened upon Michael Donald, walking by himself on a darkened street. "He seemed like a good victim," Knowles testified. "He was alone in a secluded area."

Hays pulled over to the curb. On the pretense of asking directions to a nightclub, Knowles called the nineteen-year-old technical school student over to the car, and Donald approached the vehicle. When he leaned down to speak to them, Knowles brandished the pistol and ordered him inside. Donald did as he was told.

Hays then drove to a remote rural area where only a few days earlier he and Knowles had beaten a gay man they had lured into their car in a similar way. There was little conversation among the three, but at one point Hays asked Donald whether he was familiar with the Atlanta child murders. Donald replied that he was. "Please don't kill me," he begged.

When the car stopped in a small clearing and the three men got out, Donald made a dash for freedom, knocking the gun from Knowles's hand. The weapon fell to the ground, discharging once. But Hays and Knowles managed to thwart the escape attempt, overpowering Donald and wrestling him to the ground. They subsequently began to beat him, using tree limbs and anything within reach. Donald fought back—"like a crazed animal," according to Knowles—but eventually collapsed, exhausted and semiconscious. Knowles went to the car and got the rope, and together he and Hays slipped it around their young victim's neck. To cinch it up tight, Hays put his boot on Donald's forehead and tugged. When they were through, Donald had been strangled to death.

Surveying their handiwork, the Klansmen pulled the body to the back of the car and hoisted it into the trunk. Hays then slit Donald's neck three times to make sure he was dead. After climbing back into the car, the two men retraced their route to Mobile, their mission half accomplished. Hays parked the car behind a vacant house owned by his father, and the men returned to the party. It was somewhere around midnight or shortly thereafter.

A while later, while Knowles was outside for a few moments, he caught a glimpse of Hays and Cox at the rear of Hays's car with the trunk door up, as if Hays were showing his brother-in-law the body.

About two or two-thirty Cox and Teddy Kyzar carried the cross to the courthouse and set fire to it on the lawn, as Knowles had instructed them. Sometime after that Knowles and Hays hanged the body in a small elm tree across the street from Hays's house. Shortly before dawn an early riser going for his morning newspaper found the body and called the police.

By the end of Knowles's account, Dees had his answers—at least the crucial one about the existence of a wider conspiracy. Knowing the KKK as he did, he was convinced the circle of conspirators was larger than Hays and Knowles, despite Knowles's seeming reluctance to implicate the others fully. For one, there was Frank Cox, who supplied the rope, watched Knowles make a hangman's noose with it, and later helped burn the cross on the courthouse lawn. And Bennie Hays. Dees was confident there were others.

After Knowles's testimony, we stayed at the trial only long enough to watch the remainder of the prosecution's case. Several other KKK members followed the former Klansman to the stand, including Henry Hays's ex-wife, Denise, a former member of the Unit

900's women's auxiliary, who testified that Henry had phoned a local TV station himself to report the "discovery" of the body. For the most part, their testimony consisted of recounting confessions Hays had made to them in the weeks and months after the murder.

Several days after our return to Montgomery, Henry Hays was convicted of the murder and sentenced by the jury to life in prison without parole. In an unusual move Judge Kittrell subsequently overruled the jury's sentence and ordered Hays put to death in the electric chair. Of the hundreds of people legally executed in Alabama over the years, Hays thus became only the second white in the state's history to receive the death sentence for killing a black person.

Back in Montgomery, Dees mulled over the evidence from the trial, tossing and turning it in his mind, examining it and reexamining it through the prism of federal civil rights law. As usual, he was looking for the novel twist, the unusual hook or angle that might make the suit more effective. He now felt confident going forward with the case (if the Donald family was willing, of course). But it was not enough merely to sue Hays and Knowles. Any "jackleg lawyer" (to use a favorite Dees expression) could do that, though a judgment against the two of them alone might be worth very little, either in terms of monetary damages or as a deterrent to other would-be Klan killers. Nor was it sufficient simply to identify and expose the other conspirators involved in the murder. He believed a civil suit could accomplish these goals, but he was determined that it should do more. The depravity of the killing called for it. Because the crime was at once so horrible and so classically Klannish, and because Dees viewed Henry Hays and Knowles as little more than agents of the KKK, he wanted to find a way to hold the entire organization liable and root out the evil at its source.

The outlines of a civil suit gradually began to take shape in Dees's mind. The fact that all the key conspirators were officers—a titan (Bennie Hays), a provincial klaliff (Knowles), an exalted cyclops (Cox), and a kligrapp (Henry Hays)—suggested that a legal attack on the UKA organization might be possible. From this line of thinking emerged Dees's ultimate strategy: to borrow from the world of corporate law and argue, using an agencylike theory, that

Knowles and Hays were merely acting on behalf of the United Klans when they brutally murdered Michael Donald and therefore the UKA itself should be held liable for their actions.

It was a novel idea. In the century and more of its existence, the Klan had rarely been sued. It was safe to say that it had never been sued under the theory of agency or any of its corollaries.

Agency theory was one of the fundamental tenets of corporate law, holding that a principal—an employer, for example—was responsible for his or her agent's actions if the agent committed a wrong while acting within the line and scope of his duty. Although the Supreme Court had ruled that there was no such thing as agency under the federal civil rights laws, it *had* held in an important case out of New York that a corporation nevertheless could be found liable under the civil rights laws for the actions of its employees if those actions amounted to an official custom, practice, or policy. In other words, under the Supreme Court's ruling a city could not necessarily be held liable under the federal civil rights statutes for a white police officer's wrongful shooting of a black citizen, even if the shooting was found to be negligent, but it could be liable if such shootings indicated a custom, practice, or policy. The UKA, by the same token, was not necessarily liable under the law for Hays's and Knowles's actions, particularly since the Klan was not a corporation in the usual business sense and Hays and Knowles were not its employees (even though the UKA was a for-profit enterprise). The only circumstances under which the Klan might be liable were if Michael Donald's murder were proved to be the result of an official UKA policy. Common sense dictated that it was, of course, but proving it was another matter.

In the United Klans of America we would be taking on the oldest and perhaps the largest of the three major KKK factions in the country. Of the "big three"—the Invisible Empire, Don Black's (formerly David Duke's) Knights of the KKK, and the UKA—only the UKA could trace its roots to the civil rights era. Founded in 1961, it had had only one leader for virtually its entire existence: Robert M. Shelton, a former Tuscaloosa, Alabama, rubber plant worker. Shelton, who had served almost a year in prison for contempt of Congress in the late 1960s, was of the old school. Unlike Wilkinson and Duke, he had never subscribed to the notion of a "new" KKK. For the most part, he shunned publicity and scorned his rivals for running "mail-order Klans."

Under Shelton's leadership, the UKA was the most secretive and mysterious of the major Klan organizations, and it was the one we knew the least about—except for its bloody past. UKA members had been convicted of the murder of Viola Liuzzo, the Detroit housewife and civil rights worker killed during the Selma to Montgomery voting rights march in 1965; the Sixteenth Street Baptist Church bombing, which killed four black girls in Birmingham in 1963; and the shooting death of Lieutenant Colonel Lemuel Penn, the black Washington, D.C., national guardsman murdered while traveling on a Georgia highway in 1964. In fact, the UKA had been responsible for much of the violence across the South during the 1960s. Though smaller now, and lacking the popular support it had once enjoyed, it was still a violent organization. In 1979 thirteen of its members from eastern Alabama had been convicted by the feds for a string of violent acts perpetrated against several black activists, including the state NAACP president, in Talladega County.

It somehow seemed appropriate that after confronting the Knights of the KKK in Texas and the Invisible Empire in Decatur, we should wind up going to court against this relic of the sixties' Klans. As in the Texas case, however, we had the theory and the desire to sue, but no client. For the emotional impact, Dees wanted to sue on behalf of Michael Donald's mother, but an article we had seen during the Hays trial led us to believe she might not be amenable to the idea. The report, quoting one of Michael Donald's sisters, said that Mrs. Donald had been so distraught over her son's murder that she had been unable to attend any of the proceedings. It was unclear whether she would be willing to be a plaintiff in the case or whether from the emotional or physical standpoint she even should. Dees put Randall Williams in charge of finding out.

As it happened, we needn't have worried. Beulah Mae Donald was a brave and resilient woman. Her health might be fragile—she suffered from both diabetes and high blood pressure—but her resolve was strong, and when Williams broached the subject to her through her attorney, a popular state senator from the Mobile suburb of

Prichard named Michael Figures, she accepted the offer without reservations.

Mrs. Donald's sixty-four years had been a succession of hardships: an impoverished childhood; a teenage pregnancy that cut short her education in the tenth grade; the murder of a sister; the demanding task of being a single parent after the dissolution of her marriage—all this in addition to the day-to-day struggle for survival every black Southerner faced in a frequently hostile world. Despite this, she had not permitted herself to become embittered or cynical at the hand that had been dealt her—even in the wake of the brutal slaying of her teenage son.

The youngest of seven, Michael had been the only one of her children still living at home with her in 1981. "Home" for the two was a drab cinder-block apartment in a housing project a few blocks north of downtown Mobile. Plainly decorated but neat, it was covered with pictures of Mrs. Donald's many grandchildren.

Neither vengeance nor the prospect of remuneration prompted Mrs. Donald to take us up on the offer to sue the UKA on behalf of her son's estate. Rather, she did it in the hope of bringing the rest of his killers to justice and to try to spare other families from having to endure what hers had been put through. And there was another reason: to air the full story of Michael's death once and for all.

Almost from the moment young Donald's body had been found, white officials had downplayed the possibility that the slaying might be racially motivated, notwithstanding the image of a lynching conjured up by the discovery of the youth's body hanging from a tree. The initial arrest of three young white men described by the police as "junkie types" set off speculation in the community that Donald might have been the victim of a drug deal gone sour. It was as if whites couldn't bring themselves to acknowledge that racism might be at the root of the crime, for fear of what that might say about Mobile race relations in general.

So sure was Mrs. Donald of her son's innocence of any wrongdoing that she had invited the police to search his room, and they had, taking it apart from top to bottom but finding no drugs or any other leads.

Long after the arrest of Knowles and Hays, whites had continued to play down the racial implications of the case. Mobile County Assistant District Attorney Tom Harrison, who personally (and, to his credit, vigorously) prosecuted the case against Hays, seemed to insinuate that the crime was more of a manifestation of individual racism than anything of an organized variety. "I'm not sure this was a Klan case," he stated flatly in an interview with a reporter right after the trial. "It was a deliberate, intentional homicide that happened to be perpetrated by members in the Klan."

To Mrs. Donald, who had insisted on an open casket at her son's funeral "so all the world could see"* how the killers had battered and mutilated his body, the civil suit we proposed constituted an opportunity to amend the record.

The general failure to see the case for what it was may have at least partly accounted for the long delay in solving the murder in the first place. Although the corpse was found dangling from a tree opposite a house owned by Bennie Hays, a known Klansman, and the discovery of the body followed by only a few hours a cross burning on the courthouse lawn, the Mobile police apparently never viewed the Klansmen as serious suspects, despite what many might consider telltale signs of KKK involvement. During the initial canvass of the neighborhood, the Hayses and several other Klansmen were briefly interviewed by officers in search of anyone with information about the killing, but the investigation quickly took a different tack, one apparently more in keeping with the police department's predisposition about the motives of the killers. After the case against the three original suspects collapsed, police officials connected to the case persisted in failing to pursue the most obvious lead they had.

With progress stalled, Mobile District Attorney Chris Galanos had invited the FBI to enter the investigation; but the Bureau's probe did little more than track the earlier inquiry, and it came to a similar end.

As time passed, Mobile's black community grew increasingly restive. In June 1981 one of Donald's sisters, Cynthia, picketed the Mobile County Courthouse with several supporters, and other protests were organized as the unsolved case dragged on.

---

* More than twenty-five years earlier Emmett Till's mother had used almost precisely the same words in ordering the casket to be kept open at his funeral. The fourteen-year-old Chicago youth had been visiting his Mississippi relatives during the summer of 1955 when he was kidnapped and killed for whistling at a white woman.

By virtue of the dogged determination of Senator Figures and his brother, Thomas, not to let the murder be forgotten, the case was eventually cracked. Dissatisfied with the quality of the first FBI investigation, Thomas H. Figures, an Assistant U.S. Attorney, pressed the Justice Department to authorize another one, and his request was eventually granted. A new FBI agent, James Bodman, was assigned to work with him on the case, and the pair—one black, the other white, both Southerners—launched a second federal probe into the murder. They trained their focus on the Klansmen of Unit 900, and after months of interviews they collected enough evidence for Figures's superiors in Washington to justify calling a grand jury. By that time it was early 1983.

The grand jury investigation lasted for several months. Over and over Klan witnesses—many of them without lawyers—were dragged before the panel and grilled by Figures, Barry Kowalski, and Albert Glenn, the latter two the department's line attorneys. Each time, the prosecutors picked up new facts, facts which in some cases contradicted the testimony of a previous witness or the witness himself. Using the discrepancies to play witnesses off against one another or to instill in them a fear of being charged with perjury, the prosecutors gained the upper hand. When Knowles learned that a fellow Klansman had told the grand jury that Hays had boasted about murdering Donald, the collapse of the conspiracy was imminent. Afraid Hays would implicate him in exchange for a reduced sentence and knowing that he could face the death penalty, Knowles caved in to the pressure, coming forward on June 16, 1983, to plead guilty to a felony civil rights violation.

Almost a year to the day later, we went to court on Mrs. Donald's behalf. The suit, styled *Beulah Mae Donald, et al.* v. *United Klans of America, et al.*, sought ten million dollars in damages. In addition to Mrs. Donald, the state and local chapters of the Alabama NAACP were also plaintiffs. Dees had invited them to join in the case in order to make it a class action, since that would enable us to obtain a statewide injunction barring all UKA members from future acts of violence and intimidation against any black person in the state, upon penalty of criminal contempt of court and jail.

Chapter Twelve

FROM THE start the Michael Donald suit was different from our other Klan litigation, both in its objectives and in the way we litigated it. Our ultimate goal was to take the United Klans of America for every asset it had.

Our evidentiary needs were threefold: to prove the existence of a broader conspiracy among Unit 900 members than so far had been revealed; to establish the chain of command between the corporate UKA and its Mobile chapter; and to document a history of other violent acts by UKA members in order to demonstrate that violence was, in effect, the UKA's corporate policy. The work of gathering this evidence proceeded in stages.

The first order of business, filling in the outlines of the conspiracy, was not as difficult a proposition as we had anticipated. As we began contacting the witnesses federal and state investigators had already interviewed, we found that considerable evidence of a broader conspiracy had already been unearthed. The evidence had not been fully developed, however, and because it had not been essential to proving Hays's guilt, it had not previously come to light publicly.

The first of the witnesses we approached was Teddy Kyzar. A short, rotund young man with multiple chins and curly red hair, Kyzar had been one of the handful of Klansmen present at Hays's house on the night of the murder, waiting out the verdict in the Josephus Anderson case. On Tiger Knowles's orders he and Frank Cox had burned the cross on the lawn of the county courthouse.

Only in his twenties, Kyzar seemed like one of those individuals for whom the Klan was a social club as much as a vehicle for expressing racial hostility; he came across as an essentially decent—but pathetic—person. He was a follower, and apparently an easily manipulated one at that, but one got the feeling after talking with him only a few minutes that he was a Klansman because the Klan was one of the only organizations that might extend him an invitation to join.

Kyzar had been a crucial witness in the criminal investigation, testifying at Hays's trial that Knowles and Hays had left the party at 117 Herndon Avenue after hearing the news of the hung jury and that they had returned sometime around midnight, with Knowles's shirt drenched in blood.

From Kyzar we learned that there had been a meeting of Unit 900 members at klavern headquarters on Bennie Hays's property in Theodore on March 18, 1981, a mere two nights before the killing. At this regular weekly gathering of the group, he said, there had been an open discussion about the Anderson trial, and Bennie Hays had remarked that a black man shouldn't be allowed to get away with killing a white man. Henry Hays and others had joined in the talk. At this critical juncture, however, Kyzar's recollection suddenly and mysteriously stopped, and he claimed not to remember anything else about what had been said. "When Bennie Hays started raising his voice in a mad kind of anger," he explained, "I kicked back in the chair and started daydreaming."

Although we alternately admonished and implored Kyzar to tell us everything he knew, he refused to budge from his story that he had tuned out the rest of the discussion. But a second witness, Johnny Matt Jones, filled in some of the crucial gaps. Jones, a twenty-two-year-old, had joined Unit 900 a little less than a year before the Donald murder at the encouragement of his neighbor Frank Cox, the exalted cyclops. A high school dropout, Jones, like Kyzar, was impressionable and a follower. Because many of his fellow Klansmen owned guns, often bringing the weapons to meetings, he had wanted one, and he had persuaded Cox to buy him a pistol, despite the fact he was under age. This, it turned out, was the gun Knowles had borrowed to use in the abduction.

During the summer of 1981, several months after the slaying, Jones had left Mobile and moved to Houston to be with his father, and in 1984 he was still there, employed as a mechanic. A few weeks after the suit was filed, Dees flew out to Texas to take a statement from him. Jones had already told his story to Robert Eddy, the chief investigator for the Mobile County District Attorney's office, but because his testimony had not been necessary to make the case against Hays, he hadn't taken the stand at Hays's trial the previous fall.

Jones was epileptic and was easily unsettled, so Dees arranged to go to his apartment to take the statement, bringing along a court reporter to transcribe the interview. Gradually, gingerly, Dees coaxed the story out of Jones. Seeking to put the young ex-Klansman at ease, he began with routine questions about Jones's address and date of birth. Jones quickly stumbled over his Social Security number.

At times he seemed lucid, but at other times his answers were, at best, foggy. When it came to the critical pre-murder meeting of Unit 900 on March 18, 1981, his recollection was fragmentary, but it conformed with what we had learned from Kyzar's abbreviated account.

According to Jones, Bennie Hays had addressed the entire klavern at one point during the March 18 meeting. Ordering Henry, the kligrapp (secretary), to "get this down," the elder Hays declared that if a black man could get away with killing a white man, a white man should be able to get away with killing a black man. This prompted Henry Hays to respond that "a nigger ought to be hung by the neck until dead to put them in their place," and other Kluxers chimed in their agreement. "We gonna kill a nigger," said one. Another suggested that perhaps one wasn't enough. And thus it was that the group reached the fatal consensus that if Josephus Anderson should be acquitted by the predominantly black jury hearing his case, the Klan should avenge the death of the slain white officer.

Beyond these bare bones facts, Jones was hard pressed to remember much else about the discussion. Asked about Frank Cox's role in it, he was unable to recall anything specific, but he added that Cox had expressed his approval of the plan after the meeting ended as the two Klansmen drove home together. Furthermore, he insisted that it was Cox who had advised him to lend the pistol to Knowles after Knowles, who was also under age and didn't have one of his own, had asked to borrow it.

As we retraced the investigations conducted by the FBI and the Mobile District Attorney's office, we gathered other compelling evidence about this key meeting. Several witnesses reported that a Klan member named Thaddeus ("Red") Betancourt, the keeper of a scrapbook of newspaper clippings deemed of interest to the klavern, had read aloud a clipping about the Anderson trial and that it was this act that had set off a round of threats and calls for vengeance. Still another witness attributed to the klavern's acting klaliff (vice-president), Bill O'Connor, the remark that "we ought to hang a nigger."

No one flatly came out during these interviews and said that Bennie Hays had asked for volunteers to carry out the killing or, for that matter, that Henry Hays and Tiger Knowles had openly agreed to do it. The testimony consisted mostly of finger pointing and grudging admissions. Nebulous and conflicting though the various accounts were, however, there was no question in our minds that that night there had been no idle discussion about a retaliatory murder but rather something that rose to the level of a conspiracy under the federal civil rights laws.

With high hopes we looked forward to the depositions of Bennie and Henry Hays and Tiger Knowles to provide us a clearer picture of the plot. Although the Hayses continued to maintain their innocence, Dees believed he might be able to flip one or both of them. The elder Hays was facing serious legal problems of his own: He and his wife, Opal, had been indicted on federal charges of defrauding an insurance company in connection with the June 1983 arson of their home and were awaiting trial. The fire, which destroyed the house just days after Henry's arrest, had been traced back to the old man, who had been accused of having it set to collect insurance money for Henry's attorney's fees. Dees thought he could use the couple's troubles to convince Hays to make a clean breast of his role in the crime, if only for the sake of his family.

As for Henry Hays, Dees had a slightly different approach in mind. Believing that the younger Hays had committed the murder, in part, at least, to try to please his authoritarian father, the patriarch of the southern Alabama Klan, Dees thought he could tap the resentment Henry might be harboring and get him to implicate the elder Hays.

Neither of the ploys worked, though. Bennie Hays irascibly clung to his defense that he and his son were the victims of a massive frame-up. Henry, meanwhile, refused even to state his name for the record when we attempted to take his deposition.

Knowles was a little more helpful but essentially repeated the testimony he had given at Hays's trial in December 1983. This was especially disappointing. Dees believed Knowles had been trying to protect some of his fellow Klansmen on that occasion—out of sympathy or fear—and he had been confident he could prevail upon the Kluxer to divulge the rest of the story.

Knowles had testified at the trial, for example, that Cox provided the rope with which Donald was hanged without necessarily knowing how it was to be used, despite the fact that Knowles had tied the hangman's knot in Cox's presence. He also had been vague about Bennie Hays's role in the conspiracy. He had, for example, failed to give a detailed explanation of how the murder plot had originated in the first place and had not even mentioned the discussion at the klavern meeting. These were matters we had fervently hoped to learn more about during his deposition but had not. Whether Knowles was blocking or was simply unable to recall, as he claimed, he did not add much to our knowledge of the conspiracy.

Because Knowles was the last major witness on our list to interview regarding the murder plot, we found ourselves at the end of the first phase of discovery with something less than the case we had hoped to put together. Although the evidence we had against Bennie Hays and Cox was fairly compelling, our case against the other conspirators was not nearly as strong.

Under civil law, however, the jury would have to find in our favor only by what was called a preponderance of the evidence. That meant that the jurors were merely required to conclude that the evidence demonstrated that our allegations were more likely true than not true—a substantially different standard from the one that governed criminal law, in which jurors had to be convinced beyond a reasonable doubt. The situation we found ourselves in underscored the value of the civil lawsuit as a weapon in these kinds of cases.

In the matter of proving the link between the corporate UKA and Unit 900, the second of our discovery objectives, we got help from the unlikeliest of quarters: Bennie Hays himself. Not long after the suit was filed, the sixty-seven-year-old Klansman had made an overture to Dees about cooperating with us in return for some unspecified quid pro quo.

He had sent us as a sign of good faith the original charter of Unit 900, the official document by which the national office granted authority to the local units to conduct business in the name of the organization. Tattered and frayed, printed in old English script, the sixteen-by-twenty-four-inch document would be a superb addition to our burgeoning collection of Klan artifacts. But it was of more than just archival significance. Signed by Shelton, it bore the UKA's official seal, and it came to be the first link in the evidentiary chain connecting the Mobile klavern to the corporate organization. Accompanying the charter was an invitation from Hays to visit him and discuss how we could help each other.

Within a day or two Dees and I headed off to Theodore, the town of approximately a thousand people in which Bennie Hays lived, some fifteen miles southwest of Mobile. We had no trouble locating the Hayses' residence; the twenty-five-foot-high iron cross that stood in front of it was hard to miss. The cross was not simply decorative; from time to time Unit 900 had staged recruitment rallies in the pasture adjacent to the road that ran in front of the house, and on those occasions it would be wrapped in kerosene-soaked burlap sacks and set on fire.

At the crest of a knoll fifty or seventy-five yards back from the county road stood the charred remains of the Hays house. Since the arson, which Hays had publicly blamed on anti-Klan radicals, the Hayses had lived in a mobile home located just off to the side of the burned-out structure. As Dees and I drove up the gravel driveway toward the trailer, we noticed a dilapidated wooden shed off to the left. This, we surmised, was the former headquarters building of Unit 900—former, because the heat surrounding the successful criminal probe in 1983 had led to the klavern's dissolution.

Hays met us at the door. He was a slightly stooped old man, with a bit of an oval-shaped face and thick black-rimmed glasses. Greeting us politely, he motioned us inside toward the den, where his wife was seated. Mrs. Hays, her mouth set in a grim half-smile, seemed very self-conscious and none too happy.

Hays began by thanking us for taking the time to meet with him and reiterated his desire to be of help to us. He spoke slowly and emphatically, with a distinctive, whiny drawl. Our hopes soared briefly when he revealed how he had renounced his Klan membership and had come to see the error of his ways, but as he talked on, we realized that his separation from the Klan was the result of a falling-out, not a change of heart, and that he did not intend to incriminate himself in the Donald murder. His gripe, it seemed, was primarily with Shelton. As Hays recalled it, Shelton had promised to stand by the Hays family through the legal proceedings and to help with the expenses of hiring a lawyer for Henry. Help had not been forthcoming, and now Hays had nothing complimentary to say about his former leader.

In between imprecations, he pulled out a file of Klan documents and set them on the table, inviting us to browse through them. These were among the items that had survived the fire, he said, pointing out a copy of the Klan constitution, as well as issues of the *Fiery Cross* (the UKA newsletter), a manual for new members, and miscellaneous other UKA publications. The documents were, in effect, his bargaining chips.

What he wanted in exchange for them was something we weren't prepared to give, however: dismissal from the suit and legal assistance for his son. It was now apparent that he was willing to sell out the UKA but nothing more; he had never intended to confess his role in the conspiracy. To the contrary, he adamantly maintained his, and Henry's, innocence, alternately blaming the family's predicament on Tiger Knowles or a Communist conspiracy.

Once it became clear what his terms were, the meeting concluded fairly quickly—but not before Dees made a perfunctory pitch to borrow the file, with the stipulation that we would copy it and return it to Hays the next day. But Hays didn't fall for it.

Still, within a few weeks we got our hands on the file for good. By then both Hayses had been convicted of the fraud charge. With Bennie Hays behind bars, Dees promptly subpoenaed Mrs. Hays (who had been put on probation) for a deposition, specifying in the summons that she was to bring the contents of the file with her. He warned her that if she failed to do so she would go to prison for contempt.

As we had hoped, it proved to be an evidentiary and informational bonanza. There were membership applications, flyers, financial reporting forms that each klavern filed monthly with the national office, newspaper clippings, and a raft of other items. One of the most curious was a professionally printed bookmark-shaped card with instructions for Klansmen on how to brush off inquisitive FBI agents. Another was a 1981 issue of the *Fiery Cross* that had a large front-page spread on the founding of Klanwatch. But perhaps the most unusual was a commemorative program published by the UKA on the occasion of its twentieth anniversary celebration, which had been held at the group's Tuscaloosa national headquarters building over the Labor Day weekend in 1981, some six months after Michael Donald had been murdered. Professionally printed and produced, with a color cover, it resembled in both form and content the kind of promotional literature a mainstream corporation would have prepared for a similar occasion. It was full of pictures showing the chief executive officer, Robert Shelton, hard at work in his office (including a classic, hands-on shot of him wearing his specs and seated at his desk, in shirtsleeves and tie, talking on the telephone); photographs of the organization's fancy new headquarters building, inside and out; a gilded history of the organization; even an open letter from Shelton to the membership. Curiously, it was Henry Hays's personal copy, and like a baseball program it was filled with autographs he had collected from all his favorite KKK leaders.

From the standpoint of evidence, the most important single document in the file was something called the *Kloran/Klan in Action/ Constitution* (*Kloran* for short), a multipurpose handbook containing the constitution and bylaws of the group, a section on liturgy, and another on klavern functioning and structure. Sixty-six pages long, the *Kloran* spelled out in surprisingly well-written and occasionally even lofty prose the nature of the organizational and individual relationships within the UKA. It portrayed the group as a tightly knit, cohesive unit with a military-style chain of command. This, of course, dovetailed neatly with the corporate accountability theory that was at the heart of our case.

Its evidentiary value aside, the *Kloran* made for fascinating reading, for what it both said and didn't say. Nowhere in it, for instance, did the word *nigger* appear, or any other slur for that matter, and the number of references of any sort to race were so few they might have been counted on both hands. There was a glossary of Klan terms and an explanation of the Klan calendar. There was a list of "major offenses" that constituted sufficient cause for banishment from the organization—among them treason against the United States, "disrespect of virtuous womanhood," and miscegenation.* Fully two-thirds of the manual was devoted to discussion of the structure and functioning of the local klavern and to the publication of frequently used rituals.

The UKA was a highly ritualized Klan, steeped in the tradition of the early KKK of passwords and countersigns, symbolism and ceremony. As with other societies, this emphasis on the ceremonial apparently served several purposes: to entertain, to foster unity, and to promote a self-image of a public-spirited, patriotic, Christian group. The opening ceremony of the weekly klavern meeting provided a good example of these purposes at work. It revolved around the "preparation" of a "sacred altar"—a table upon which rested a vessel of holy water, an open Bible, an American flag, and a sword. The altar was "prepared" by the main officers of the klavern, in what was the equivalent of a kind of presentation of the colors, and was accompanied by prayer and the singing of patriotic songs.

A casual reading of the book would have almost left the impression that the United Klans was a civic group, like the Rotary Club or the Jaycees; its motto was *Non Silba Sed Anthar,* or "Not for self but for others." Under the subheading "Organizations of Local Klans," there was the Welfare Committee, whose responsibilities included administering the Klan charity fund; the Religious Activities Committee; the Vocational-Trades-Labor Committee, set up to

---

* In the course of our various investigations into the Klan we ran across several KKK members who admitted having had sexual relations with nonwhites, suggesting that it was not that rare an occurrence. One of the female members of the Decatur Klan who participated in the May 26 conspiracy later dropped out of the group and subsequently took up housekeeping with a black man.

"promote vocational Klannishness among all Klansmen"—i.e., to encourage Klansmen to trade and do business with other Klan members—the Sick Committee, whose members were to visit the sick (both Klan members and non-Klansmen) on behalf of the klavern; the Athletic Committee; the Entertainment Committee (" 'All work and no play' is not only dull—it is unhealthy"); the Educational Committee ("One of our glories is that the Klan from year to year, and almost from day to day, envisions wider horizons and nobler purposes"); and the Civic Committee. The darker side of the Klan was only hinted at by the inclusion of the Military Committee and the Intelligence Committee, the "eyes and ears of the Klan Army."

The acquisition of the charter and the *Kloran* was a big boost to our case, helping us verify through the UKA's own official documents the ties that bound the corporation to its chapters, and this second phase of the case began to come together nicely. Link by link, we thus forged a chain between the national organization and Unit 900.

Just when everything seemed to be going our way, however, we collided head-on with a procedural obstacle erected by the Klan, a barrier known in legal parlance as a corporate veil. It happened during the early part of 1985, as we were preparing for Robert Shelton's deposition. One day, while doing a records search to identify the UKA's assets, a title researcher we had employed discovered that the handsome new seventy-two-hundred-square-foot Butler building in rural Tuscaloosa County that served as the United Klans' national headquarters and that we had come to believe was the organization's chief asset did not technically belong to the United Klans at all. It was owned instead by a legally distinct corporation, also headed by Shelton, called the Anglo-Saxon Club.

Although the Anglo-Saxon Club was foreign to us, its name and Shelton's position with the group suggested that it was little more than a front for the Klan, a corporate veil behind which to hide the UKA's assets. Both the national UKA and many of the local chapters were known to use front names and d/b/a's in conducting their public business, and we concluded that Anglo-Saxon was another of these.*

The ramifications of the ownership question for our lawsuit were extremely serious. Unless we were able to pierce this corporate veil and demonstrate that the UKA and the Anglo-Saxon Club were one and the same, we would be unable to seize the building to satisfy any judgment we might win against the corporate Klan at trial. In other words, the UKA organization would have effectively rendered itself judgment-proof, and the primary objective of the lawsuit—to hold the corporate Klan accountable for the wrongdoing of its members—would have been thwarted. Suddenly, unexpectedly, we had a crisis on our hands, and for the next several weeks we dropped everything else and threw all our investigative time and resources into learning more about this club and its relationship with the UKA.

Our initial findings were not encouraging. According to the club's incorporation papers, the group had been organized in 1958, more than two years before the UKA was even founded, a fact that, of course, cast serious doubt on Anglo's ability to have been established as a front group for it. Furthermore, Shelton had not even been among its original officeholders or incorporators, suggesting that he may have had less influence in the establishment of the group than we had assumed. On top of that, nowhere in the document was there the slightest reference or allusion to the Klan. From these and other facts it became clear that the Anglo-Saxon Club was considerably more sophisticated than the typical Klan front and that the job of piercing the corporate veil would be more formidable than we had at first anticipated.

Dees was soon at work devising a multipronged investigative attack. He subpoenaed the UKA's bank records (which were filed under yet another d/b/a, the Alabama Rescue Service), assigned me to track down and interview as many of Anglo's incorporators as possible, and then turned his attention to learning more about

* The use of a d/b/a—short for "doing business as"—was a perfectly legal practice borrowed from the business world. UKA klaverns employed d/b/a's more than any other Klan group. Among the more interesting front names we came across were the McCalla (Alabama) Young Men's Social Club, the True Blue Gun Club of Nicholasville, Kentucky, and the Grafton Fellowship Club in Newport News, Virginia. Among women's auxiliary units, the most distinctively named was the Wayne County Sewing Circle in Goldsboro, North Carolina.

Shelton's pre-UKA Klan activities. As a student during the 1950s at the University of Alabama (which was also located in Tuscaloosa) Dees had become aware of Shelton, who was then the fiery Alabama grand dragon of a Georgia-based KKK faction called the U.S. Klans, led by a man named Eldon Edwards. Knowing what he did about the founding of the Anglo-Saxon Club, Dees now began to suspect that the club might have served initially as a front group for Edwards's Klan.

In light of the Anglo-Saxon controversy, Shelton's deposition loomed even larger in importance than it had originally. On April 15, the date on which it was scheduled, Dees and I left Montgomery about midmorning to drive to Tuscaloosa, armed—as we always were those days—with the pistols and bulletproof vests that had become standard equipment for us, like briefcases and tape re- corders.

Shelton was now a grim-faced, dour man of fifty-six. The crew cut of the hawk-faced young Klan leader of the sixties had given way to a longer, contemporary look; the open-necked, short-sleeve shirts, to a three-piece suit. Those concessions to the times aside, Shelton seemed worlds apart from Wilkinson and the other leaders of the "new" Klan: cold; aloof; humorless; seemingly oblivious of his im- age. Rumor was that he hadn't been the same since the sudden death of his college-age daughter in the late 1970s from a sudden illness. Shelton rarely attended Klan rallies anymore; some ques- tioned whether the fire was still there.

Once the deposition began, however, he proved to be anything but a pliant witness, responding with terse, elusive answers to Dees's inquiries, volunteering virtually nothing, and forcing Dees to frame his questions with surgical precision. Less than five minutes into the examination, Shelton brought the deposition to a halt when he refused to respond to a question he considered invasive, and before his attorney had a chance, he had cited the constitutional bases for doing so.

When Dees brought up the matter of the Anglo-Saxon Club, Shelton grew contentious. He denied that it was a Klan front or had anything to do with the Klan, asserting that it was merely a social club formed by his parents and some other Tuscaloosa citizens. But as Dees persisted, an array of additional facts began to emerge, and with it an altogether different picture of the group. Not only did it turn out that Shelton was the president of Anglo-Saxon, but the club's secretary-treasurer, Lewis Perkins, was none other than the national secretary-treasurer of the UKA. The only other club officials were their wives.

Shelton tried to repair the damage done by these revelations by suggesting that some of the offices had been left vacant by death and simply had yet to be filled, only to have Dees elicit the fact that the group hadn't held a business meeting in almost ten years. When Dees inquired about the existence of any minutes of meetings or other corporate records, Shelton, now on the defensive, came back with an answer that ultimately led to the unraveling of the whole ownership question. In an effort to demonstrate that Anglo-Saxon had held meetings and conducted business and was a legitimate enterprise, he cited the existence of minutes of a meeting the club had held during the middle 1970s to ratify the sale of a piece of property it had then owned on the south side of Tuscaloosa.

It was the first we had heard of any additional assets the club might have had. Dees abandoned his scripted questions to pursue the lead. Where was this property? Who had bought it? How long ago had it been sold? What was the purchase price? Were the proceeds deposited in a bank? Which bank? Were the funds expended? The barrage of questions went on for several pages.

When the session was over, we had the elements of a solid circumstantial case that the Anglo-Saxon Club had indeed operated as a front group for the UKA for the purpose of hiding the Klan's financial assets.

As Dees had suspected, the relationship between Anglo-Saxon and the United Klans predated the construction of the new headquarters building in the late 1970s. In fact, it went all the way back to 1961, when Shelton emerged as the imperial wizard of the newly formed UKA and relocated it from its birthplace in Georgia to Tuscaloosa, his home. From that time until 1977, when the sale to which Shelton had referred in his testimony took place, the UKA had had free use of the Anglo-Saxon group's ostensible "clubhouse," a modest concrete-block structure built on 4.2 acres of land the club had purchased in 1958. And prior to 1962, according to

Shelton's own testimony, his Alabama Knights of the Ku Klux Klan had occasionally met there.*

Against this backdrop it was obvious that the sweetheart deal the UKA now had with Anglo-Saxon was only a continuation of a prior arrangement. In exchange for essentially unrestricted, rent-free use of the headquarters building, the UKA had only to pay the utilities and property taxes and perform necessary maintenance, as per an agreement made between Shelton as president of Anglo-Saxon and Shelton as president of the UKA.

There was still more evidence: the fact that the Alabama realm of the UKA used the new headquarters building for its monthly state-wide gatherings and the national organization for its annual Labor Day weekend "klonvocation"; the fact that the Anglo-Saxon Club had never held a single meeting there; the fact that the only sign identifying the building was one standing at the entrance to the grounds and bearing the words *United Klans of America*; the fact that the *Fiery Cross* and other UKA publications touted it as the organization's headquarters, without so much as a single reference to Anglo-Saxon.

The smoking gun, however, turned up in the Anglo-Saxon Club's own corporate records—records that Shelton had testified he had been unable to put his hands on but that Dees, on a hunch, located several days later at a Tuscaloosa bank. The clinching piece of evidence was a 1958 letter to Anglo-Saxon's attorney from one of the club's charter members, a Tuscaloosa CPA who also happened to be a member of the Klan. The letter writer strongly insinuated that the Anglo-Saxon Club had been incorporated primarily for the purpose of owning real estate. Furthermore, he indicated that the organization's membership was confined to members of the Syca-more Club, the front name for one of the chapters of the Tuscaloosa Klan.

This letter and the three corporate resolutions in the file—all dealing with real estate transactions—made it apparent that the primary business Anglo conducted was buying and selling land for the KKK.

We believed that together with the other facts we had gathered,

---

* Shelton's testimony was unequivocal on this point, although within minutes of so testifying he denied that that was what he had said. The Alabama Knights were formed by Shelton in 1958, after he had quit or was expelled from Eldon Edwards's U.S. Klans.

this was ample evidence to prove that Anglo-Saxon was a front for the UKA. With immense relief and a sense that we had dodged a disaster, we went back to work on the central issues of the case.

The history of the civil rights era was littered with the victims of UKA violence, and it appeared at first that to fulfill our remaining evidentiary objective, proving that violence constituted a corporate policy of the United Klans, we might be obliged to do little more than obtain certified court records of those Klansmen who had been tried and convicted of the crimes (the few who had been taken to court). But as Dees took a closer look at federal court rulings applicable to the Donald case, he realized that more would be required than simply compiling a laundry list of UKA atrocities. To prove to the satisfaction of the courts that violence was officially sanctioned by the UKA, it would be necessary to demonstrate that the Klan corporation or its top officers had promoted or instigated it.

Lacking documentary proof, evidence of this sort could come only from the testimony of a former Klansman, someone who had traveled in the highest circles of Klan leadership and—this was a big "and"—was willing to testify to what he knew.

The only person we knew of who fitted this profile was a former Birmingham UKA member named Gary Thomas Rowe, the same Tommy Rowe whose testimony had helped convict two United Klansmen in the murder of Viola Liuzzo. Rowe, an FBI informant deep inside the UKA during the 1960s, had actually been in the car from which the fatal bullets were fired, and the information he provided had led to the quick arrests of the killers. After coming out from undercover to finger his former colleagues, he was placed in the Federal Witness Protection Program, given a new identity, and relocated to another state. We had no idea where he was then living or what his new name was.

As was often the case, however, Dees just happened to know someone who had the information we needed, in this instance a Montgomery lawyer friend who had once represented Rowe in a legal matter. The friend obliged by relaying a message to Rowe, who called Dees. Though initially reluctant, Rowe finally agreed to come to Montgomery to give a deposition.

In the meantime, I flew to New York on a hunch that the Anti-Defamation League, having monitored KKK activity several decades longer than we had, might have some documentary evidence that would illustrate the corporate UKA's racial animus: newsletters, flyers, or other publications. When it came to the United Klans, our files were thin.

The trip proved well worth it. On my second day in the ADL files I found precisely the kind of information we were looking for, yet even I was taken aback by its content. It was a ghastly, macabre two-panel drawing in the *Fiery Cross* depicting the lynching of a black man. The first panel, which was located at the bottom of a right-hand page, consisted of a drawing of a white man addressing the reader, accompanied by the caption "IT'S TERRIBLE THE WAY BLACKS ARE BEING TREATED! ALL WHITES SHOULD WORK TO GIVE THE BLACKS WHAT THEY DESERVE!" An arrow instructed the reader to turn to the next page, on which appeared the picture of the black man, his neck obviously broken, his body dangling grotesquely from a rope tied in a hangman's noose. It was a repulsive piece of Klan journalism, and it amounted to nothing less than incitement to murder. The fact that it appeared in a 1979 issue of the newsletter made it likely that Hays and Knowles had seen it; at any rate, its proximity in time to the killing of Michael Donald would give it weight as evidence. When I later described the drawing to Dees, he was as amazed as I had been. Over the years we had seen plenty of vile Klan literature, full of epithets and slurs, but this sketch was the single most graphic call to violence we had ever encountered.

During the last weekend of April 1985 we flew Rowe into town for his deposition, expecting it to produce some compelling evidence of the UKA's corporate liability. Rowe had already confirmed in his phone conversation with Dees that Robert Shelton had been personally involved in the planning of the attack on the Freedom Riders in Birmingham, and he had suggested that other high-ranking members of the UKA were also engaged in the conspiracy. Tantalized at the possibilities Rowe's testimony held, we could hardly wait to get him under oath and begin.

Tommy Rowe was a short, stocky man with close-cropped hair and a ruddy complexion; he looked nothing at all like the tall, trim former pro football player (nicknamed Dandy Don) who had portrayed him several years earlier in a made-for-television movie about his experiences. Though talkative, he was not open, nor was he particularly warm.

What he *was* was extremely controversial, reviled by the Klan and by civil rights activists alike, who blamed him for not preventing the Liuzzo murder. The Liuzzo children had named him as a defendant in an unsuccessful suit they had brought against the FBI in connection with their mother's death more than a decade after the slaying. During the late 1970s the district attorney of Lowndes County, where the slaying had occurred, had filed murder charges against him (eventually dismissed) on the strength of accusations made by two of the Klan members originally convicted in the killing, who claimed Rowe had actually been the triggerman. The years since Rowe's exposure as an FBI informant had seemingly brought him as much condemnation as acclaim.

The deposition was scheduled for 10:00 A.M. on April 27, but by 9:45 no one had yet made an appearance for the Klan; 10:00 arrived, and there was still no sight of John Mays, the Klan's lawyer, or Shelton.

We had already had a hint that they might not show up. A few weeks earlier, when Dees had informed them during Shelton's deposition that we intended to take Rowe's testimony, Mays had disdainfully remarked that he didn't even want to be in the same room with Rowe, and Shelton had concurred. By coincidence, Mays, a high-ranking officer in the Alabama National Guard, was scheduled to be on a mission abroad that day but he had never sought a postponement of the deposition and apparently had not seen fit to send Shelton or a replacement to cross-examine Rowe. So when the clock struck 10:15, Dees decided to go ahead and begin without them.

Rowe's testimony could hardly have been more damaging if we had scripted it ourselves. He portrayed Shelton as an activist leader, keenly involved in the goings-on of the local klaverns, a leader who not only condoned violence but aggressively encouraged it, even to the point of personally directing the notorious attack on the Freedom Riders at the Birmingham bus station on Mother's Day, 1961.*

But while the Freedom Riders attack provided the most flagrant

* This incident, one of the most infamous of the civil rights era, involved the collusion of the Klan and the Birmingham police, who left the protesters unprotected for fifteen minutes after their bus arrived in order to give the Klansmen time to carry out the attack. Rowe, who had been present at a meeting between police and Klan higher-ups to work out the details of the conspiracy, testified that Shelton himself had been in attendance and that a police

illustration of Shelton's personal promotion of Klan violence, it was not the only one. According to Rowe, the imperial wizard had earlier urged some of his followers to "do something" about blacks organizing a sit-in movement to protest segregated conditions at Birmingham's lunch counters. A few days later a group of Klansmen, known in UKA circles as a missionary squad, jumped several demonstrators ("sinners") sitting in at the local Woolworth store and beat them.

Rowe also tied Shelton to the Liuzzo murder. While he was unable to testify that Shelton had actually ordered the killing, he asserted that the UKA leader had given his most trusted aides the green light to "do what you have got to do" about the volatile situation in Selma on the eve of the voting rights march.

With the first attempt to march to Montgomery having ended in tear gas and beatings at the hands of the Alabama state troopers and a Dallas County sheriff's posse, the leaders of the Selma movement had issued a call for nationwide support for another march two weeks later. Between the time of the aborted march, March 7, and the second attempt, on March 21, it became clear to many people—apparently including members of the UKA—that the demonstrations had the potential to become a pivotal event in the civil rights struggle. Within the Klan the march was the subject of a flurry of meetings all across central Alabama. Following the regular weekly meeting of Rowe's klavern, Shelton huddled with a handful of his closest aides (including his Alabama grand dragon, Robert Creel) to talk about the Selma situation. The rank-and-file Klansmen had already gone home, and the members of this informal inner circle had remained to discuss what action the Klan should take. At one point during the conversation, Rowe testified, Shelton remarked that "dammit, we had to go down there and get that shit taken care of, it was getting out of hand down there."

representative, Lieutenant Tom Cook, had assured the Klansmen that his officers would not interfere. "You have got time to beat them, kick them, burn them, kill them, I don't give a shit, we just don't care," Rowe recalled Cook as saying. "We don't ever want to see another nigger ride on the bus into Birmingham again." The incident left several of the protesters seriously injured and one of their number wheelchair-bound for life.

Rowe claimed that he had informed the FBI of the conspiracy after the meeting with Lieutenant Cook and was assured that the attack would never be allowed to happen. As events unfolded at the bus station, he was bewildered to see FBI agents standing and watching. He was later told that the Bureau had passed on his warning to state officials and was reminded that the FBI was an investigative, not a law enforcement, agency.

On several occasions in the days leading up to the second march, Rowe accompanied several high-ranking UKA members to Selma to "scout out" the areas where the demonstrators might spend their nights along the route since they would be at their most vulnerable after dark. But it was not until the final day of the march, he said, that he learned what had been decided upon, and even then, only in stages. The word had come down from Bob Creel, the grand dragon. On the morning of March 25, the day the marchers arrived in Montgomery, Creel had called Rowe and instructed him to rendezvous with a small group of Bessemer, Alabama, Klansmen who were headed for Montgomery. Creel declined to be more specific, but Rowe could tell something big was going on. "His exact words to me [were], 'Tommy, this is probably going to be one of the greatest days of Klan history, probably be one of the days you will always remember until the day you die, you will always remember today,'" Rowe recalled.

Rowe immediately called his FBI control, who phoned his superiors in Washington in turn; their instructions were for Rowe to go along.

At that point in the story, having gotten from Rowe all the evidence he possessed against Shelton and the corporate Klan, and with only the telling of the murder itself remaining, Dees let Rowe continue uninterrupted. Rowe was an effective witness, and Dees knew his description of the grim events surrounding the murder (events that called to mind the Donald case) would make a greater impact on the jury if told without the seams created by a question-and-answer format:

> Most of the morning we spent there, most of the day we spent in the Montgomery area. Later in the evening . . . Gene Thomas [with Collie LeRoy Wilkins and E. O. Eaton, the other UKA members in the car besides Rowe] says, "Hey, we need to take a ride, we've got to go some place." We all loaded back up in the vehicle. We ended up in Selma. We went in to a little cafe . . . and ordered a few beers.
>
> Gene Thomas excused himself from the table, went over and talked to a group of men and brought one of them back over, kind of a tall fellow, probably in his late 20s, early 30s. And he says, "Hey, gang, I want you to meet so and so." [The man] was the one they [had] arrested for attempted murder or murder of a priest. . . .
>
> [Later] when we started to leave, that same individual came back

and . . . slapped us each one on the shoulder and patted us on the
back and said, "Well, boys, I did my job, you guys go do yours." . . .
Gene Thomas turned around and said, "We fully intend to. It's going
to be a big day for us."

We all . . . got in the automobile and . . . started cruising the
streets—I wasn't sure what the hell was happening at that point. The
first place I recognized was a black church. There must have been 200
blacks and whites mingled standing out around this church. I recall
Gene Thomas saying, "Hey, Wilk, look brother, Wilk, look over there,
this is it." And he started rolling his window down, Gene Thomas
did. . . . And I looked around and I said, "Aw, shit."

About that time Wilkins says, "Hey, look, let's get them two son-of-
a-bitches right there." It was a very attractive-looking white woman
and kind of an older black guy, probably in his 30s. And the woman
wasn't no more than 19 or 20, in a pair of short shorts. Looked real
good. The black man had his arm around her waist and they was
standing there and Wilkins said, "That's it, let's take them."

. . . Gene started heading the car toward them and I said, "Holy
shit." Just off to the side was a military jeep with three MPs standing
by it, mounted with a .30-caliber machine gun on the back. I said
"Goddam, Wilk, look over there, let's get the shit out of here. They
have got fucking troops over there with goddam machine guns, fool,
let's get the hell out of here before we get in trouble."

He says, "Hey, this is your goddam day and my day, this is the
biggest day we will ever have, Tommy, don't you worry about it, today
is the day."

Gene said, "Well, he's right, look up." And you could see more
troops mingling in the crowd. So we aborted and I said, "Thank God
for that." I thought that was the end of that.

. . . We drove out of th[e] area. I recall seeing in front of me a big
high steel bridge. . . . We were sitting at a red light and a car pulled up
beside us, to my left. . . . I was in the back seat. To my left a car pulled
up and there was a big black man in the car. . . . And there was a—we
could tell it was a blond-headed white woman in the car with him
driving. And Eaton was the one, I believe Eaton was the one that said,
"Goddam, look over there." . . . And Wilkins said, "I'll be a son-of-a
bitch, look at that, let's take them."

At that point, the light changed. The car pulled in front of us in the
left lane and then turned and went across the bridge. . . . At the next
red light just before . . . going over the top of the bridge, they stopped
again and Gene Thomas said, "You guys get down in the back, get
down in the back." And Wilkins and I were sitting in the back, we

leaned over each other. Gene didn't want the people in the car to see all of us. . . .

I was trying to see what the hell was going on. I eased my eye up and I looked and this black man was looking directly over at the car. . . . He had a black furry-looking cap and a green sport coat and a white shirt and tie and they went across the bridge. At that point, Gene said, "You guys can get up; they are going across the bridge."

As we went across that bridge we got to speeds, hell, 80, 90 miles an hour easy and she kept getting faster. At that point, Gene says to Wilkins, "This is it, let's do it." Gene Thomas reached in this little compartment between the two seats . . . and he took out a pistol and handed it to Wilkins. He handed it right over in front of me. . . . Wilkins took the pistol. I said to myself, "Oh, shit." And Wilkins said, "Hey, baby brother [Rowe's Klan nickname], when we get that mother-fucker up there and get him stopped somewhere I'm going to get that sport coat for you." I will always remember that. He said, "It will just about fit you." . . .

So as we got faster and faster they got faster. At that point, Gene says, "Hey, they know we're back here." And the lady just hauled ass, I mean she put the gas to it. As we went across the bridge and some curves I remember seeing a Jet Drive-In Restaurant on my righthand side. I seen the brakes to the car just flash one time and I thought she was going to stop there. She didn't stop there, she in fact give it more gas. . . .

There were some highway patrolmen on the left over there, had a van stopped. We passed those highway patrolmen and those people in that van at about 80 miles an hour. And they couldn't help but see us, they couldn't help but see us, because we had already been stopped over in that area earlier in the evening by the troopers. And I said, "Oh, God, they have seen us," but they didn't come, nothing happened.

We kept pursuing them further and as we went around a curve the woman—she was just erratic. She began to drive fast and erratic and at that point I seen a sign that said [Craig] Air Force Base. . . . The lady started to turn the car in, you could just tell the way she swerved her car, and for some unknown reason she swerved it back out and stomped the gas and got up to 80, 90, 95 miles an hour. She passed that.

We went across a little concrete bridge shortly after that, not too far, and we began to gain on the car. And it was pitch black out behind us but . . . I remember seeing a pair of headlights and I said, "Hey, hey, Gene, there's somebody coming up behind us, probably the goddam troopers chasing us. Let's get the hell out of there, man, let's get the hell out of here."

And he said, "Here, Wilky, do it, I'm going to take them." At that point he accelerated. And when we passed the car Wilkins rolled the window down. We got pretty much even with the car and the lady just turned her head solid all the way around and looked at us . . . and her mouth flew open like she—in my heart I've always said she was saying, "Oh, God," or something like that, you could tell she was just startled.

At that point Wilkins fired a shot. The first shot hit the glass but it didn't appear to penetrate it. He fired three or four more shots. [I saw] what appeared to be blood running down the side of the lady's face. . . . [The] black man kind of fell over towards the dash of the car, over her shoulder, and slumped down toward like in her lap over the wheel. At that point she just fell right down toward the wheel. And the car veered—I thought the car was going to shoot off the road. It didn't. The car went straight as a board for 500 feet. It didn't turn, it didn't stop, it went down the road. I said, "Jesus goddam Christ, look at that, let's get out of here." And Gene Thomas said, "Goddam, I don't believe it." At that time the car just very casually—it just didn't curve abruptly—very casually ran off the road into some bushes.

Chapter Thirteen

MONTHS BEHIND schedule the SPLC moved into its sleek new glass-and-steel headquarters building during the final week of May 1985—almost two full years after the muggy July morning that had found us huddled against the dawn in front of the burned-out office on Hull Street. Perched on the side of a hill in the heart of downtown Montgomery, the new Law Center had a panoramic view of the business district and the state government complex and, a little farther to the north, the Alabama River, flowing languidly past the city toward Mobile. Stylishly modern, the building stood apart from the prevailing architectural tradition of downtown Montgomery, just as Dees had desired. Yet while it also imparted a sense of permanence and institution, a kind of visual affirmation that the SPLC would have to be reckoned with for many years to come, there was no disputing the fact that it was a flashy home for a public interest nonprofit law firm. Dees's detractors quickly dubbed it the Southern Affluence Law Center.

If the construction of the new headquarters building seemed to transform the image of the SPLC from a storefront law office to something more institutionalized and mainstream, it also had the effect of formalizing the patchwork security system that had been implemented, piece by piece, at 1001 South Hull, our old address. With the threats against Dees and the SPLC continuing unabated (on the eve of the move the Alabama Bureau of Investigation warned us that a Pennsylvania Klansman had vowed to level the building before we could occupy it), elaborate security measures were built into the structure, from closed-circuit television equipment to electronically operated magnetic door locks to a sophisticated motion detection system. Outside, an iron security fence was erected around the back of the property to keep unwanted visitors out of the staff parking lot, access to which was limited to passage through a remote-controlled gate. Adding to the fortress effect, a guard shack was installed for the benefit of the security personnel we still found it necessary to employ.

Even under ordinary circumstances, the new headquarters building would have caused a stir within the organization. There were some staff members who thought the corporate look, color-coordinated decor, and nine-hundred-thousand-dollar price tag excessive. The circumstances at the SPLC, however, were anything but normal just then. The enormous pressures generated by the security situation—Beam's visit to the office the previous fall, the death threats, the transformation of the SPLC from a walk-in office to a virtual armed compound, the intense glare of the media spotlight—all had taken their toll, exposing long-simmering tensions between Dees and the rest of the legal staff about the way the Center was run and its litigation priorities. The consensus among the staff was that the Klan cases, and the Klanwatch Project itself, were taking up more space on the SPLC's agenda than they warranted, draining resources that otherwise would have been spent on the SPLC's other civil litigation. The Project had never been very popular with the legal staff, and aside from assistance he received from former Legal Director John Carroll and Stephen Ellmann (both since departed), Dees had essentially carried the litigation ball by himself. The other attorneys generally did not perceive the KKK as a significant problem or thought it was not the SPLC's mission to combat it.

The physical act of moving seemed to bring the disaffection to a head. Dees and several members of the legal staff clashed openly about his intention to streamline the Center's caseload, a plan that included drastically paring down the SPLC's work in the field of death penalty defense, as well as a pullback on voting rights cases and other traditional civil rights litigation. Although Dees insisted that the program changes were merely the product of changes in the legal landscape, not retrenchment, some among the legal staff believed Dees's ultimate goal was to stop handling non-Klan cases altogether, since the Klan litigation had made the long-maligned Law Center more popular in and around Montgomery and had proved to be a potent fund-raising issue.

Behind the conflict at hand, however, the issue was one of control. As cofounder of the SPLC and its guiding force through the first decade and a half of its existence, Dees had an almost paternalistic concern for its welfare and for assuring its future. While staff attorneys might come and go, he reasoned, he would always be there, and by virtue of his special relationship with the organization he believed he was uniquely qualified to recognize what was best for it in the long run. Part of the problem was, the authority that flowed from Dees's special relationship with the SPLC was not reflected in a formal title (his only official post, that of chief trial counsel, was primarily for public identification purposes), and the fact that he lacked clearly delineated executive powers fueled his colleagues' resentment of his actions. He remedied the problem by asking the Center's board of directors to invest him with the title of Executive Director.

Within eighteen months of the move into the new headquarters, the Center's entire legal staff of four attorneys (excluding Dees) had resigned. Joining them in leaving was Randall Williams.* The departure of the five bright young staffers concluded a brief, tumultuous chapter—and a sad one—in the history of the Center.

By the time the episode was over the summer of 1986 had rolled around, and there was still no resolution to either the Decatur criminal case or the civil one. The on-again, off-again criminal prosecution was on again—after a fashion. Although the Court of Appeals for the Eleventh Circuit had reversed Judge Acker's deci-

---

* At the time Williams was no longer the Klanwatch Director, having resigned the post and made a lateral move within the SPLC to head the organization's new Education Division. I had been appointed director of the Project in his place.

sion to throw out the evidence we had turned over to the feds, Acker had gotten the case back, only to hold new hearings and "find" new evidence of "collusion." He had subsequently tossed the evidence out again and ordered the Justice Department attorneys to prepare to try each of the defendants separately—meaning nine different trials. The only good news was that Derane Godfrey, the van painter, had pleaded guilty to a felony conspiracy charge. In the closing months of 1986 and early 1987, however, Acker wreaked further havoc on the case, dismissing the charge against David Kelso because the government refused to try him without being given the chance to appeal one of the judge's pretrial rulings and overturning a jury verdict of guilty against Ricky Lynn Creekmore, the first of the ten defendants actually to go to trial. It looked as if justice would never be done. With each additional ruling and each passing month, the prospects for achieving justice in the criminal case appeared bleaker and bleaker, summoning to mind images of the sixties, when Klansmen attacked civil rights activists with impunity. Only back then the federal judicial system had played an important role as a court of last resort. As for the lawsuit, it was awaiting the outcome of the criminal case.

One evening in the midst of all this, I was relaxing at home when the phone rang.

"Bill, this is Pete Taylor," a mellifluous bass voice drawled from the other end of the line. Taylor was a captain in the intelligence division of the Alabama Bureau of Investigation. He had never called at home before. "Garry is dead." Garry was Garry Nungester, our longtime source and, as it happened, Taylor's cousin.

In the split second before Taylor went on, I wondered whether the Klan had found Nungester out, whether he had been murdered. He had long been suspected in some corners of the white supremacist movement of being an informant. In 1983 his film had been confiscated, and he had been tossed out of the annual World Aryan Congress at Aryan Nations headquarters in Idaho when Bill Riccio, the radical young Alabama Klansman, accused him of being a spy. In recent years, as he came into contact with more and more radical elements, his concern about his safety had grown to the point where he had reluctantly begun packing a gun.

Taylor, however, said that there were no signs of foul play. It appeared that Garry had died of natural causes, in all likelihood from heart failure. Still, at the request of the family, Taylor was going to Decatur the next day to talk with the investigators, and he invited me to make the trip with him.

There was a cruel irony about Nungester's death. Four days earlier he had shown up at the SPLC, his files loaded in his car, to announce that he was quitting undercover work. What had begun as an exercise in civic responsibility in reaction to the coming of the Klan to his hometown (and to the fact that his father had been a POW in Nazi Germany) had burgeoned into an all-consuming preoccupation. It had taken a toll on his marriage, his life-style, and (he noted presciently) his health. He wanted out. Depositing the files in my office, he had departed, saying he would phone in a few days. Now, these few days later, his cousin and I were on our way to Decatur to satisfy ourselves that his death was not a homicide. (Indeed, the results of the autopsy pointed to death by natural causes.)

A strange thing happened on the night before the funeral. As a colleague and friend of Nungester's I had been asked by his wife to serve as a pallbearer and had gone up to Decatur ahead of time to pay my condolences to his parents. I wished to tell them how valuable his contribution had been to our work—in the Robinson case, the Decatur suit, the arson investigation—and how the information he had provided us about the threats against Dees, coming as it had before the warnings from the FBI, had possibly saved Dees's life.

My girlfriend and I had been at their home less than a half hour when the doorbell rang. Garry's father went to answer it, and when he opened the door, there stood Don Black, the grand wizard of the Knights of the Ku Klux Klan, dressed in his familiar three-piece suit and looking like a successful young executive. Dr. Nungester seemed to recognize his name, invited him in, and introduced him to the circle of family and friends gathered in the living room. Suddenly it was very quiet.

When it was my turn, Black and I shook hands and looked briefly into each other's eyes. I knew he knew who I was, if only by name, but he never expressed surprise or in any way acknowledged that he did. Nor did I. He stayed for only a few minutes, expressed his regrets, then left as cordially as he had come.

*   *   *

A few months after Nungester's death, on February 9, 1987, the Michael Donald lawsuit, potentially the most important Klan case we had undertaken, went to trial in Mobile. The setting was a wood-paneled, high-ceilinged courtroom in the United States Courthouse for the Southern District of Alabama, an imposing gray edifice located in the downtown section of the city.

For the first time since her son's murder, Mrs. Donald attended court to confront the members of Unit 900 face-to-face. Her silent, dignified presence at the counsel table infused the proceeding with a moral tone quite unlike that of any of our previous trials, and even though she did not testify—she spent much of the trial gently rocking back and forth in her chair, listening to the gruesome testimony with her eyes closed—she was the central figure in the courtroom.

Seated about ten feet away from her, at the adjacent counsel table, were Robert Shelton, the imperial wizard, and most of the individual Klan defendants, plus the Klan's lawyer, John Mays. Henry Hays, who had never even responded to the complaint and thus had technically defaulted, remained on death row; his accomplice, Tiger Knowles, sat apart from the other defendants, next to the wall opposite the jury box, with his U.S. marshal bodyguards.

The defendants were a motley group: Bennie Hays, the stooped, white-haired patriarch of Unit 900; Red Betancourt, the husky, ruddy-complected keeper of the Klan scrapbook whose reading of a newspaper clipping drew the klavern's attention to the Josephus Anderson murder trial; Frank Cox, Henry Hays's baby-faced brother-in-law, the supplier of the rope and, indirectly, the pistol; William O'Connor, an overweight, balding shipyard worker whose remark that "a nigger ought to be hung" if Anderson was acquitted had fueled the conspiracy; and Teddy Kyzar, the chubby little social outcast who admitted attending the meeting where the retaliation murder was discussed. Seated around the counsel table, most dressed in street clothes, one or two in coat and tie, they looked more pathetic than threatening.

By contrast, Shelton appeared almost urbane in his light gray business suit, color-coordinated tie, and wire-rimmed glasses. Though he shared the counsel table with his former followers (according to courtroom custom), he wanted no part of them now. The strategy of the corporate Klan was to dissociate itself from the Mobile klavern. Thus it was that the thirty-nine-year-old Mays, the longtime counsel for the UKA, came to represent the corporation alone and none of the individual defendants.*

Opening arguments provided a glimpse into Mays's strategy. In a two-minute statement, he deplored the killing of Michael Donald as a "disgusting, horrible" crime that offended the sensibilities of Klan officials, and he pleaded ignorance, on behalf of the corporation, of any aspect of the conspiracy that led to it.

"I don't know what sort of evidence you're going to hear about who did what, who covered up what, who threatened who, who obtained what, who thought it was humorous, who didn't," he told the jury. "I do know this: You will hear no evidence that Robert Shelton or any other national officer in the United Klans of America killed anybody, threatened anybody, [or] obtained anything that was involved in the atrocity that was committed."

Dees, keenly aware that the burden of proof rested squarely on our side of the aisle, addressed the all-white jury for the better part of a half hour, seizing the opportunity to present a detailed overview of our case. He knew to return a judgment against the national organization—our primary goal—the jurors had to understand not only the facts of the murder but the theory of corporate liability.

Beginning with the Anderson trial, Dees described how the highly unusual composition of the jury, eleven blacks and only one white, and the nature of the charges had grabbed Unit 900's attention and set the conspiracy in motion. Highlight by highlight, he went on to illustrate how the plot progressed from thought to fruition: the meeting between Tiger Knowles and the Hayses; the elder Hays's qualified support for the plan; the sanctioning of the plot by the other members of Unit 900 at the March 18 klavern meeting; the gathering at Henry Hays's house to await the Anderson verdict; the trip to Cox's mother's house to borrow the rope and to

* By their own choice, the individual defendants who were contesting the suit—everyone, in other words, except Henry Hays and Tiger Knowles—were all proceeding pro se; that is, they were representing themselves. For Mays's part, there was reason to believe that he was more than just an attorney for the UKA; he had been referred to on several occasions in UKA literature as the "imperial klonsel." According to the UKA constitution, the imperial klonsel is identified as an officer of (and therefore I assume a member of) the Klan organization. Both Mays and Shelton have denied that Mays was a member and have insisted the multiple references were the result of a printer's error.

Johnny Matt Jones's for the gun; finally, the murder itself and the subsequent cross burning on the lawn of the county courthouse. When Dees finished, he briefly explained how, under the agencylike theory we were using, the Klan itself could be held liable. The jury listened and stared back dispassionately, as juries often do.

Having completed the preliminaries, we called our first witness: Robert Shelton.

Dees's object in beginning with Shelton was to set the stage for the testimony about the Donald conspiracy, to establish that the members of Unit 900 had not been operating in a vacuum. Using the *Kloran*, Dees referred Shelton to the passages that detailed the links between the local units and the national organization and described the UKA's military command style. In addition, he had him validate the Unit 900 charter Bennie Hays had turned over to us and read an excerpt from an oath each Klansman was required to take, pledging the swearer to help preserve white supremacy.

Shelton proved to be an argumentative witness, accusing Dees of distorting the meaning of phrases like "fighting army of the Klan" and comparing the secrecy surrounding his group with that of the Masons and other fraternal organizations. He was plainly unintimidated by the interrogation. Dees refrained from cutting the imperial wizard off, however, for he was only too happy to let him voice his protestations. As the examination was coming to a close, Dees handed Shelton the copy of the *Fiery Cross* showing the drawing of the black man with the noose around his neck. He directed Shelton to read to the jury the words that accompanied it. "It's terrible the way blacks are being treated," Shelton read in an emotionless, matter-of-fact voice. "All whites should work to give the blacks what they deserve."

"What do you see on the other page?" Dees asked.

"It is a black with a rope on it . . ." Shelton replied, before immediately launching into an explanation. He protested vigorously that he had not known about the drawing prior to its publication, blaming its inclusion on a Klan official in Louisiana who oversaw the printing of the *Fiery Cross*. When the issue came out, Shelton said, he had called the official right away to express his "concern" and was told that it had been used as filler material. He was assured, he testified, that it would never happen again.

It was a plausible explanation, one that tended to lessen the exhibit's impact; Dees, concerned that there be no confusion among the jurors, struck back. He pulled out Shelton's deposition, the one we had taken two years earlier, and pointed out that the imperial wizard had given no such explanation when asked about the drawing at that time. Shelton had no response.

Then Dees showed Shelton the newspaper again and asked one final question. "Now, Mr. Shelton, this came out of the *Fiery Cross* dated 1979 and it says down here Robert Shelton, editor *and* publisher. Is that right?"

"Yes," Shelton conceded.

Satisfied that he had undercut the Klan leader's explanation, Dees returned to the counsel table. The UKA attorney, John Mays, then walked toward the witness stand and picked up the paper. Standing at Shelton's elbow, he leafed through it, asking the Klansman about the other contents of the issue. There was nothing else to approximate the tone or tenor of the drawing; in fact, the rest of the paper was devoted largely to stories on current politics and social issues, the kinds found in many a mainstream right-wing publication. Finally Mays asked Shelton if the sketch—Mays called it a cartoon—had appeared in any other issue of the *Fiery Cross*, before or since. Shelton replied that it had not.

Dees got in the final word, however. During redirect examination he asked Shelton if he had ever published a retraction. The answer was no; the damage was done.

Tactically the introduction of the lynching sketch into evidence at the start of the trial was a perfect lead-in to the testimony about the conspiracy to kill Michael Donald. Nothing could have exemplified the corporate Klan's espousal of violence as a policy more dramatically or convincingly.

So, immediately following Shelton, we came back with the testimony of one of our most compelling witnesses, Johnny Matt Jones, the epileptic young ex-Klansman who had been present at the March 18 klavern meeting. His deposition was read into the record since we had determined before the trial (in view of his fragile condition) not to force him to take the stand. The Federal Rules of Civil Procedure permitted this to be done when a witness lived more than a hundred miles from the courthouse, and given the fact that Jones lived in Texas, we decided to exercise this option available to us. Coming hard on the heels of Shelton's testimony, Jones's account of the March 18 meeting—at which, he said, Bennie Hays had promoted a retaliation murder in the event Josephus Anderson was set free—gave credence to the notion that high-ranking Klan officials like Hays were merely voicing a UKA policy when they advocated violence.

After putting Red Betancourt on the stand briefly to tell about reading the newspaper clipping, we called our other main witness on the conspiracy, Tiger Knowles. By then twenty-three years old, Knowles had undergone a complete transformation since we first saw him at Henry Hays's trial in 1983. A good twenty-five pounds lighter, he was no longer the burly young man he had been then. Besides the excess weight, gone were the long sideburns, and his hair, which had once been straight and greasy, now looked as if it had been permed.

Intent on establishing that the chain of command described in the *Kloran* had its parallel in real life, Dees began his examination of Knowles by questioning him about the lines of authority in the UKA. Knowles confirmed the group's essentially military character and indicated that his office, province klaliff, placed him directly below Bennie Hays, the titan, and above Frank Cox, the exalted cyclops. He noted, furthermore, that Hays was answerable directly to Shelton. Eventually Dees worked his way around to the conspiracy, specifically to the discussion Knowles had had with Henry and Bennie Hays a few days before the murder. Against the backdrop of the testimony about the UKA's tight organizational structure, Dees wanted to show the jury that the conspiracy was not a rogue operation but a project of the highest-ranking officials in the Mobile area, acting in the line and scope of their authority.

As Knowles's testimony continued, there was less and less room to doubt that it could have been anything else. When he explained the motive for hanging the body rather than secretly disposing of it— that it would "get the message across . . . that the Klan didn't want black people on juries"—it had to be clear to everyone in the courtroom how that related to the oath every UKA member took to preserve white supremacy. In the same way it became apparent that the randomness of the murder and the attempt to make it appear a lynching were intended to reap the greatest possible intimidation from the slaying.

A stillness settled over the courtroom as Knowles began testifying about the events surrounding the murder. The jurors, absorbed by the story, sat almost motionless, while around the defense table Knowles's former Klan colleagues stared intensely or took notes; even Judge Alex Howard seemed to lean forward at one point.

When Knowles reached the point about the conspirators gathering around Henry Hays's TV set to watch for word of the Anderson verdict, Dees paused and motioned to Danny Welch, one of our new investigators, to set up the video recorder. To make the testimony more vivid, we had decided to show the jury a videotape of the ten o'clock news from the night of the murder, hoping it would stimulate the jurors' imaginations to visualize what had happened at 117 Herndon Avenue that night.

The broadcast began with a reporter announcing the mistrial. There followed a short sequence showing Anderson, a tall, muscular black man dressed in a business suit and tie, walking out of the courtroom, declaring that he should have been found not guilty. Then came a brief interview with the prosecuting attorney, lamenting the fact that the state had no eyewitness who could identify Anderson as the killer. According to Knowles, the report had produced a hostile reaction among the Klansmen and their friends.

"All right," Dees went on. "Now would you tell the jury, what, if anything, you did after you saw the news conference [*sic*]?"

"Well, Henry Hays and myself went and got Henry's car," Knowles replied laconically. "We had the gun and the rope and we went out looking for a black person to hang."

Just as he had at Hays's murder trial, Knowles recounted the circumstances surrounding the murder without once betraying any emotion; it was difficult to tell whether he simply didn't feel any or whether he was suppressing it. He whipped through it so fast, in fact, that Dees had to slow him down. Dees was intent on putting every grisly detail in front of the jury. He prodded Knowles to describe the manner in which Henry Hays had taunted young Donald with allusions to the Atlanta child murders and how Donald had begged for his life. And in the wake of Knowles's terse description of the homicide itself, Dees obliged him to give a detailed account of the brutal assault that preceded it: how the two Klansmen had beaten young Donald senseless and slipped the noose around his neck, then beaten him some more when he stood up to defend himself; how Hays had placed his boot on Donald's face to cinch up the noose and had slit his throat three times with a razor knife to make sure he was dead. This was by far the most grueling part of the proceeding for Mrs. Donald. I heard a quiet sniffle from her direction, and when I glanced down the counsel table, I saw her, seated, her eyes closed, clutching a tissue. She was gently rocking in her chair from the waist up, doing her best to stay composed.

As far as the corporate Klan was concerned, however, the most damaging moment of Knowles's testimony was not his description of the murder. Rather, it occurred as Dees was bringing his examination to a close. Having approached the exhibit table, Dees picked up the copy of the *Fiery Cross* with the lynching sketch in it and handed the paper to Knowles. When he inquired if Knowles had seen it before, Knowles indicated he had.

"Now, when you saw this piece of information, how did you interpret that coming from Robert Shelton, editor-in-chief, as a Klan official?" Dees asked.

"That that's what blacks deserved, to be hung . . . and that that's what we should do, go out and hang people, black people," was Knowles's answer.

It was a devastating admission against the UKA organization, and later, when it was Mays's turn to cross-examine Knowles, he skipped over the former Klansman's other testimony entirely and immediately zeroed in on the sketch. Groping to neutralize its impact, he sought to build on the anomaly defense put forward by Shelton earlier, forcing Knowles to concede that he had never seen the drawing or anything resembling it in any other issue of the *Fiery Cross*. Fortunately, however, Dees had already proved that Shelton had done nothing to repudiate the publication of the sketch, blunting the impact of Mays's attack.

Still, Mays scored at least a couple of points in his cross-examination of the young Klansman. The first related to Shelton's personal conduct. Under persistent questioning, Knowles admitted that on the many occasions he had attended state and national meetings at the group's headquarters in Tuscaloosa he had never actually heard Shelton advocate violence, a fact that certainly militated in the organization's favor.

The Klan attorney also achieved some success in challenging our portrayal of the conspiracy as an official UKA activity. Focusing on the three-way meeting between the Hayses and Knowles at which the idea of the killing apparently was hatched, Mays sought to characterize it as a social gathering, not a Klan meeting. Pressing Knowles for details, he elicited the fact that the three were friends outside the Klan, that Knowles and the younger Hays often went out drinking together, and that the former was a "regular visitor" at the Hayses' house on occasions wholly unconnected to Klan activities. In addition, Mays forced Knowles to concede that the meeting had not even taken place in the klavern building, as was supposed to be the case whenever official Klan business was to be discussed. Overall, however, Knowles weathered Mays's brief cross-examination relatively well, emerging from it with his credibility still intact.

Since all the individual defendants were representing themselves in the case, they were each given an opportunity to take their turns at Knowles after Mays had finished. Accorded wide leeway by Judge Howard in the kinds of questions they could ask, they sometimes went far afield to discredit their former colleague, making for highly unusual courtroom theater and at times briefly turning the trial into a forum of allegations and countercharges. Bennie Hays went first, attacking Knowles in a rambling, disjointed way and at one point dredging up the matter of a twenty-dollar bounced check that Knowles had written him several years earlier. But none of the Klansmen scored many strikes in his attack on Knowles, and the exercise seemed more to confuse than to enlighten the jury. Thanks to a major miscalculation by Hays and some quick work at the plaintiffs' table, Knowles's credibility was, if anything, strengthened by the episode.

Hays, a wily old man, set out from the start of his cross-examination to cast Knowles as a liar. Figuring no one for the wiser, he challenged him about a statement Knowles had made during direct examination concerning the existence of a junior Klan. Knowles, in response to a question from Dees, had indicated he joined the UKA youth organization before eventually graduating to the adult group. Rising from his chair to begin questioning Knowles, Hays recalled the statement and, addressing his comments to the jury, stated flatly that there had never been such an entity. Then he turned to other areas of questioning. Before concluding, he returned to the subject and drove home the point once more: There was no junior Klan; there had never been one. After a final exchange with Knowles on the subject, he sat down.

As one of the other defendants began to pose his questions to Knowles, Dees and I conferred hurriedly at the counsel table. Both of us recalled seeing an article about the disputed organization in one of the issues of the *Fiery Cross*; in a matter of minutes I had located the publication.

After all the defendants had had a chance to examine Knowles, Judge Howard asked Dees if he wanted to take advantage of redirect examination to ask any additional questions. Eager to turn the tables on Hays, Dees walked over to the witness stand and handed Knowles the newspaper, directing him to read a headline on page one. Knowles read it very deliberately. "The Junior Order of the United Klans of America by Mr. Robert M. Shelton, Imperial Wizard," he said.

"O.K. Is this the group you first got in with?" Dees asked, seeking to milk the point for all it was worth.

"Yes, sir," Knowles replied, "it is."

Whatever damage had been inflicted against Knowles through the cross-examination was quickly repaired. Bennie Hays had gambled and lost. In doing so, however, he had undermined not only his own cause but that of the other defendants, including the corporate Klan. If the jury harbored any doubts about whether Knowles had testified truthfully concerning the lynching sketch and its influence on him, its doubts had now been laid to rest.

One by one we called the remaining defendants to the stand; happily for us, each one had something damaging to say about the others with regard to culpability in the conspiracy. Bill O'Connor, who, along with several of the other conspirators, had stood in front of 117 Herndon watching the police go about their investigation on the morning Donald's body was found, recalled Bennie Hays pronouncing the dangling corpse "a pretty sight or pretty picture." Hays turned right around and implicated O'Connor, testifying it was he who had first suggested that a "nigger" ought to be killed if Anderson were acquitted. Teddy Kyzar swore that Bennie Hays had implied that he, Kyzar, would be "dead within eight hours, twenty-four at the most" if he ever told the police what he knew about the murder plot.

Everyone, it seemed, had something damaging to say about everyone else—everyone, that is, except Frank Cox. Cox declined to testify at all, repeatedly invoking the Fifth Amendment to questions put to him by Dees. Dees had sought to probe Cox about his involvement: whether he had been the exalted cyclops of Unit 900 at the time of the slaying; whether he had traveled with Hays and Knowles to get the rope from his mother's house, as Knowles had sworn; whether he had seen Knowles tie the hangman's noose; and whether he had burned the cross on the courthouse lawn with Teddy Kyzar. Each time Cox pleaded the Fifth. Dees continued to fire questions at him for several minutes, aware that it made Cox appear as if he were trying to hide something. Finally, in order to ensure that the point had been made with the jury, Dees asked Judge Howard to explain the purpose of refusing to answer. Only then did he permit Cox to come down.

The very next witness was Cox's mother, an attractive, soft-spoken woman who was very fashionably dressed and who seemed quite middle-class. Ironically, Sarah Cox had been cooperating since 1983 with federal and state authorities investigating the Donald slaying. Brought to their attention by Knowles, who had identified Frank Cox as the provider of the rope, she had confirmed critical portions of Knowles's story: that her son, accompanied by his two buddies, had come to her house on the night before the murder to borrow a rope, explaining that they needed it to pull Knowles's mother's car, which they said was disabled on a nearby highway. The next day, after hearing about the Donald hanging, she had asked her son where the rope was and was told that it had split into so many pieces that there "wasn't anything left to return."

The impact of her testimony was enormous. So, too, was that of Beatrice Knowles, Knowles's mother, a plain, unpolished woman, who followed Mrs. Cox to the stand. No, she told the court— somewhat wearily, it seemed—her car had not been stalled along the highway in March 1981.

Once we finished the last of the testimony about the Donald murder, we still had two witnesses to call before resting our case, two of our best witnesses against the corporate Klan. The first was Gary Thomas Rowe, the ex-FBI informant, whose testimony about Shelton's personal advocacy of violence during the 1960s contrasted sharply with the image the imperial wizard had earlier tried to project to the jury. Rowe told all about how Shelton had conspired with the Birmingham police to attack the Freedom Riders and had encouraged other acts of violence against blacks in Alabama during the heyday of the civil rights movement. And because of a clever stratagem Dees had employed, reading Rowe's deposition into the record rather than calling him to appear in person, there was nothing Mays could do to refute the testimony. It went into the record undisputed, leaving the jury no alternative but to regard it as true.*

Rowe's testimony was nearly perfect. The only thing it really lacked was timeliness. To the jury (as to some of us on the plaintiff's side) it was ancient history, an account from another epoch, another South, the stuff of textbooks and documentary films. Dees knew it was a gamble to expect the jurors to hold the corporation liable primarily on the strength of Rowe's testimony. Without similar testimony of a more recent nature, he feared that the jury would perceive the Donald murder as the handiwork of a few Klan hotheads in Mobile and let the corporate UKA go.

Shortly before the trial, therefore, Dees had directed me to come up with another informant, somebody more contemporary, who could back up Rowe's testimony. I, in turn, had passed the matter on to our newest addition to the Klanwatch staff, Joe Roy, who was a former Montgomery policeman, like Danny Welch, and had once owned a detective agency. Roy had a reputation as one of the slickest investigators in Alabama. No matter how formidable the task, he always had a way of getting the job done. Once, in a hotly contested divorce case, he had been hired by the estranged husband to follow his wife on a trip to a large midwestern city to see if she was carrying on an affair there. Booking a seat on the same flight as the woman and befriending her, Roy had laid the bait by confiding to her his fictitious marriage problems. By the time the plane arrived at its destination, the woman not only had admitted she was having an affair but had given him her boyfriend's business card. On another occasion he had gained access to a highly restricted Strategic Air Command missile base in Nebraska, with its vaunted security, by posing as a contractor bidding on a construction project.

* After Mays opted not to attend Rowe's deposition in Montgomery in 1985, Dees decided to introduce the deposition as evidence rather than subpoena Rowe to appear at the trial. In essence, Mays forfeited his right to cross-examine by choosing not to make an appearance at the deposition, since Rowe, who lived more than a hundred miles from the courthouse, like Johnny Matt Jones, was under no obligation to testify at the trial in person.

To find Randy Charles Ward, our final witness, Roy had to draw on his best investigative skills. Ward, a former exalted cyclops of a UKA unit in eastern Alabama, had been one of the ringleaders behind a campaign of violence and intimidation against black activists in Talladega County, east of Birmingham, in 1978. Along with approximately twenty other UKA members, he was indicted on federal civil rights violations. Subsequently he turned state's evidence and pleaded guilty. After testifying against the other Klansmen, Ward entered the Federal Witness Protection Program, was given a new identity and Social Security number, and was relocated to another part of the country. When Joe Roy set out to track him down (at the suggestion of Henry Frohsin, the former Assistant U.S. Attorney from Birmingham who had prosecuted the case), there was no longer a trace of him or any of his family in Talladega County.

Using every investigative tool at his disposal, Roy finally located Ward's parents and paid them a visit. Shocked that they had been traced and wary of Roy's vow—little more than an empty bluff though it was—to keep hunting until he had located their son, they agreed to convey the message that we wanted to talk to him. In a couple of days Ward phoned, and Roy coaxed him into helping us.

Ward's testimony buttressed our case against the UKA in several important ways. As a former unit leader he was in a position to testify knowledgeably, and credibly, about the structure and operation of the group, and his affirmation of its military-style chain of command gave the jury the opportunity to hear that characterization from yet another source.

Even more critical was what Ward had to say about violence and its official sanctioning by Shelton and other UKA leaders. He testified that the titan over him had once remarked that Ward's unit "was being ran [sic] like a bunch of old men sitting around a campfire."

"Intimidation," Ward quoted the official as saying. "Said that was the best policy, to put the fear of God in the people."

Ward and his klavern took the titan's remarks as a green light to become more militant, he testified, and not long afterward he and fellow members of the Military Committee, the klavern's leadership, put their newfound militancy into action. With the advance approval of the titan, the Kluxers shot up the homes of two area NAACP officials involved in trying to get the towns of Childersburg and Sylacauga to hire black police officers, after earlier carrying out a similar attack on the home of a local white woman rumored to be dating a black man.

Far and away the most critical portion of Ward's testimony had to do with Shelton, however. Ward had been present at a weekly klavern meeting when Shelton was in town and had been mesmerized, like the rest of the unit, while the imperial wizard told "war stories" from the sixties, including boasts about his role in the attack on the Freedom Riders in Birmingham. "Everybody was fired up," Ward testified. "When Mr. Shelton came around, people would follow him through hell if it came to it."

A one-on-one conversation Ward had had with Shelton after the Talladega arrests provided still more evidence of Shelton's personal espousal of violence. Ward called the imperial wizard to find out what he should do, and Shelton assured him the Klan would provide financial assistance and a lawyer. "He said to talk to the guys and tell them that everything was all right, that they would help us—help our unit raise money for the lawyer's fee or whatever, for bail, and to tell them that they weren't kicked out of the Klan, but just not to attend and stay low."

Shelton's remarks were tantamount to sanctioning violence and added to the growing mountain of evidence that intimidation and violence were not only the hallmarks of the UKA but the corporate policy as well.

When Ward stepped down from the witness stand, we felt a surge of confidence in our prospects for prevailing against *all* the defendants in the lawsuit, including the one we were most interested in prevailing against, the corporate Klan. Ward's testimony, like Gary Thomas Rowe's, represented that of someone with no direct stake in the outcome of the case, and we believed it would have a profound effect on the jury. On that note we rested our case.

In essence, the trial was over. To our amazement Mays announced that the United Klans would present no witnesses: The UKA was resting its case. Most of the individual Klan defendants followed suit.* Only Bill O'Connor chose to put on a defense, and the only witness he called was himself. In a brief, rambling statement he professed his innocence and then sat down. With that the testimony phase of the trial abruptly and prematurely came to an end.

This totally unexpected turn of events caught nearly everyone off guard. Judge Howard, who had not yet prepared his charge to the jury on the assumption that the trial would run at least another day, put the court in recess until the next morning.

Dees and Richard Cohen, the new SPLC legal director, along with Senator Figures, were shocked at Mays's decision not to respond to the evidence we had presented. It made no apparent sense. Rowe's and Ward's testimony about Shelton's advocacy of violence stood completely unrebutted; no one had taken the stand to contradict a word they had said.

All Dees could figure was that Mays and Shelton either failed to comprehend the legal theory under which we were proceeding—wrongly believing, perhaps, that we were obligated to show that Shelton had somehow been personally involved in the Donald conspiracy—or were simply confident that the all-white jury would automatically rule in the Klan's favor, as all-white Southern juries frequently had done in the past.

On Thursday, February 12, the fourth and final day of the trial, closing arguments were given. Dees and Figures split the two hours allotted to each side, Dees emotionally arguing the facts in the case and Figures meticulously explaining the law. In turn, Mays and each of the individual defendants were given an opportunity to make their cases to the jury. As a matter of course, Judge Howard asked Tiger Knowles if he wanted to address the jurors, and Knowles, despite the fact that he had already admitted his guilt, indicated he had something to say. Rising from his seat against the far wall of the courtroom, directly opposite from where the jurors were seated, Knowles walked past the counsel tables and approached the jury box. He wore a solemn, almost grim, look on his face.

---

* There was one fewer defendant at the counsel table now than there had been at the beginning of the trial. With the permission of Judge Howard we had dropped Teddy Kyzar from the suit. Kyzar had always seemed less culpable than the other members of Unit 900. Moreover, the cooperation he had shown the feds had helped them crack the case in 1983.

"Ladies and gentlemen," he began slowly, "I've got just a few things I want to say. I know that people's tried to discredit my testimony. But I want you to know that everything I said is true. . . ."

Suddenly all the emotion he had been suppressing for so long welled up inside him. "I've lost my family. I've got people after me. Everything I said is true. I was acting as a Klansman when I done this," he said, his body shaking. "And I hope that people learn from my mistake. And whatever judgment you decide, I do hope you decide a judgment against me and everyone else involved. . . ."

By now Knowles was sobbing, and so were a lot of other people in the courtroom. He turned toward Mrs. Donald, who was crying audibly, and addressed her directly. "And I can't bring your son back," he said. "But I'm sorry for what happened. And God knows if I could trade places with him, I would. I can't . . ." His voice trailed off.

Clutching a tissue, Mrs. Donald spoke back to Knowles, in a scene that no one who saw could ever forget. "Son, I forgave you a long time ago," she said in a voice barely above a whisper.

Regaining his composure, Knowles turned back to the jury. "And I do hope that you find a judgment against me and everyone involved. Because we are guilty. If we weren't guilty, I wouldn't be up here doing this, I wouldn't be in the Witness Protection Program, and I wouldn't be wasting your time or anyone else's. And Mrs. Donald wouldn't have the loss of her son, if this wasn't true. That's all I've got to say."

Jurors aren't supposed to be swayed by their emotions, and perhaps the jury in the Donald case would have found in Mrs. Donald's favor anyway. The facts were there, and because of Mays's tactical decision, they stood in bold relief.

Later that evening, after approximately four hours of deliberations, the five-woman, one-man, all-white jury returned judgments of liability against the UKA itself and each of the individual Klan defendants. They were ordered to pay Mrs. Donald $7 million in damages.

Epilogue

THE UKA gave up its national headquarters building without a fight, and one day a few weeks after the trial had ended the keys and the deed to the property arrived at the SPLC, rather unceremoniously, in the morning mail. With that, ownership of the building officially passed into Mrs. Donald's hands. It was—it almost goes without saying—a first in the history of the KKK.

Out of curiosity several of us from the office, accompanied by Senator Figures, drove to Tuscaloosa to have a look at the place, but other than bricks and mortar and aluminum siding there was little to see. Shelton or his subordinates had stripped it of everything Klannish, including the three iron ceremonial crosses that had once stood at the entrance to the property and a painstakingly carved cypress sign donated by the Florida realm. The story was much the same on the inside, so that the building looked less like a Klan headquarters than an abandoned warehouse or factory. The only real testimony to its past was a wooden wall plaque, hanging in the lobby, which had the words *KKK Yesterday Today Tomorrow* burned into it. So was the once-mighty United Klans of America brought to its knees by a humble black cleaning woman.

At Mrs. Donald's request we put the building up for sale. Because of its location at the end of a dirt road out in the country, few prospective buyers came forward, and although it was appraised at roughly $125,000, it eventually sold for only about half that figure. With the proceeds of the sale Mrs. Donald bought a house in downtown Mobile, not far from the housing projects she had called home for nearly thirty years. It was the first house she'd ever owned.

Publicity about the case reverberated for months. News of the verdict and of the Klan's surrender of its headquarters ran in virtually every daily newspaper in the country and was followed by feature pieces in *People* magazine and on the ABC News program "20/20," among others. The *New York Times Magazine* did a cover story on Mrs. Donald; *Ms.* magazine named her one of its "Women of the Year" for 1987.

The avalanche of media attention prompted a huge outpouring of support for the "woman who beat the Klan," as the *Times* called her, and it manifested itself in hundreds of letters from well-wishers across the country—so many that "the mail lady was mad," Mrs. Donald half-jokingly confided to one reporter. Although the display of concern was deeply gratifying to her, it could not ease her pain; the burden of Michael's horrible death was always with her. She suffered a stroke in June 1988, rebounded briefly, and died on September 17. She is buried next to Michael in Whispering Pine Cemetery, north of Mobile.

Happily, she lived long enough to see both Bennie Hays and Frank Cox indicted for murder in the case. The charges, brought by a Mobile County grand jury in August 1987 at the urging of District Attorney Chris Galanos, were a direct result of the success of the civil suit, and this time the prosecutor's office tried the case as a Klan killing. In May 1989 Benjamin Franklin Cox was convicted by an all-white jury of being an accomplice in the slaying and was subsequently sentenced to life in prison. At this writing Bennie Hays, reportedly ailing with heart problems, is still awaiting trial.

As for Tiger Knowles and Henry Hays, both remain incarcerated. Knowles, serving a term of ten years to life in a federal penitentiary, will be eligible for parole in 1993, the year he turns thirty. Hays, who recently marked his sixth year on Death Row, continues to appeal his conviction in an attempt to avoid execution in Alabama's electric chair.

Opal Hays died of a massive heart attack she suffered at Holman Prison in Atmore, Alabama, after a visit with Henry. Before her death she had become active in a Death Row mothers' support group, many of whose members were black.

The Decatur cases, both the criminal prosecution and our civil suit, were still stuck in legal limbo when I left the Center in the fall of 1987. In the three years since my departure, both cases have finally snaked their way through the courts to resolution.

On June 7, 1988, the U.S. Court of Appeals for the Eleventh Circuit unstuck the criminal prosecution in dramatic fashion when it decided—in response to the government's appeal of a number of off-base rulings by Judge William M. Acker—to remove Acker from the case and turn it over to a new judge. In a lengthy written opinion accompanying the decision, the appeals court cited numerous misapplications of the law and erroneous findings of fact in Acker's rulings and suggested that he was biased against the prosecution beyond the point of being able to try the case fairly. The language of the opinion was unusually blunt, climaxing in the court's assessment that Acker simply was "no longer able to view these cases impartially," a damning professional rebuke for a jurist.

In one fell swoop the circuit court undid most of the damage Acker had inflicted to the case, reversing his decision to dismiss the indictment against David Kelso, reinstating the conviction of Ricky Creekmore, and ruling for the second time (as it had on the government's previous appeal in 1985) that the Justice Department could use the evidence we had turned over to its prosecutors, Craig Shaffer and Dan Rinzel, in 1983. The Klansmen subsequently appealed the decision to the U.S. Supreme Court, but the High Court let the ruling stand. A new judge was promptly appointed to hear the case.

With Acker out of the picture, the long holdout among the Klan defendants tellingly collapsed like a house of cards. Terry Tucker, the exalted cyclops of the Cullman klavern and leader of the Klan Special Forces, was the first to strike a deal with prosecutor Al Moskowitz, who had taken over for Shaffer. Just days after the Supreme Court's rebuff, Tucker entered a plea of guilty to a misdemeanor charge of conspiring to violate the civil rights of the marchers. One after another, the others followed. David Kelso was next, then Grand Dragon Roger Handley. Finally, on January 9, 1989, just minutes before their trial was scheduled to begin, the four remaining defendants—William Johnny Mason, Lenwood White, Ray Steele, and Bill Riccio—pleaded guilty to the misdemeanor conspiracy charge, with Steele and Riccio entering pleas to an additional single felony count of obstruction of justice for encouraging Klansmen to lie to the FBI during the Bureau's failed 1979 investigation.

One of the longest-running Klan prosecutions in American history was, at last, itself history. A whole decade had passed since the attack at Bank and Lee streets, five years since the indictments themselves, and all ten Klansmen the feds had brought charges against stood convicted (nine of them via guilty pleas).

Because the conspiracy charge to which most of the Klansmen pled was only a misdemeanor, the sentences handed out were relatively light, ranging from probation for Kelso to three months and five-hundred-dollar fines for Mason and White. Steele and Riccio received two years and a thousand-dollar fine each for the obstruction of justice charge.

With the criminal case at last out of the way, the civil suit moved to center stage, and it was resolved on a similarly positive note several months later, in July 1989—without ever going to trial. In light of the disposition of the criminal case and the fact that the lawsuit had accomplished its primary purpose of righting the wrong committed against the Decatur marchers, we elected (with their consent) to settle out of court rather than go to the time and expense of a lengthy trial. Of the seventy or so Klansmen we had sued, there were only about a dozen defendants left in the case. (Over the previous few years we had gradually whittled down the number to streamline the case for trial. Trying a case against seventy defendants would have been a logistical and procedural nightmare, for the court as well as for us.) The vast majority of the Kluxers—fifty-five or sixty—had already signed consent agreements, releasing them from liability in exchange for a formal pledge not to rejoin the Klan for at least five years and to refrain from harassing any minorities for that same period.*

The settlement provisions Dees hammered out with the final dozen or so defendants followed roughly the same outlines: a ban on membership in white supremacist groups (ten years in the case of most defendants) and an agreement not to engage in racial harassment. There were several additional wrinkles: fifty hours of community service for some; monetary damages for others, ranging from $500 from Ray Steele to $2,000 in the case of Roger Handley—whatever Dees managed to squeeze out of them. The total amounted to $11,500.

Five of the defendants agreed (albeit reluctantly and only after Dees had threatened to take them to trial) to attend a special two-hour class on civil rights that was to be led by Dr. Lowery of the SCLC. The class was designed not to be punitive but to facilitate dialogue by engaging the Klansmen to sit down in a room and meet with black people face-to-face, the hope being that the Klan members might begin to view blacks as people, with many of the same cares and concerns that they themselves had.

On May 12, 1990, the class was held behind closed doors in a Birmingham hotel conference room. When the session was over, it was evident that the experience had had no effect on some of the participants. Roger Handley called it "a wasted two hours." Another Klansman, holding a newspaper in front of his face to avoid being photographed, responded to a reporter's question about what he had learned with the wisecrack: "To always carry a newspaper."

But Terry Tucker, the former Klan Special Forces leader, emerged talking about common ground, and there were reports that several of the Klansmen had held hands and prayed with the civil rights activists.

On those notes, Case No. CV-80-HM-1449-S of the United States Court for the Northern District of Alabama officially ended.

---

* Although some might argue that we let the civil defendants off too easy, we were satisfied that we had made them pay a hefty price for their participation in the effort to block the march: a decade's worth of anxiety, plus legal fees and lost wages. Furthermore, the settlement carried the full force of a court order, so that if any of the defendants violated it, they could be prosecuted on criminal contempt of court charges.

*   *   *

By the time the final chapter of the Decatur episode had been written, circumstances in the Klan world had changed dramatically from what they had been in 1979. The resurgence that was then just picking up momentum had now played itself out. Indeed, in mid-1990 combined KKK membership had dropped to about fifteen hundred people, the lowest it had been in nearly two decades; activity was sporadic; the grandiose-sounding Invisible Empire consisted of a small network of loosely associated klaverns scattered around the South and was without effective leadership.

Even in North Carolina and Georgia, long the hot spots of organizing during the 1980s, the Klan was on the decline. Glenn Miller, the onetime leader of the Carolina Knights, was out of circulation altogether, having pled guilty to a federal charge of using the U.S. Postal Service to solicit the murder of Dees. Miller had been angry at us, especially at Dees, for successfully prosecuting him on a criminal contempt of court charge for violating the consent agreement he had signed in 1985 (the one in which he had agreed not to operate a paramilitary army). In a highly unusual development Dees had been appointed a special prosecutor by the federal court and, with the assistance of the U.S. Attorney in Raleigh, Sam Currin, a Jesse Helms protégé, had won criminal contempt convictions against Miller, his Klan group, and the group's second-in-command in the summer of 1986. The case had exposed Miller's role in the Order, his acceptance of two hundred thousand dollars in stolen money from Order founder Robert Mathews, and the involvement of active-duty U.S. military personnel in Miller's Klan. As a result of the prosecution, the Klan group folded, and in the wake of its demise Miller sent out a letter to five thousand members and supporters declaring war on the U.S. government and calling for Dees's assassination.

The decline of the KKK in one of its other main strongholds of the 1980s, Georgia, owed much to strict law enforcement at all levels of government, as well as to several Klanwatch lawsuits. The most important of the latter ended with a multimillion-dollar judgment against the ringleaders of the Klan-led mob that attacked peaceful civil rights protesters in Forsyth County in a widely publicized incident in January 1987. (About thirty thousand dollars in damages have been recovered so far from three KKK leaders.)

Perhaps the most telling commentary on the Ku Klux Klan's status as the last decade of the twentieth century began to unfold was the fact that other, more radical white supremacists had begun to ridicule it openly, deriding the robes and hoods, the funny titles, and the march-and-protest strategy that characterized what was left of the KKK. That is not to say that the more radical wing of the white supremacist movement was in much better shape. Since the federal government's offensive against the Order in 1984 and 1985, groups such as Aryan Nations had been faring little better than the KKK itself. In 1987 the Justice Department brought indictments against Aryan Nations' leaders Louis Beam, Richard Butler, and Robert Miles on seditious conspiracy charges for their alleged participation in the Order plot to overthrow the U.S. government. The three were acquitted by an all-white jury in Fort Smith, Arkansas, in 1988, however.

It remains to be seen, of course, whether the Klan's decline will turn out to be permanent or not. Earlier predictions of its demise have proved notoriously premature, and in the South, where tolerance for the group among whites has always been high—somewhere down the line practically every white Southerner has a great-granddaddy or uncle who was in the Klan, and most adult whites still believe the KKK saved the South from the carpetbaggers—anything is possible. In all likelihood, however, future historians will look back upon the resurgence of the 1970s and 1980s as a minor revival, a kind of last gasp of the once-fearsome hooded order.

Whether the Klan is finished or not, its recent resurgence has proved, ironically, just how much the South has changed since the 1960s. That a group calling itself Klanwatch could have survived for long in the Deep South during the civil rights era is highly debatable. Even if the authorities hadn't put it out of business, it is inconceivable that the Klan would have allowed it to exist. Moreover, it seems unlikely that an all-white jury could have been found anywhere in the region that would have returned a judgment in favor of black plaintiffs against the KKK in those turbulent, watershed times. The fact that a group of white jurors in Mobile, Alabama, rebuked the Klan in the 1980s is truly a milestone for race relations in the South, as well as a legal landmark.

Today, when the Klan marches, the services of the police are sometimes required to protect it from confrontations with counter-demonstrators. When it seeks a permit to conduct activities on public property, it runs into opposition even from white politicians, newly mindful of their black constituents. White ministers are now more likely to denounce the Klan from the pulpit. Civic leaders are more inclined to speak out, too. Sentiment against the KKK is stronger than ever before and manifests itself in a variety of ways.

All this is not to suggest that sympathy for the organization has completely dried up, or that depriving the Klan of its constitutional rights is the proper way to respond to its hatemongering activities, or even that the KKK is no longer a threat, but it does denote a sea change in white attitudes in the two decades since the civil rights movement came to a close.

Would that the story could end here. Although the Klan has been on the decline, there is less good news on other fronts. In 1989 David Duke, the former grand wizard, won a seat in the Louisiana senate; in the fall of 1990 he came amazingly close to pulling off an upset when he drew 44 percent of the vote against incumbent U.S. Senator J. Bennett Johnston in the general election. In Arkansas a neo-Nazi turned in a respectable showing in the 1990 race for the Republican nomination for lieutenant governor. Outbreaks of racial tension are reported on an increasing number of college campuses from coast to coast. The incidence of random hate violence—acts of racially, religiously, ethnically, and sexually motivated bias committed by individuals with no organizational ties—shows no signs of letting up. If anything, in fact, the problem may be getting worse.

Perhaps the most disturbing development of all has been the rise of a new, extremely militant racist organization that threatens to supplant the Klan and the Nazis as the leading hate group in the country. Comprised of shaven-headed young white males in their teens or early twenties, the aptly named skinheads are every bit as violent as their robed counterparts, and their distribution is much wider, encompassing not just the South but the whole country. Since 1986 at least a half dozen racially or ethnically motivated murders committed by skinheads have been reported in states stretching from Oregon to Florida. Nationwide membership in the loosely knit group is estimated in mid-1990 at about three thousand and growing.

With the Klan on the wane, Dees and Klanwatch have turned their sights on the skinheads and other violent racists. In 1989 the SPLC and the Anti-Defamation League of B'nai B'rith joined forces to file a civil suit against three skinheads who clubbed to death an Ethiopian refugee in Portland, Oregon, in November 1988. Using the agencylike theory first employed in the Michael Donald case, the attorneys for the two groups set out to prove that the killers had acted at the instigation of the leaders of a California-based racist group called WAR (White Aryan Resistance). For the second time the strategy proved successful; in the fall of 1990 a civil jury in Portland returned a multimillion-dollar judgment against the murderers and against WAR leaders Tom and John Metzger. The Metzgers have signaled their intention to appeal the verdict.

The rise of the skinheads in the United States (they originally hail from Europe) suggests that organized racism is by no means in danger of disappearing from American society. Extremist groups, after all, are merely manifestations of a powerful current of racism that suffuses American life. While litigation has its place in the fight against this activity, all the lawsuits in the world won't make it go away. Ultimately the only answer is to change attitudes, and the place to start is with the young.

Resource Organizations

ANTI-DEFAMATION LEAGUE OF B'NAI B'RITH
823 United Nations Plaza
New York, NY 10017
(212) 490–2525

CENTER FOR DEMOCRATIC RENEWAL
P.O. Box 50469
Atlanta, GA 30302
(404) 221–0025

KLANWATCH
Southern Poverty Law Center
P.O. Box 548
Montgomery, AL 36104
(205) 264–0286

NATIONAL INSTITUTE AGAINST PREJUDICE AND VIOLENCE
31 South Greene Street
Baltimore, MD 21201
(301) 328–5170

SIMON WIESENTHAL CENTER
9760 West Pico Boulevard
Los Angeles, CA 90035
(213) 553–9036

Acknowledgments

IN THE course of writing this book I have received help from many quarters, and I welcome the opportunity at long last to say a public thank you.

For their encouragement and guidance through the initial stages of the process, I owe a special debt of thanks to Michael Shapiro and Ellen Sklarz. My agent, Russ Galen, and my publisher, Grove Weidenfeld, both took a chance on an unpublished author. Mark Polizzotti went about his work of editing the manuscript in a constructive, supportive way that made me appreciate both him and his craft. In addition, I want to single out Jim Moser and Susan Tillack at Grove for all their help as well.

My former colleagues at the Southern Poverty Law Center have assisted me immensely through the many ups and downs of such a project. At the risk of leaving someone out, I wish to thank Pat Clark, who succeeded me as Klanwatch director, Danny Welch and Joe Roy (investigators par excellence), JoAnn Chancellor, Betty Powell, Mamie Jackson, Richard Cohen, Sheila Rhodes, Dave Watson, Linda Stringer, and Lillie Mays. My thanks also go to Morris Dees, who first encouraged me to write this book, and to all of the Law

Center's donors, without whose generous support the Center's important work would be impossible.

To Tom Oliver, my high school journalism teacher, and Randall Williams, an old friend, I express my gratitude for encouraging me to write.

Finally, I wish to acknowledge friends and family for their constant support all along the way. In addition to my parents and my brother and sister, I am especially grateful to Jennifer Johnston, Tom Gardner, Dennis Balske and Joan Van Almen, Faith and Cyrus Johnston, Nancy Ansheles and Steve Cohen, Jill and Bob Checkoway, Buzz and Gail Ansheles, Beth, Carole, and Joan Ansheles, and Elizabeth Dodge.

And most of all to Cath—my wife, kindred spirit, and best friend.

Photographs have been provided by and are reproduced by kind permission of:

THE SOUTHERN POVERTY LAW CENTER: pp. iv (bottom; photo by Bill Stanton), v (top; photo by Chuck Livingston), viii (bottom; photo by Morris Dees), x (bottom; photo by Bill Stanton), xi (top; photo by Paul Robertson, Jr.), xi (middle; photo by Randall Williams), xii (top and bottom), xiv (top; photo by Bill Stanton), xvi (top; photo by Bill Stanton), xvi (bottom; photo by Danny Welch). GARRY NUNGESTER (COURTESY OF THE ESTATE OF GARRY NUNGESTER): pp. i, vii (top), x (top), xi (bottom). CHRISTOPHER BELL/*Huntsville Times*: pp. ii (top), iii (middle), vi (bottom), vii (bottom). LINDA WARREN LIND: pp. iii (bottom), v (bottom), viii (top). JIMMY ELLIS (COURTESY OF THE ESTATE OF JIMMY ELLIS): p. ii (bottom). JOHN GODBEY/*Decatur Daily*: p. iii (top). ROBERT DUNNAVANT (COPYRIGHT © BY ROBERT DUNNAVANT): p. iv (top). MICHAEL P. SMITH: p. vi (top). JOHN R. VAN BEEKUM: p. ix (top). WIDE WORLD PHOTOS: p. ix (bottom). MOBILE (ALABAMA) POLICE DEPARTMENT: p. xiii (top). ESTATE OF BEULAH MAE DONALD: p. xiii (bottom). JOE ROY: p. xiv (bottom). *Mobile* (ALABAMA) *Press Register*: p. xv (top). OFFICE OF THE UNITED STATES MARSHAL: p. xv (middle photos). ANTI-DEFAMATION LEAGUE: p. xv (bottom).

Index

Knowles, James Llewellyn ("Tiger"):
  (*continued*)
  as Klan officer, 199, 200
  motivation of, 194, 203, 238
  sentencing of, 248
  testimony of, 194–195, 209, 211,
    232, 236–240, 241, 246
Kowalski, Barry, 204
Ku Klux Klan (KKK):
  age range in, 5
  anti-Catholic attitude of, 83
  anti-Semitism of, 36–37, 79, 110,
    135
  arson used by, 84, 93, 152–163,
    169–170, 179, 186–188
  author's views on, 23–24
  bombings by, 84, 92, 110
  calling cards of, 93, 95, 125
  ceremonies of, 39–40, 213
  children's participation in, 36
  civil rights movement opposed by,
    84
  civil rights violated by, 75–76, 78
  civil vs. criminal prosecution of,
    75–76, 150, 165, 174–175, 209–
    210, 229–230
  constitutional rights of, 174–176,
    254
  cross burnings by, 34, 35, 39–40,
    61, 83, 93, 167
  decline of, 83, 252–254
  documentation on, 24
  drug-peddling operations of, 110,
    180n
  electoral power of, 83–84
  factions of, 37, 81–82, 200
  FBI investigations of, 34, 58–59, 69,
    75, 76, 113, 118, 180–181, 212,
    219, 221, 223
  finances of, 86, 110–111, 138
  founding of, vii, 83
  as fraternal society, 83
  gambling operations of, 110
  history of, 80, 82–87, 253
  infiltration of, 77–78, 110,
    135–136, 219

  informants on, 169, 219, 221, 223
  injunction against harassment by, 75
  insignia of, 40
  intimidation by, 23–24, 75, 86
  klaverns of, 81, 213
  "klonvocations" of, 218
  lawsuits against, 75–76, 150
  leaders of, 25, 85–87, 130–131
  legal fees of, 110, 111
  literature distributed by, 50, 81
  mail-order operation of, 85
  marches organized by, 166–167,
    254
  masks used by, 35, 53
  membership of, vii, 83, 84, 86–87,
    121, 122, 252
  miscegenation and, 213n
  mock-lynchings by, 87–88, 128,
    193–194
  monetary damages exacted from,
    75, 78
  monitoring of, 76–77
  oath of secrecy for, 102, 122
  organizational principles of,
    130–131
  paramilitary units of, 61–62, 93, 97,
    100–101, 111–113, 188–189,
    214, 252
  paraphernalia sold by, 36, 86
  police infiltrated by, 27–28
  police surveillance of, 35, 52–53
  political agenda of, 34, 38, 254
  press coverage of, 38, 76, 77, 80,
    85–86, 87, 177
  pseudo-Christian basis of, 36–37,
    39, 79, 82, 98
  public image of, 85, 110, 200–201,
    216
  race war expected by, 86, 112, 180
  rallies of, 6, 34–41
  recruitment by, 38, 50, 81, 84, 112
  resurgences of, vii, 76, 82–83,
    84–85, 252, 253
  SCLC compared with, 176
  seasonal activities of, 110
  shootings by, 84

About the Author

A SEVENTH-GENERATION Southerner, Bill Stanton was born in Arkansas in 1953. He was educated at Hendrix College in Arkansas and at Emory University in Atlanta, Georgia, where he received a master's degree in History. From 1978 to 1987 Mr. Stanton worked at the Southern Poverty Law Center in Montgomery, Alabama, devoting most of his energies to the Klanwatch Project, of which he became the director in 1985. He currently works for an alternative sentencing program in New England and is associated with the National Coalition to Abolish the Death Penalty.